D1606144

THERAPY, IDEOLOGY, AND SOCIAL CHANGE

Comparative Studies of Health Systems and Medical Care

General Editor
CHARLES LESLIE

John M. Janzen, *The Quest for Therapy in Lower Zaire*
Paul U. Unschuld, *Medical Ethics in Imperial China: A Study in Historical Anthropology*
Margaret M. Lock, *East Asian Medicine in Urban Japan: Varieties of Medical Experience*
Jeanie Schmit Kayser-Jones, *Old, Alone, and Neglected: Care of the Aged in Scotland and in the United States*
Arthur Kleinman, *Patients and Healers in the Context of Culture: An Exploration of the Borderland Between Anthropology, Medicine and Psychiatry*
Stephen J. Kunitz, *Disease Change and the Role of Medicine: The Navajo Experience*
Carol Laderman, *Wives and Midwives: Childbirth and Nutrition in Rural Malaysia*
Victor G. Rodwin, *The Health Planning Predicament: France, Québec, England, and the United States*
Michael W. Dols and Adil S. Gamal, *Medieval Islamic Medicine: Ibn Riḍwān's Treatise "On the Prevention of Bodily Ills in Egypt"*
Leith Mullings, *Therapy, Ideology, and Social Change: Mental Healing in Urban Ghana*

Therapy, Ideology, and Social Change

MENTAL HEALING IN URBAN GHANA

Leith Mullings

UNIVERSITY OF CALIFORNIA PRESS

Berkeley   Los Angeles   London

University of California Press
Berkeley and Los Angeles, California

University of California Press, Ltd.
London, England

Library of Congress Cataloging in Publication Data

Mullings, Leith.
    Therapy, ideology, and social change.

    (Comparative studies of health systems and medical
care)
    Bibliography: p. 233
    Includes index.
    1. Psychotherapy—Ghana.   2. Mental healing—Ghana.
3. Healing—Ghana.   I. Title.   II. Series.   [DNLM:
1. Psychotherapy—Ghana.   2. Medicine, Traditional—
Ghana.   3. Social change.   4. Mental health.   WM 420
M959t]
RC451.G45M85   1984   362.2'09667   83-18072
ISBN 0-520-04712-5

Printed in the United States of America

1 2 3 4 5 6 7 8 9

TO MY PARENTS
Lilleth and Hubert Mullings

Contents

Acknowledgments

THIS book would not have been possible without the cooperation of the people of Labadi. To the market women, farmers, patients, healers, ritual specialists, and many friends, who taught me about the customs although I no longer had my name, I am deeply indebted. Special appreciation goes to Nii Anyetei Kwakwranya II, Ataa Leyteyfio, Mrs. Janet Tetteh and Reverend Tetteh. I would like to thank the Sociology Department of the University of Ghana at Legon for sponsoring my research. I am especially grateful to Dr. J. A. Bossman for his support.

The manuscript benefited from the helpful comments of Professors Charles Leslie, Roger Sanjek, William Shack, Joan Vincent, Dr. Kofi Appiah-Kubi, James Ocansey, Lydia Torgbor, Christian Beels, M.D., and June Jackson Christmas, M.D. I owe special thanks to Professor George Bond for his careful and critical readings, and unflagging encouragement.

For assistance in the preparation of the manuscript, I would like to thank Sydney Gluck, Karen Hanson, Gloria Mike, Sandra Mullings, and Bill Rose.

I could not have completed this work without the support of my immediate and extended family, in matters ranging from typing to child care. Special thanks to Jarvis, Pansy, and Pauline; Alia, Michael, Colby, and Keith.

The original field research was supported by grants from the African Studies Committee of the University of Chicago, the Danforth Kent Foundation and a Public Health Service Special Predoctoral Nursing Fellowship (#5 F04 N027080-06). A postdoctoral fellowship from the Hastings Center, Institute of Society, Ethics and the Life Sciences, allowed me time to think about cross-cultural mental therapy.

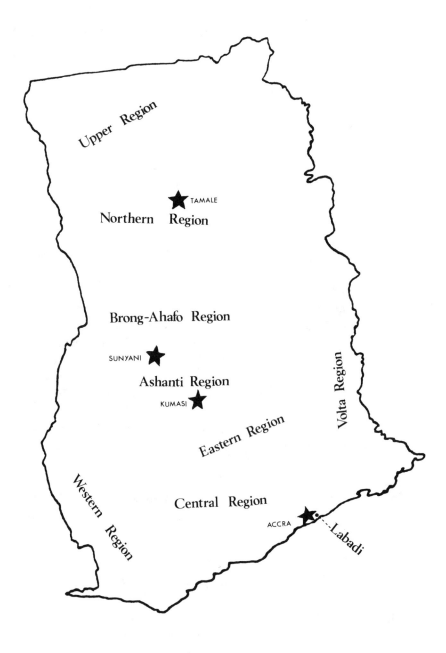

Map 1—Ghana.

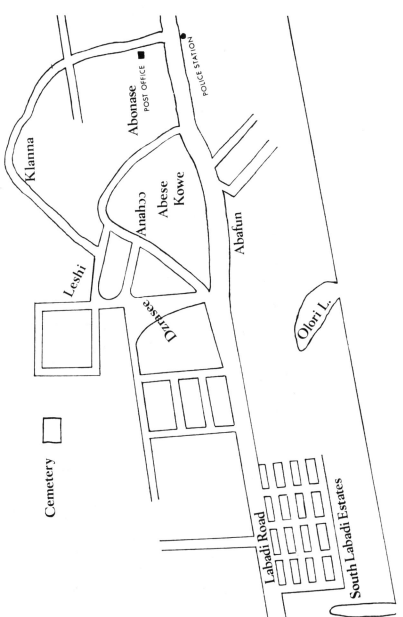

Map 2 — The seven quarters of Labadi.

Introduction

IN all societies the ability to manipulate healing can be used to reinforce selected social relations, classes, and ideologies. While this is most obviously the case in psychotherapy, which entails premises about what behavior should be, numerous studies demonstrate the way in which other forms of medicine can be involved in the management of society (see Parsons 1951; Ehrenreich and Ehrenreich 1974). Therapies may align themselves with the interests of specific classes and groups of a given society, may mediate and reinforce certain ideological elements. They are created within a given social order, but also reproduce that order. An essential issue is which set of values is being transmitted and in whose interests.

This concern was evident in the 1979 press release of the World Health Organization (WHO) urging governments to support "traditional[1] medicine," to eschew total reliance on Western medicine, and to strive to integrate Western and traditional medicine to meet the health needs of their countries. This recommendation, which represented a departure from previous positions that placed emphasis on the implementation of biomedical facilities, was based on a number of preliminary inquiries. In 1974 a joint study by UNICEF and WHO recommended the mobilization and training of practitioners of traditional medicine, and in 1977 a resolution calling for the promotion and development of training and research in traditional medicine was passed by acclamation in the World Health Assembly. Subsequently, several seminars and regional conferences resulted in pragmatic recommendations and proposals designed to implement this new policy (Bannerman 1977:16).

The position taken by WHO was, in part, a response to a generalized critique, or at least a rethinking, of the notion that biomedicine is universally superior. In the United States this is reflected in a new surge of antimedicine movements, as well as in the growing recognition that the health sector is in crisis. In developing countries we find questions being raised about the value of importing Western biomedicine as a whole, criticism of the basic premises of biomedicine, and a reevaluation of traditional medicine. Most such critiques point to the necessity for attention to the socioeconomic conditions that produce health and disease, primary care as the center of health planning, the popular participation of collectivities in health planning (Bibeau 1979:183), and some to fundamental structural changes as a prerequisite to real changes in the health care delivery system (Gish 1979:208). Such a direction reflects a rejection of colonialism and the domination of European forms of organization and ideological systems. While others hesitate to formulate the problem so sharply, implicit in their positions are questions about the underlying ideologies of Western biomedicine, challenging such basic premises as the nature of health, the causes of illness, and the relationship of the individual to the collectivity.

There is no consensus endorsing WHO's direction. Critics of traditional medicine point to the problems of charlatanism and second-class health care. Most do agree, however, that indigenous medical systems require more study. In delineating WHO's program for the implementation of traditional medicine, Bannerman stated, "Investigations will also be conducted into the psychosocial and anthropological aspects of traditional medicine . . ." (1977:17). To date, most studies of traditional medicine undertaken for WHO have focused on the investigation of autochthonous pharmacopoeia.

Indigenous psychotherapy in Africa remains a relatively unexplored area of African medical practice, despite the fact that the majority of psychotherapy is undertaken by indigenous practitioners. Swift and Asuni (1975:200), for example, note that "both groups [traditional healers and healing churches] serve as a kind of protective screening device to prevent the psychiatric and general hospital from being swamped with patients who have psychological problems." My study attempts to expand our knowledge of African medical systems by presenting a study of indigenous psychotherapeutic systems in Ghana.

Psychotherapy represents an area in which the challenges to the cross-cultural validity of biomedicine become most acute. Because most mental illnesses are diagnosed on the basis of deviant behavior, psychotherapy continues to be an approach to correcting deviant behavior. Thus, even more sharply than other aspects of medicine, all forms of psychotherapy are intimately linked to a particular set of moral premises.

It has been noted that some form of psychotherapy exists in most cultures. Studies by Sargant (1957), Frank (1961*a*), Kiev (1964, 1972), Torrey (1972*a, b*), and Prince (1980) have emphasized the similar features that allow different forms of healing to be considered as psychotherapies within the same conceptual framework. In emphasizing the commonalities, these scholars were, very properly, repudiating the ethnocentric view that Western psychotherapy, based in "science" rather than "culture," was distinct from "primitive" forms of therapy and was cross-culturally applicable.

Yet grouping all "non-Western" forms of healing into one category and then posing a simple dichotomy between non-Western and Western healing was itself ethnocentric. What becomes important, particularly in light of the critique of biomedicine and the reevaluation of indigenous therapies, is to trace the way in which all psychotherapeutic systems are linked to the structure of a given type of society. As Press suggests, this is the necessary next step in the study of medical systems in general. "Ultimately we must aim for an appreciation of the range of functions which medical systems can fill, and the manner in which medical systems are derived from generalizable societal, cognitive, and adaptive processes. Here, the continuing search for societal dependencies and paradigmatic models . . . is essential" (1980:55). While scholars such as Kleinman (1980) have set out categories for the comparison of medical systems, their concern has tended to focus on the structural-functional dimensions, rather than on how these systems relate to the larger society. The interrelationships of medical systems and societies, of course, have important implications for countries considering the importation of biomedical systems.

One of the central arguments presented in this study is that an adequate explanation of therapeutic systems must include analysis of the infrastructural conditions, particularly the class relations that accompany the emergence, persistence, and decline of medical systems. Such an approach is premised on the assumption that the social relations (and hence the medical systems) within the society are conditioned by the international context in ways that go far beyond the mere introduction of technological change.

This approach differs in emphasis from most ethnographic studies of mental therapeutic systems, which have emphasized cultural themes, linking such systems to ideology or religion. Thus Reynolds (1976) discusses Morita psychotherapy with reference to the "Japanese personality"; therapy in the United States has been explained in terms of the premises of Protestantism (Davis 1938); spiritism among Puerto Ricans in New York has been linked to Catholicism (Harwood 1977);[2] Wittkower and Warnes (1974) relate the differences in psychotherapeutic systems of the United States, Japan, and European socialist countries to different cultural and ideological systems.

These studies reflect the dominant theoretical trends in medical anthropology, where the emphasis on medical systems as cultural systems continues to dominate cross-cultural studies. Kleinman, for example, envisions the unique contribution of medical anthropologists as that of "systematically developing cultural analysis . . . ethnomedicine would take the context of *meaning* within which sickness is labeled and experienced as its central analytic and comparative problem" (1980:379). Fabrega (1974), too, in pursuing a paradigm that would allow for cross-cultural comparability of medical systems while retaining cultural meaningfulness, has tended to ignore the material links (see Hopper 1979).

These works have made invaluable contributions to our understanding of medical systems. By beginning with the premise that illness and medicine are products of sociocultural settings, they assert the integrity of cultural systems. Such a framework laid the groundwork for the analysis of biomedicine as a medical system embodying cultural premises and assumptions to the same extent as any other (see especially Kleinman 1973 and Fabrega 1974).

Clearly, culture significantly influences all medical systems. As Kleinman (1980) has noted, healing is a cultural process; illness is culturally constructed from disease in that it is the function of medical systems to translate biological and psychological dysfunction into meaning and experience for the patient and social group. Thus, Kleinman notes that new healing processes are based on reconstructions of ideology—the development of new values and new ideologies. In psychotherapy, the ideological system is, perhaps, even more salient than in systems concerned less exclusively with "the education of a person" (Kovel 1976:46).

To note, however, that psychotherapy and, indeed, all medical systems are cultural is only one step in the analysis. One must explain the occurrence of the "new values" and "new ideologies" — the ways in which cultural systems are linked to the social relations of the society.

An exception to this direction in medical anthropology has been the evolutionary-adaptation approaches that move beyond the explication of indigenous categories in approaching culture as an adaptive response to environmental pressures (e.g., Alland 1970). While allowing for the analysis of interaction of the population and environment, work such as Alland's is limited by a tautological use of "adaptation" and by a rather naturalistic conception of environment that excludes such external relationships as those of colonialism and neocolonialism. It seems appropriate that medical anthropology, which must now deal with societies within the context of a world system,[3] develop analyses that specify the way in which infrastructural relations, conditioned by the world system, mediate between the organism/population and the environment, shaping the structure of the therapeutic system as well as the occurrence and distribution of disease.

This study concerns itself with the former, comparing the two major forms of indigenous psychotherapy currently coexisting in Ghana. Both forms of therapy can be considered to be ritual healing in that they occur within a religious context — traditional religion and spiritualist Christianity. We will find that both therapeutic systems (as well as Western psychiatry) have many similarities, but also differ significantly. I suggest that the categories of "Western" and "non-Western" are inadequate; the way in which therapies structure the meaning of illness, the techniques and processes they employ, and the goals characteristic of each type of therapy can not be adequately explained without analysis of the international social relationships that condition them.

In examining the meaning of illness, we will note that in all forms of therapy the identification and labeling of the illness is part of the initial treatment process. It accomplishes the function of assigning an idiosyncratic phenomenon a cultural meaning, thus placing the behavior in a cognitive framework. That labels influence the perception of experience and shape the somatic experience and symptomology of illness is evident in culture-specific disorders, such as *susto, windigo,* and others. The process of naming the illness lifts to the conscious and socially recognized level much that was previously unconscious, or perhaps more accurately, unidentified (see Lévi-Strauss 1963 for a seminal example of this process).

We will find that while the specific techniques of psychotherapies differ, there are underlying processes common to several forms of therapy. The "dramatic healing ritual," for example, is thought to be characteristic of most forms of non-Western healing and to distinguish these therapies from Western approaches. The dramatic healing ritual is characterized by the conscious manipulation of symbols as part of the healing process. While it has been repeatedly demonstrated that symbol systems function to promote transformations in behavior, the relationship between ideology and social behavior remains somewhat unclear. Mental therapy has as its professed goal the molding of a concept of person, the restructuring of the perceptual framework of the deviant individual into that of the well (acceptable) one. Therapeutic systems embodying culturally defined notions of the individual differentially structure the meaning of illness and health, and employ specific techniques, symbolic and otherwise, to transform the idea into the reality.

It is perhaps with respect to the goals of therapy that various psychotherapies clearly differ most profoundly. Kennedy (1973) and others have noted that "non-Western" therapies diverge significantly from "Western psychiatry" in the lack of emphasis on "ego-strengthening" as a goal. We will explore the bases of dissimilar goals of therapy among what are called non-Western systems, as well as differences between African and biomedical therapies.

In comparing the major forms of psychotherapy existing in Ghana, this study attempts to go beyond the empiricism of some of the earlier studies by raising questions about the way in which therapeutic systems are embodied in social formations. It also differs from most investigations of indigenous African medicine in being an urban study, in contrast, for example, to Ngubane (1977) and Janzen (1978).

My research was conducted from 1970 to 1972 in Labadi,[4] a neighborhood of Accra, the capital city. Labadi, with a population of 26,000, is now part of Accra, although it was one of six original coastal towns settled by Ga-speaking peoples in the sixteenth century. It reflects many of the characteristics of more recent urban forms, while at the same time maintaining the traditions of a long-settled town. Like the other Ga coastal towns, Labadi includes its own dependent villages and is a semi-independent political unit. Although I shall take healing in Labadi as the point of departure, it will be evident that many of the processes described have their counterpart in other areas of Ghana and perhaps beyond.

Ghana, a state of ten million, faces problems typical of many postcolonial countries attempting to improve the health of their people. Despite efforts to expand its health facilities, beginning in 1957 when Ghana was the first sub-Saharan African state to break the relations of colonialism, disparities in access to health care established under colonialism continue. Given the finding in 1977 that 70 percent of the population was without convenient access to health care in the biomedical sector and that the general health status in Ghana had not improved, the National Health Planning Unit recently recommended the recruitment and training of community level primary health workers. Recognizing that traditional practioners had been central to the delivery of health care, the Ministry of Health has begun supporting the training and recruitment of indigenous healers with the inauguration of Primary Health Training for Indigenous Healers (PRHETIH) in Techiman (Warren 1979:11-12). As we have noted, psychotherapy is one area in which the majority of health care still occurs in the context of nonbiomedical healing institutions, undertaken primarily by traditional and spiritualist church healers (Twumasi 1972, 1975; Jahoda 1961).

This book contains three parts. In the first, I attempt to sketch the setting in which therapy occurs, laying the basis for discussing the relationship of forms of therapy to social structural formations. The first chapter discusses the changing mode of production and the particular urban form that characterized Ghana at this point in its development. Chapter 2 discusses the range of medical options and the way in which they are related to other institutions in the society.

Part II consists of the ethnography of therapy—a detailed account of traditional and spiritualist healing. Each type of therapy was approached as a system, in the sense of functionally integrated entities of intercommunicating parts. In general, Press's definition of a medical system as a "patterned, interrelated body of values and deliberate practices, governed by a single paradigm of the meaning, identification, prevention and treatment of sickness" (Press 1980:3) applied. I agree with Press that treating coexisting systems as "ideally true" systems allowed for comparison without implying that each system was internally homogeneous.

I relied primarily on the case study approach; in addition to interviewing and observing the healer, I followed the cases of specific patients, noting what people did about illness and healing and how they rationalized it, within the context of the disease theory system. Despite the well-known disadvantages of case study data, this approach proved most useful for this type of study. Even where wide-scale comparison is the goal, such comparison can only proceed successfully if the context of the cases to be compared is understood. Thus, descriptive case studies are often the first step for laying the basis for more wide-scale survey comparisons. In the study of cross-cultural mental illness and therapy, we often do not possess enough data to isolate intelligently the variables to be emphasized. Because significant aspects of illness and therapy are not yet understood, it would have been difficult to determine the correct questions or the accuracy of responses necessary for survey methodology. Thus, despite the fact that this approach limits the numbers that can be studied, long-range detailed descriptions of cases and treatments are an important first step in cross-cultural studies of mental disorders.

Part III attempts to relate the findings to a larger body of literature, with the purpose of discussing some of the basic issues surrounding cross-cultural mental therapy. By exploring issues concerning mental therapy and social structure, we raise questions, not only about mental therapy in developing countries, but about medicine and social structure in the United States. Those readers less interested in the ethnographic detail might glance at this section first.

PART I

THE CONTEXT OF ILLNESS AND THERAPY

Introductory Note

In the first two chapters, I seek to acquaint the reader with the social context within which illness and healing occur. Chapter 1, a description of the changing society, lays the basis for subsequent discussions of therapeutic systems and social relations. Chapter 2 examines medical pluralism in Labadi, surveying the range of healing options available.

1

The Setting

Men make their own history, but they do not
make it just as they please; they do not make
it under circumstances chosen by themselves,
but under circumstances directly encountered, given and transmitted from the past.
— Karl Marx

PERHAPS it is the copious evidence of circumstances given and transmitted from the past that leads observers to remark that Labadi is
the most "traditional" of the Ga coastal towns. When one walks
through the streets, however, it is Marx's description of the emergence of manufacture—new forms appearing side by side with old
forms, but gradually bursting them asunder—that comes to mind.
The myriad stores, stands, street vendors, indoor and outdoor markets sell everything from traditional drums to Japanese radios, from
indigenous herbs to penicillin. The day begins before 6 A.M., when
the paved and unpaved roads fill with people calling out morning
greetings on their way to the farms, markets, to the ocean to fish, or
to jobs in Accra.

The interweaving of new and old is also evident in religious phenomena. Near the two main streets connecting Labadi with central
Accra five miles to the west and Tema (the port town) ten miles to
the east, the modern edifices of the Presbyterian, Catholic, and
Anglican churches tower over scores of *gbatsui*, the conical, straw-
topped dwellings of the indigenous gods whose priests and mediums
heal by time-proven means. On several of the many unpaved roads,
signs advertising at least ten spiritualist "healing" churches may be
seen at any given time.

The conventional Christian churches are generally found in

more recently constructed sections of town. In these areas, which house Ghanaians from other regions of the country as well as Labadians, there tend to be nuclear family dwellings, often supplied with electricity and internal plumbing. In the centrally located seven quarters — the original site of settlement, where the highest concentration of gbatsui is found — rectangular cement-covered buildings consisting of individual rooms built around a courtyard constitute extended-family dwellings. Some of the old houses now have electricity and an internal water supply, but the majority of inhabitants use kerosene lamps and collect their water in buckets from the town's public water faucets. Here, from their vantage point on the Atlantic Ocean, generations of Labadians have witnessed the comings and goings of the Portuguese, Swedes, Dutch, and English, and the advent of independence.

It is said that the La people migrated to the Accra plains from Benin, Nigeria,[1] around the sixteenth century.[2] The migrants, who intermixed with the people already in the area, arrived in extended kinship groups under the leadership of a *tse* (father/owner),[3] who occupied the roles of family head, holder of the land, and priest of the family gods. They brought with them their gods (*dzemawọdzii*) and incorporated the gods of the aboriginal peoples. Not surprisingly, concepts of the sacred made reference to the production and reproduction of society. The sacred office of *shitse* (owner of the land) was vested in the autochthonous people, and their descendants continue to hold that office. Later, as fishing became a significant subsistence activity, the office of *woleiatse* (father/owner of the fish) and the priest of the god Afrim was invested in the lineage group reputed to have brought fishing to Labadi. The sacralizing of the lineage was represented not only in the ritual power of the tse, but in the lineage gods (dzemawọdzii) in their charge. Today the ritual activities of the dzemawọdzii continue to make reference to ensuring the reproduction of crops, livestock, and townspeople, and are an essential aspect of traditional healing.

The coastal people, subsisting by cultivation and later by fishing, were gradually drawn into the wider economy of West Africa. For example, salt extracted from the ocean and the lagoons became an important item in the development of inland trade. As the Ga-speaking peoples interrelated with other African groups through trade and military activities, they defined and redefined their own group, eventually developing federations and towns. The interchange among African groups was reflected in the Ga pantheon, which expanded to include other African deities, and regional and individual cults.

The process of territorial aggregation was, to some extent, organized around the *mangtse* (literally, "owner" of the town). Later this office acquired the connotation of "chief," and the mangtse occupied the "stool," the symbol of leadership of the town. However, as Field notes (1940:71-84)—and all Labadians I encountered agreed —the Ga were originally governed by priests; the mangtse was originally a war medicine associated with specific periods of military organization.

It is likely that the pattern of social relationships that gradually emerged and that continues to exist in some form in much of rural West Africa was akin to what we now call the village community (Magubane 1976:173). Typically, village production is carried out by small independent farmers and is characterized by a relatively low level of technology. The degree of commercialization is slight, and tools are relatively simple and generally available. Classes, as defined by ownership of the means of production—in this case land —do not exist. While this does not preclude forms of differentiation based on age (see Dupré and Rey 1973; Meillassoux 1964), gender (see Mullings 1976), and differentiation of kinship groups based on ritual claims of ownership (see Horton 1972), common access to land, organized through the lineage, is the basis of the high degree of collectivism and egalitarianism found in such societies. This form of social organization often existed side by side with stratified state societies.

Although there are difficulties inherent in any attempt to reconstruct precolonial forms of social structure, the existence of the village community has been documented in much of West Africa. Elements of this pattern of social relations are found in contemporary Labadi. Seven maximal lineages—the four original founding lineages and three others that later migrated to the area—are the basis of the social organization of the town. Each maximal lineage continues to be associated with a house of origin and two sets of names for alternate generations. All seven lineages are represented on the chief's traditional council that is responsible for governing the town; their duties range from making decisions on land sales to hearing cases involving "traditional" law. The major lineages continue to be the nominal holders of land and other lineage property; rights to land, a room in the lineage house, and succession to lineage and town offices continue, at least nominally, to be available to eligible members of the major patrilineage as their birthright[4] (see Mullings 1975 for details). Every year almost all the townspeople participate in *homowo,* the central public ritual celebrating the lineage gods and ancestors.

The Portuguese first established a fort at Elmina in the early 1480s, but permanent European settlement of Accra began in 1650 when the Dutch built what is now known as Ussher Fort. In 1657 the Swedes built Christianborg Castle, two miles west of Labadi (which they lost to the Danes a few years later), and in 1673 the British built James Fort in Accra. The arrival of the Europeans became a factor in accelerating the development of stratification. As the Europeans had difficulty penetrating beyond the coast, the initial trade was indirect, resulting in the development of a new class of African middlemen, serving as intermediaries between African and European traders (Daaku 1970:115 ff.). The European presence also created a demand for new types of African skilled and unskilled labor, producing a class of African wage workers (Daaku 1970:103; Reindorf 1966:41).

The imposition of the slave trade in the seventeenth century had massive and far-reaching effects on the population, laying the basis for the dismemberment of Africa in the nineteenth century. The slave trade had the impact of strengthening state structures; the introduction of firearms made large-scale raiding possible (Wallerstein 1976:34; Daaku 1970:27-33) and made the acquisition of firearms a necessity for survival. The consolidation of military states was, of course, reflected in religious forms, which assumed a more warlike character (DeBrunner, 1967:45). The areas around the European forts became major slave-trading centers. The chaplain of the Danes at Christianborg, near Labadi, described the transportation of slaves to the coast in 1710:

> The slave-trade is the most horrible and detestable trade imaginable. Traders bring slaves to the castle or trading posts for sale. All the slaves are tied together, yet without iron chains or fetters around the feet. A very long strip of cloth (usually bark cloth) is employed to tie them together. The band is fastened round the body of the first slave; subsequent slaves are only fastened round their right upper arm. The In-

dian file of tied slaves is driven by their owners like cattle. When I have
to witness this, my eyes shed tears, and I remember what is written in
II Timothy, chapter 2, verse 26: "that there are men ensnared in a
similar way by the devil, after being captured to do his will." (Cited in
DeBrunner 1967:47)

The La people, like others in the area, were forced to organize
into defensive towns for mutual protection. Thus, by 1732, Barbot,
a slaver and explorer, described Labadi as a walled settlement (Barbot 1732:185). One can still find evidence of the disruption caused
by the buying and selling of human beings. People remember that
the dwelling of the Lakpa, the major deity of Labadi, became a
sanctuary for those fleeing capture, and that the office of priest for
that god (which, as we shall note, is now of major ritual importance)
was charged to a freed slave.

As the priorities of the Europeans shifted from a demand for
slaves to a demand for land and cash crops, palm oil export gained
importance, eventually becoming a factor in the colonization of the
Gold Coast. For the West, particularly the British, who had gained
hegemony, the mercantile period became one of accumulation of
capital through the exploitation of African resources and labor to
be reinvested in the West (Rodney 1972; Magubane 1976). While
the bulk of the African population continued to be involved in the
traditional economy of the village community, a small stratum of
Ga merchants and wage workers with individual access to money
had now become institutionalized.

Christianity was the major cultural arm of the European presence. In the early 1840s, the Basel mission opened a school at Christianborg, the town adjacent to Labadi. Reindorf (1966:221) reports
that in 1855 H. L. Rottman, "the energetic missionary merchant,"
opened a factory at Christianborg. In 1857, the Basel Mission instituted a workshop to train locksmiths, blacksmiths, wheelwrights,
carpenters, shoemakers, and other artisans. This labor force was
then employed by the mission in a "factory," but also became a
source of skilled African labor for the entire West Coast (Szereszewski 1965:8; Kimble 1963:7; Reindorf 1966:222). The association between the religious institutions and the development of economic
incentives and orientations is unwittingly revealed by Reindorf, an
early Ga convert and missionary, in the following discussion of the
workshop at Christianborg.

Our Committee think that it is not only right but their strict duty to make our Christian from the Gentiles partakers of the social blessings, which Europeans abundantly derive from Christianity. To effect this purpose, industrial establishments were opened in Christianborg for joiners, wheel rights, carpenters, lock-smiths, blacksmiths, shoe-makers, and bookbinders. Our industrial missionaries had to sur-mount many difficulties with their workshops; and we are thankful to state that, in this branch also our mission has not labored in vain. After many trials, the different establishments became self-supporting and all these different trades tended to produce Christian diligence, honesty and sobriety. These workshops have not only enabled the Europeans to build more salubrious and comfortable dwellings than those they first inhabited; but the natives, following their example, have improved upon their former style of house; in fact, all the social changes, which this branch of our work brought to the Gold Coast are generally appreciated and speak for themselves to every one possessing eyes to see and sense sufficient to observe and compare past and pres-ent. (Reindorf 1966:223)

This interesting intertwining of economic endeavor and religion, to which we will return later, is also noted by Kimble (1963:7), citing evidence given by Reverend E. Schrenk of the Basel Mission in 1865, who "welcomed the effect of trade in 'enabling the native people to see different European articles which must enlarge their views,' and thus provide an incentive to enterprise."

As early as 1874, Basel missionaries became involved in a dis-pute with the chief of Labadi, Maale Dada III, when they attempted to build a church in the area of Labadi now known as Emmaus. After gaining a court ruling in their favor, the missionaries pro-ceeded with the building of the church, but the opposition of the townspeople forced early Christians to withdraw from the rest of the town and to build their houses around the chapel. The early conflict between the missionaries and traditional authorities is evident in an "enquiry into circumstances mentioned in a letter of complaint from the chief of Labadeye" [*sic*],[5] dated 1883. The chief com-plained that two missionaries had interfered in the marriage of a young woman from Labadi by sending a letter to him stating that she had signed up for baptism and therefore must not be given to this "fetish-man," though the young woman had expressed her desire to proceed with the marriage.

Opposition to Christianity was only one form in which resistance occurred. In 1852, when a poll tax of one shilling per man, woman, and child was levied, Labadi, Christianborg, Teshie, and other small villages refused to pay and were bombarded by the British ship HMS *Scourge* on September 13, 1854, during the celebration of the annual *homowo* festival. Townspeople also resisted attempts to make the land a commodity (something that could be bought and sold) and to alienate it. The records of the national archives are replete with suits brought by the people of Labadi against political officers and elders for the sale of stool land and unauthorized use of funds obtained from these sales. The level of resistance, however, was not sufficient to alter the course of events. As monopoly capitalism superseded competitive capitalism, political control was imposed on the Gold Coast. By 1872, the Gold Coast had been declared a British colony, although it was not until 1902 that the British were able to subdue the Ashanti and incorporate Ashanti and the Northern Territories.

In 1877 the British moved the capital of the colony from Cape Coast to Accra, developing an administrative city that incorporated the original Ga towns. The infrastructure of the city was oriented toward expediting the export of cocoa, the principal cash crop. As Accra became a center of manufacture as well as administration, migrants came to the area, settling both in central Accra and in outlying neighborhoods, such as Labadi, which became part of Greater Accra. The complex of new one-family dwellings (called housing estates) built in the 1940s at Christianborg and Labadi, as well as in other areas in response to the 1939 earthquake, gave impetus to the growing heterogeneity of the area.

The colonial economy conditioned the way in which the class structure developed, creating, in addition to a rapidly growing sector of urban and rural self-employed, a small working class in transport and construction. Large-scale expatriate firms, able to move inland as the transportation network developed, expanded at the expense of small European firms and African traders. By 1930, Compagnie Française de l'Afrique Occidentale (CFAO) and Societé Commerciale de l'Ouest de l'Afrique (SCOA), dominated by United Africa Company (UAC), handled the majority of West African trade (Hopkins 1973:198-199). The coastal people, therefore, have been involved for many generations in contact, trade, development, and transformation. Yet the slave trade and colonialism were pro-

cesses that had major and extensive effects on the structure of coastal society.

Domination inevitably brings a response; the movement for
independence developed. While Kwame Nkrumah and the Conven-
tion People's party (1951-1966) successfully attacked the political
structure of the colonial system, the basic economic structure, being
in the interests of the then dominant world system, was not so easily
changed. Following the coup that ousted Nkrumah and the Conven-
tion People's party, Busia's Progress Party, voted into power in
1969, reversed many of Nkrumah's attempts at creating economic
independence, cut back social services, and froze wages. By 1970,
one-quarter of the registered labor force was unemployed, and the
cost of living in April, 1971 was up 100 percent from March, 1963
(Marshall 1976:56). The crisis increased as cocoa prices plummeted
to their lowest level since 1965 and the currency was devalued 44
percent. In 1971, Busia was deposed by the National Redemption
Council.[6]

Having given a brief outline of the history of this part of the
coast, we now turn to a discussion of the local area and its development. Labadi, which became part of the Accra municipality in
1943, is best conceptualized as a neighborhood of the Accra-Tema
urban complex, the repository of the infrastructure developed by
the colonial administration to expedite the exportation of cocoa.
Yet it is a great deal more than that, being also one of the original
Ga towns, populated by lineages that have been in the area since the
sixteenth century. This means that although Labadi contains a significant migrant population, characteristic of all West African
urban areas, it also has a relatively large nonmigrant population. In
1960,[7] of a population of 25,939, 16,211 (62.5 percent) reported
that they were born in Labadi, 1,611 (6.2 percent) in the region but
not in Labadi, and 6,805 (26.2 percent) in a different region (5.1
percent did not answer the question) (1960 Population Census of
Ghana). The large proportion of indigenous people, along with the
nominal ownership of the land by the lineages, created the foundation for the continued existence of those social institutions intertwined with lineage organization.

By 1970 to 1972, however, the chief estimated that approximately three-fifths of Labadi land was no longer under the jurisdic-

tion of the stool or the lineages, having been alienated from the community and used for government or private purposes. While the remaining land continued to be, in form, collectively owned, the struggle for access to and use of land (as we shall discuss, access to land for farming is key in this type of social structure) was greatly affected by the relationships of capitalism, although the mechanisms of distribution were governed by lineage principles.

The process by which land became a commodity is instructive. Social institutions of the village community mode of production that facilitated distribution of the land were drawn into the service of the colonial state. To serve the needs of indirect rule, the office of "chief" was created by the colonial government in the image of the Ashanti, a much more centrally organized state. The content of political offices was transformed as the political officers and elders, who held ritual power over the land, were given the power to alienate land from the stool (primarily to the British during colonialism), thus facilitating the emergence of class divisions out of traditional differentiation. The colonial records retained in the Ghana National Archives attest to the opposition of the people of Labadi to these policies, that opposition often erupting into bitter struggles over political leadership (see Mullings 1975, for examples). These confrontations, which were often manifested on the ritual level in struggles over the celebration of homọwọ, the annual ritual, were still occurring in 1970 to 1972.

The presence of such disputes, which often figures in incidents of illness, reflected the continuing importance of access to and control over land, despite the fact that the population was increasingly divorced from agriculture. In fact, it is perhaps this particular form of development, found in other West African and "developing" cities (see Gugler and Flannagan 1978) and labeled by Magubane as the "Colonial Capitalist Mode of Production" (Magubane 1976), that gives the struggle for land its salience. Despite the move towards wage work, proletarianization is incomplete—workers in nonfarming sectors of the economy continue to grow food on the side, both for consumption and the market. Recently, with the general economic decline, people have returned to farming in greater numbers. Labadi land is, of course, of strategic importance, being near enough to the city center for people to work in both sectors. Both non-Labadians and Labadians farmed the land, but Labadians were able to do so in greater numbers.

Although a smaller percentage of the inhabitants of Labadi were involved in agriculture than the national average (three-fifths of the national labor force was in agriculture in 1960 [Caldwell 1967:57]), in actuality, the proportion of indigenous Labadians engaged in agriculture was probably somewhat greater than the census figures indicate. While the 1960 census reported only 5 percent of the population engaged in agriculture (see table 1), in the

TABLE 1
EMPLOYMENT IN LABADI

	Male	Female
All industries	5,582	3,350
Agriculture, forestry, hunting, and fishing	403	22
agriculture	140	18
field crops, foodstuff production	115	14
cocoa growing	25	3
fishing	248	1
Mining and quarrying	31	77
Manufacturing	708	329
food	16	58
beverage	15	2
textile goods (wearing apparel)	123	248
furniture and fixtures	155	2
transport equipment	211	2
Construction	1,317	34
Commerce	700	2,472
Transport, storage, and communication	711	14
Services	1,570	397
government	811	58
community	279	142
business	101	3
All occupations	5,582	3,350
Professional, technical, and related	304	120
Clerical	889	108
Sales	230	2,447
Farmers, fishermen, loggers	409	19
Workers in transport, commerce	2,487	398

Source: 1960 Population Census of Ghana Special Report A—Statistics of Towns. Census Office, Accra, 1964.

central areas of town, where the original seven quarters are located and the population varied from 53 to 88 percent "born in Labadi," 11 to 28 percent of the employed men worked in agriculture. This contrasted with the outlying areas, where the population was only 26 to 36 percent Labadian. There from 4 to less than 1 percent of the employed men worked in agriculture (see Appendixes 1 and 2).

Thus, while the bulk of Labadians were employed in other sectors, a sizeable minority remained in agriculture. The vast majority of agricultural products in Ghana, whether for sale or consumption, were produced with the traditional implements of the hoe and the cutlass (although most Labadians rent tractors to clear the land). Okra, cassava, tomatoes, watermelon, pepper, and eggplant were the crops most frequently grown in Labadi, both for sale and for consumption.

In 1970-1972 most small farmers in Labadi worked land that continued, in principle, to be collectively owned. In order to procure the use of stool land, an individual was required to make the request through the lineage head, who would then approach the head of the maximal lineage or quarter (*akutso*). The *akutshotse* (head of a maximal lineage) might grant the request, on the condition that the chief be informed and sent the customary drink. Although most farmers continued to farm communal stool land, the collective aspect of farming had narrowed considerably. Labor had rapidly become more individualized. The majority of farmers worked the land themselves—clearing, planting, weeding, and harvesting—with help from their nuclear family (wives and children) during some phases of the agricultural cycle, notably during harvest. The wealthier stratum of farmers might employ laborers from the north on a seasonal basis. The farmers that I interviewed, aged fifty to sixty, reported that in their fathers' generation brothers often farmed together; or, if each brother had his own farm, they cooperated on several agricultural tasks. This is substantiated by Field's report in 1940 that every married man had his own farm, but the members of an extended family group aided one another in clearing the land (1940:62). At the time I did research, the farms around Labadi were worked individually, but the extended family continued to be the unit of production in many of the outlying villages. The farmers stated: "In the old days, they understood themselves. Now everybody paddles his own canoe . . . nowadays, you just give money. Things have changed."

The farmers themselves were stratified, a few being relatively well-off, but most engaging in small-scale, often rather precarious, farming. The few who were able to engage in commercial capitalist farming hired laborers, owned large holdings, and often engaged in other agricultural enterprises such as livestock raising. We can infer that this group was not very large from the statistics of the Report on Ghana Sample Census of Agriculture 1970 (see tables 2 and 3). Labadi was included in the statistics for Greater Accra, where although 64 percent of all holdings were used to grow crops mainly for sale, only 11 percent of holders employed "permanent or other" labor.

TABLE 2
HOLDINGS BY TYPE — DISTRICTS

	Subsistence only		Mainly subsistence		Mainly sale		Total	
	No.	*%*	*No.*	*%*	*No.*	*%*	*No.*	*%*
Ghana	111,100	14	289,700	36	404,400	50	805,200	100
Eastern Region	2,700	2	34,900	23	110,600	75	148,200	100
Greater Accra	500	2	9,300	34	17,400	64	27,200	100

Source: Table VII 14, Report on Ghana Sample Census of Agriculture 1970.

TABLE 3
HOLDERS EMPLOYING PERMANENT AND OTHER LABORERS

	Number	Percentage
Greater Accra	3,000	11
Eastern Region	21,400	14
Ghana	97,200	12

Source: Table VI, Report on Ghana Sample Census of Agriculture 1970.

Other farmers privately owned small pieces of land (usually about five acres). Although they might hire some laborers, it was usually on a temporary or seasonal basis, and often they worked alongside them. The poorest group of cultivators usually farmed under five acres of land. Their plots were not, as a rule, privately owned property, but stool land to which they had obtained usufructory rights. The more prosperous in this group might hire laborers to drive the tractors and to help with the weeding, but the predominant unit of labor was the farmer and his family. Farming was extremely precarious: land allocated to this poorest group was often inferior, perhaps located at the bottom of a hill where the crops were frequently threatened by flooding. If there was an overabundance of production and prices dropped drastically, the farmers found themselves unable to sell their crops. Farming was often combined with other occupations, such as fishing or unskilled or semi-skilled work, in an attempt to make ends meet. See Appendix 3 for examples (from my field notes) of the various categories of farmers.

Despite the fact that land was collectively owned and most tools were relatively simple, in 1970-1972 farming was individual and competitive; it was part of the commodity economy and dependent upon market forces. In addition to the fact that most holdings were cultivated primarily for sale, the farmer was required to become involved in the market in order to cultivate at all. Farmers were dependent on the market not only for the sale of their produce but also for the purchase of articles for personal consumption and for the payment of taxes. Tools, fertilizer, and sometimes seeds had to be bought, and tractors had to be rented to clear the land. While most Labadian farmers hoped to use seeds from last year's crop, if these were not available and could not be borrowed, they were purchased at the market. Farmers forced into this position ran the risk of purchasing a set of seeds that had been mixed with "bad" seeds, and becoming victims of "looting," a practice in which the seeds to be sold were boiled in order to ruin the crop and reduce competition.

While many Labadians combined the traditional occupations of farming and fishing, the 1960 census reported that one woman and 248 men were fishermen (see table 1). These figures appear to reflect a decline since 1936, when it was reported that 400 to 500 men engaged in fishing (Brown 1936:12).

The fishermen stated that in the past, men fished in family groups or singly, in their own canoes. By 1970 to 1972 fishing, like farming, reflected the growing trend toward individual ownership on one hand and wage labor on the other. Although some fishermen purchased larger canoes cooperatively, in many cases the canoe and nets were owned by someone other than the fishermen, and the fishermen were, in effect, wage workers. A report researched in 1936 indicates that this process was already fairly well advanced:

several of the canoes were owned by clerks, artisans, traders, and others (Brown 1936:13). The catch was divided into four parts, with one part allocated to the owner of the boat, two parts to the owner of the nets, and the remainder divided among the fishermen, who were usually related to the owner of the boat. Each fisherman usually gave his fish to his wife, or if he did not have one, to his mother, to be sold at the market. Family production continued in the practice of *nǫbua,* an institution where men who fished together, usually part of an extended family group, also worked one another's farms in turn. This cooperative arrangement was reported to be practiced in 1936 (Brown 1936:29). According to an informant, it ceased around 1960. Before commercial construction of fishing vessels, canoes were built on the coast by those who were going to use them. In 1936, a large canoe cost approximately the equivalent of twenty-eight cedis. (In 1970-1972 one cedi was worth one dollar.) Boats are now made inland and transported to the coast. In 1971, the larger fishing vessels that held twelve men cost approximately seven hundred cedis, in addition to the three hundred cedis for an outboard motor and two cedis for the net. Fish caught by the fishermen were packed into cartons and given to the wife of the owner of the boat (if she marketed fish), who would then pay the fishermen a set price. Part of this amount was given to the owner of the boat and net, and the other part was divided among the fishermen, who may or may not be related. In 1971, a box of herring measuring approximately 2 ft. in width, 3 ft. in length, 6 in. in depth usually brought about five cedis in season and eight cedis out of season. Most fishermen, then, were essentially wage laborers.

The declining land base and the other processes of urbanization have conditioned the modification of the lineage and its functions. The lineages continue to be the nominal holders of the land and to give the individual rights to the town offices; they continue to bestow names and perform rites of passage. Other major functions, however, of the lineage — education, law enforcement, and adjudication — have been assumed by regional and national organizations. Large numbers of individuals have moved from lineage houses and set up nuclear family dwellings (see Azu 1974:126 ff. for discussion of such dispersion). One frequently heard, "your own house belongs to you, while your family house belongs to the whole family," as the reason for the change.

As lineage members dispersed, lineage solidarity and authority have generally weakened, but not disappeared, as the meaning of lineage membership has been reworked. Although some authority continued to be vested in the elders, and those lineage members who resided in a lineage compound continued to meet regularly to make important decisions regarding the welfare of the lineage (such as inheritance), lineage councils contained a relatively small proportion of the eligible individuals. Formerly, the responsibility of the major lineage for individual members was manifested in collective responsibility for debts incurred by members and lineage assumption of responsibility for care of the children in case of the father's death. In 1970-1972 the lineage was no longer held responsible for the debt of an individual, although voluntary contributions might be expected. Though the lineage was expected to care for minor children of deceased members, this did not always occur in practice. While the lineage continued to play a role in life cycle rituals, such as birth, marriage, and death, the nuclear family was assuming more and more of the responsibility. Whereas only a generation ago a funeral was the responsibility of the entire major lineage, in 1970-1972 it was the task of members of the immediate family to provide awnings, lights, the funeral fee (*tegbamọ*), the coffin, drinks, and mortuary fees. As we shall note, the shifting locus of responsibility applied to illness as well. While it used to be said that "the lineage inherits" and property was divided (with some exceptions) among two generations of patrilineal relatives, in contemporary times contradictions between collectively-owned lineage property and privately-owned self-acquired property often result in serious disputes, accusations of witchcraft and sorcery, and incidents of illness (see Appendix 4).

Some of these patterns have been documented by Azu in her study of changing kinship patterns in Labadi. She administered a questionnaire to a random sample of 120 people, using the results to compare two quarters in Labadi—Klanna, an old sector "less affected by change," and Emmaus, "the new sector which is undergoing rapid change" (Azu:4). The data she collected substantiated her thesis that while traditional patterns remain, they are being modified by the new patterns of social relationships. She documented significant variation of residence patterns by comparing what she calls the "modern" and "traditional" sectors. In Klanna only 19.3 percent of the married women in the sample resided with their husbands, although many no longer adhered to the traditional pattern where males lived in lineage houses with patrilineally related men and females lived with matrilineally related women. In Emmaus, where 51.9 percent of the married women in the sample resided with their husbands, the residential nuclear family appeared to be emerging, although a large proportion of women (42.4 percent) continued to remain with their mothers.

Patterns of reciprocity, too, seemed to be changing. Azu's comparison of the rates of remittance to parents from children demonstrated significantly less remittance to males in Emmaus than in the more traditional Klanna. In Emmaus only 23.8 percent of the males claimed to receive remittance from children while 42.8 percent claimed they did not receive any (23.8 percent claimed to refuse it). In Klanna, on the other hand, 61.1 percent received remittance and only 27.7 percent said they did not. Of interest is the fact that the figures for females differed very little between Emmaus and Klanna, with 73.3 and 75 percent receiving remittance (Azu:75). Although Azu's study is somewhat limited by her "traditional" versus "modern" dichotomy, her findings do demonstrate the way in which lineage relations persisted, while being adapted and modified. As we shall discuss, questions about mutual aid among extended family members are increasingly raised as the individualization of wage labor and legal contract in the market economy develop.

The rapidity with which the long-established occupations of farming and fishing declined and new ways of making a living emerged can be gleaned from examination of the census reports. The first official census of Labadi in 1891 reported the total population of Labadi to be 7,008, the primary occupations being farming and fishing, with petty trading "on the increase." By the 1960 census, the last census to report Labadi as a separate area, 72 percent of the population reported themselves employed in mining and quarrying, manufacture, construction, commerce, transport, storage, and communication—jobs that did not exist as primary occupations half a century earlier—compared to only 5 percent engaged in agriculture (see table 1). In this section, we shall look a little more closely at how people made their living. We shall find that, as in many former colonial countries, there was the emergence in Ghana of what has been called the "protoproletariat," who appear to be especially vulnerable to psychosomatic disorders, so often treated by healers.

The manner in which the occupational structure developed was largely conditioned by the social and economic needs of colonial capitalism within the world system. An important outcome of this situation was the growth of individualization of enterprise without the proletarianization that might, under other circumstances, provide the basis for new forms of solidarity. For example, mining, created to serve the needs of Great Britain, is dominated by modern capital-intensive establishments producing for the world market. Despite its importance as a national export industry, it only employed 2 percent of the national labor force in 1960 (Caldwell 1967: 57). Alongside this capital-intensive mining sector, however, another 16 percent of the national labor force, reported as employed in mining and quarrying (the collection of stones to be sold to construction companies) were independent diggers, utilizing calabashes (primarily in the Western and Eastern regions) (Szereszewski 1966: 73).

The predominance of the small-scale self-employed was evident in manufacturing. Steel (1977:47-48) reported that between 1957 and 1971 manufacture was the most consistently fast-growing sector under both public and private ownership. The 1960 census reported that in Labadi 12.7 percent of employed males and 9.8 percent of employed females were working in manufacturing. While most females were involved in textile manufacture (7.4 percent), primarily dressmaking, and also in food production, the largest proportion of men employed in this area were engaged in manufacturing transport equipment, furniture, and fixtures. The majority of persons working in the manufacture of food, beverages, textile goods, furniture, and fixtures were self-employed or employed in small concerns. This was not incongruent with the national situation, where manufacturing was dominated by technologically simple concerns that did not include paid employees (Caldwell 1967). By the time of the 1970 census, 90 percent of workers in food, wearing apparel, beverages, and furniture were employed in small-scale concerns (Steel 1977:57).

In construction, the wage laborers outnumbered those who were self-employed, suggesting that small family businesses were less numerous. Nevertheless, there was a high proportion of small concerns: nationally, 59 percent of the establishments had no paid employees in 1960 (Killik 1966:277). Wage laborers were employed primarily by the large-scale European concerns and the Ghana National Construction Corporation, which were responsible for the bulk of public construction, employing 35,000 workers in 1962. The fact that much of the large-scale construction in Ghana occurred in the Accra area (the main sector producing commodities in Accra Central District was construction [Szereszewski 1966:94]) suggests that a significant portion of the 23.6 percent of the male work force in construction consisted of wage laborers.

In 1960, 12.7 percent of the employed males in Labadi worked in transport, storage, and communication. Since nationally one-half of the workers in transport were connected with the mammy lorries (buses) and other trucks (Caldwell 1967:57), it is likely that this percentage was even greater in Labadi, where the numerous lorries are the main form of transportation. Again, these lorries were primarily individual concerns. As Field (1960:135 ff.) has suggested, the inscriptions that grace every vehicle reflect the fears and aspirations of the owner:

> I am laughing because I have been able to buy a lorry, but other people are crying because they can't.
> If anyone knew what a lot of money I was making he would envy me.
> Those who envy me are those of my own house.
> I am well protected, so if envious people plot my downfall, they won't succeed.
> No one likes me to have this lorry; they envy me.
> People have been wondering how I got the money to pay for this lorry.
> Oh, God, help me to pay for this lorry.
> I am sure that some day I shall be able to pay for this lorry.

Services, a very heterogeneous category including government, administration, health, and domestic services, provided employment for 28 percent of the employed men and 11.8 percent of employed women in 1960. In Labadi, as in Ghana as a whole, the government was the major employer of wage laborers in this sector. Included in this category were clerks, civil servants, bureaucrats, intellectual and military elements. There was a wide range of opportunity in this sector, with some white-collar workers beginning at close to the minimum wage and others having the potential to develop an "elite" lifestyle (also see Sanjek 1981:54). The privileged position of some strata of this sector derived from the fact that income was often unusually high due to the shortage of trained personnel, that the salary scale was often adjusted to the expatriate scale, and that many in this group participated directly in local and national policy, thus adding the dimension of power. Education, which has been historically attached to Christianity, was seen as a channel for obtaining wealth and power, and became very significant for entry into these strata (see Owusu 1970:92). It has been suggested that education has the potential for transforming status distinctions into measurable economic class distinctions (McKown 1976:177), and that the way out of poverty lies in the bureaucratic and entrepreneurial ladder, which is linked to educational achievement (Hart 1976:496). As we will note in the course of this study, much of the "anxiety" we encountered in incidents of illness seemed to focus around the question of obtaining an education and, through that, being able to advance to positions of wealth and power. In fact, a complex of symptoms — including somatic complaints such as pain, burning, and numbness in the head, fatigue and sleepiness; sensory impairment, such as visual difficulties; and intellectual impairment, such as poor retention and an inability to grasp the meaning of the printed and sometimes the spoken word — was so common that it has been labeled "brain fag syndrome" (Prince, 1960) and identified in much of West Africa (see Wintrob 1973). Such stresses were aggravated by the fact that, with the recent constrictions of the economy, the rate of upward mobility has been curtailed (Sanjek 1981:17).

It is what the census refers to as commerce that perhaps most accurately expresses the overriding character of the town. In 1960 it included 12.5 percent of the employed men and 73.8 percent of the employed women. In Labadi, commerce is primarily small-scale marketing of agricultural goods, cloth, food, and personal items. Labadi women, who personify the West African market woman, sell at any of the markets in Accra, Labadi, or in between these points. Most of these markets seem to have been established in the early decades of the century. The independence and individualism of Labadi market women is well known. While the husband and wife may cooperate to some extent, particularly if the husband is a farmer, there was general agreement among market women that their profits were their own. Husbands universally complained that their wives retained a larger proportion of the proceeds from sales than they had agreed, and that they had no recourse in correcting this because they had no way of knowing the prices for which their wives sold their products. Women candidly agreed that they misled their husbands, claiming that their profits from marketing were their own business.

This general picture has led observers to conclude that the West African market woman has gained an enviably independent and secure position vis-à-vis men as colonialism has expanded market opportunities. It appears, however, that this improvement in status was illusory, as women were not equally represented in the wage-earning sectors of the economy (see Mullings 1976; Robertson 1976). This trend has been documented; in 1970, although women represented 45 percent of the total employed in Ghana, only 11 percent of employees in large-scale establishments were female (Steel 1977: 59).

Profits from marketing, usually applied to the care of the woman and her children, were precarious and uncertain in 1971. While women marketing farm produce sometimes made ten cedis or more a week, at other times profit and capital were lost and the women were plunged into debt. As we shall see, the vicissitudes of marketing were frequently implicated in illness.

How all this fits together into a class structure has been the subject of several interesting analyses of class in Africa (see Magubane 1977; Cohen 1977; Kitching 1972). We will not go into that discussion here, but rather focus on those aspects that seem to be most relevant to our discussion of illness and healing. Most significant is the predominance in Labadi of the stratum referred to as the "proto-proletariat." Armstrong and McGee (1968), for instance, have distinguished between the capital-intensive, firm-created "formal" sector and the labor-intensive, bazaar-centered "informal" sector. The formal sector involves wage employment in multinational and local firms. The informal sector includes a wide variety of small-scale producers and distributors of goods and services, including small traders, middle traders (wholesale), hawkers, and craftsmen and women. The informal sector usually involves lower wages and longer hours, and is often based on family labor and traditional relationships. Hart (1973) suggests that the distinction between these two sectors is largely one between wage earning and self-employment. These investigators suggest that one result of the colonial mode of development, involving development without industrialization through the orienting of the economy to the production of a cash crop, is that the protoproletariat is a substantial sector of the occupational structure and probably will remain so for some time in Ghana and other former colonial countries. In Ghana, slightly less than one-fifth of the labor force is composed of wage employees (Hart 1976:496).

In Accra, and certainly in Labadi, informal sector activities increased throughout the 1960s. Hart (1973:62) estimates that in 1960 they accounted for nearly one-half of all employment. The fastest growing area of employment in Ghana in the 1960s was services, followed by manufacturing. In both area, it was the informal sectors that increased. By 1970, services in Accra, of which Labadi is a part, accounted for one-third of all employment. Between 1960 and 1970, manufacturing increased 59 percent, with petty production estimated to account for the majority of the increase (Sandbrook and Arn 1977:27-28). In other words, the structural development is such that large proportions of people are involved in the small-scale production of goods and services and the distribution of commodities.

The informal sector is not, however, peripheral to the formal sector. Numerous scholars have commented on the way in which the informal sector functions to support the formal sector: that the labor-intensive traditional sector provides a "sense of employment" for those who are often underemployed (Armstrong and McGee 1968:354); that the availability of cheap goods and services, often a function of greater exploitation in that wages are lower and hours longer, permits a larger share of the economic surplus to be transferred to larger firms (Sandbrook and Arn 1977:23-24); that self-employed petty traders often serve to enrich the manufacturers whose goods they distribute (Sanjek 1981:13). Further, the existence of work in the informal sector that can supplement low wages means that employers can get away with lower wages in the formal sector.

Economic decline has grave ramifications for the informal sector, particularly urban petty commodity production and distribution. In the course of the 1960s the real minimum wage fell by about 45 percent (Sandbrook and Arn 1977:29). Workers in the informal sector depend for their survival on those customers who work in the formal sector, so that the decline that occurred in real wages for skilled and semiskilled workers directly affected them. While profits of market traders varied, the income of street sellers, who make up the bulk of Labadi traders, was estimated to be quite low, with many having a marginal product of zero (Sandbrook and Arn 1977: 31).

Within this sector, the boundaries between employment, under-employment, and unemployment are consequently somewhat unclear. Unemployment in 1960 was reported at 11 percent both for Labadi and for Accra as a whole. However, the meaning of this figure remains disputed. Some suggest that the unemployment statistics are misleading, reflecting primarily first time job seekers who, as middle or primary school graduates, are awaiting white-collar jobs for which they feel themselves qualified (Hart 1976:494; Steel 1977:8). It is suggested that the informal sector provides alternate sources of income to urban dwellers and migrants who seek, but do not find, jobs in the wage sector.

Despite this function, the fact remains that the conditions of employment in the informal sector in which the bulk of Labadians seem to participate can be extremely harsh and precarious. The fact that people must employ a variety of measures to mitigate the effects of unemployment and underemployment helps to explain the persistence of traditional relationships even as the capitalist mode of production propels relationships in more individualistic directions. As we have seen in the case of the farmers who also engaged in skilled and unskilled work, urban workers retained rights to land through lineage membership and farmed it for consumption and market. Non-La urban dwellers purchased, rented, or occupied plots of land that they farmed as a sideline (see also Hart 1973:70).

People relied on exchange and reciprocity among kin in times of crisis and need. In describing another neighborhood of Accra, Hart notes (1973:65):

> Not surprisingly, faced with the impossibility of making ends meet, the urban worker of 1966 often ran up considerable debit accounts, used some of his pay to settle a few bills, went on a short-run binge until penniless, and spent the majority of the month in penury and increasing debt, relying on extended credit facilities and a wide range of putative kin and friends to provide occasional meals, and even lodging, if necessary.... The number of dependents laying claim on a single wage is rendered highly variable through the continuous exchange of personnel, goods, and services within an extended kin-group resident in both urban and rural areas.

Reciprocity based on kinship ties extended beyond the times of crisis. People also utilized it to help with upward mobility. Oppong (1974) found that 54 percent of a sample of Akan civil servants had provided for the education of children of relatives. Similarly, Caldwell (1968:60) found that four-fifths of a sample of Ghanaian college graduates who had already found employment felt that they were obligated to provide at least one-tenth of their income to relatives. In Labadi, Azu (1974:75) found that salaried workers were most involved in giving aid to the parents' and grandparents' generation.

The necessity for reciprocity, however, is most intense in situations of need and crisis, which seemed to be frequent for the urban self-employed. The fact that people had access to land through the village community mode of organization and that they drew on kinship obligations to get by seemed to have a great deal to do with the persistence of traditional forms of organization. Yet, we must note that these so-called traditional relationships had been transformed by, and supported, the capitalist sector. We have noted that officeholders of the village community often became vehicles for manipulating and facilitating the sale of land. We shall see that the traditional healer, while utilizing relationships characteristic of the village community form of organization, often functioned as a private practitioner. While traditional relationships were affected by and interdigitated with the capitalist sector, it was also the case that people used these relationships to mitigate some of the hardships produced by capitalist relations.

The basic transformation—the development of a market economy and capitalist relations of production—took a specific form characteristic of colonial societies. While capitalist development in Europe was accompanied by wide-scale proletarianization, in Ghana we have the emergence of a large sector of self- and family-employed small-scale producers and distributors. This sector of the population, concentrated in urban areas, is perhaps the most adversely affected by the insecurity of the market economy. Occasionally individuals prosper, but it is more often the case that existence is marginal. With the vagaries of the market economy, which has the appearance of a capricious, unknowable force, accusations of witchcraft and sorcery, said to induce illness, flourish.

It is not surprising that there is some evidence people in this sector (Inkeles and Smith 1970), as well as those in lower level bureaucratic positions (Jahoda 1966) and students, as stated previously, seem to be particularly vulnerable to psychosomatic symptoms linked to stress.[8] Although the increased frequency of psychosomatic disorders (and thus the profusion of healing institutions) has been linked to increased anxiety resulting from social change, modernization, and urbanization (see Field 1960; Christensen 1959), the Harvard Project on the Social and Cultural Aspects of Development, carried out in six countries, including Nigeria, seems to indicate that exposure to urban life does not of itself produce psychosomatic symptoms. It is instead the status of individuals within the urban system that seems to condition the occurrence of these phenomena. In Lagos, for example, men between eighteen and thirty-two were questioned about a wide range of psychosomatic symptoms: difficulty in sleeping, trembling limbs, nervousness, beating of heart, shortness of breath, sweating palms, headaches, frightening dreams, and perceiving themselves as affected by witchcraft. No differences were found among several categories of cultivators and urban dwellers. However, when farmers were compared with a sample of nonindustrial workers, including for the most part those in the informal sector as described above, the urban group showed a significantly higher incidence of stress (Inkeles and Smith 1970).

The view that it is the status of individuals within the urban system, not the process of urbanization itself, that is most relevant to understanding social factors in illness is supported by the findings of Beiser, Collomb, Ravel, and their colleagues. They undertook a series of studies among the Serer, a rural Senegalese people, conducting mental and physical examinations of 300 rural Serer and 269 migrants to Dakar (Beiser and Collomb 1981). They found that the hypothesis that urbanization creates mental health risks was not confirmed.

> Thus, in revising our too simplistic theories about the effect of social change, we must take care to distinguish between situations of change which confer subordinate status, powerlessness, joblessness, and frustration upon people, from those which offer openness and real opportunity. (Beiser, M., et al. 1978:86-87)

The way in which therapeutic systems — the response to illness — develop reflects many of the societal processes described above. The emergence of individual wages for labor, individual ownership, and the individualization of legal contracts have ideological ramifications. Alternative ways of conceptualizing and evaluating the person and the relationship between the individual and the collectivity develop with the new pattern of market relations (see Dumont 1965, 1970). The ideological development of new concepts of the individual is given impetus by the predominance of the petit bourgeois stratum and its characteristic commitment to notions of individual effort and destiny. As we shall discuss, ideological frameworks congruent with such views, such as those presented by the spiritualist healer, are embraced and manipulated as they both precipitate and provide the rationale for certain forms of action.

At the same time, harsh conditions, including economic insecurity and ill health, require that people mobilize reciprocal relationships. Traditional healing often provides a context for rallying such resources. Thus, although individualism is increasing, people create and use collective social institutions to confront adversity.

The Healers

ANY observer of contemporary Ghana is immediately impressed by the variety of interpretations of illness and opportunities for treatment available to the sufferer.[1] Today healing in Labadi, and in Accra as a whole, is carried out in three different settings, involving distinct ideologies about the nature of illness, the process of disease, and appropriate therapy. Although there is overlap and continuity, each type of healing is characterized by its own regularities and premises. Autochthonous or traditional healing draws on the indigenous cosmological system for a framework of illness and therapy. Spiritualist therapy is carried out in the setting of the spiritualist churches, utilizing their variation of the Christian world view to construct a framework for illness and treatment. Biomedical therapy is imported via the West and takes place in a formal institutionalized setting, utilizing biomedical explanations and techniques.

One of the most significant differences between these general categories of healing is the extent to which healing and illness involve the kin group. Unschuld has observed that plural medical systems within one society often reflect differential control over medical resources, that historically this process involves "a continuous shift of control over resources from the individual family to the community and then to outside groups and organizations" (1975:306). As one might expect from the decline in lineage corporate functions described in the preceding chapter, the progression of contemporary therapy systems in Ghana reflects this shift away from the family. In this chapter, we will examine the range of therapeutic situations available to the population.

TRADITIONAL HEALING

There are several types of traditional practitioners. Given the variety of practitioners and the different historical points at which they emerge, one might question the validity of placing them in one category labeled "traditional." The term *traditional* is further stigmatized by connotations of immutability and stagnancy. As I shall demonstrate, not only is it true that healing roles have evolved and changed but many practitioners, far from being hidebound, often utilize empirical experimental approaches, varying treatment as new circumstances arise. Because of the large and ever growing body of literature referring to traditional healing, however, I will retain the term to be used in contradistinction to spiritualist and biomedical healing.

In the 1930s, Field (1937:127) distinguished between practitioners who used their powers for good and those who used them for evil. *Wọngtsẹ* (owner of the *wọng*) and *tsofatse* (owner of medicine) were both thought to be concerned with curing, while the *wọngtsulọ* was considered to be primarily involved in killing and harming. By 1955, Acquah's (1958:123) survey counted 274 practitioners in Accra, for 167 of whom healing was their sole or main source of income. She described the following types of practitioners: the herbalist, who has a broad knowledge of herbs and who may also use Western drugs and magico-religious cures; the medicine man, who possesses *ju-ju* and whose clients generally seek success; the Muslim healers, who may be of several types; the "fetish" priests and priestesses, who divine through a particular god; and the soothsayer, who is only concerned with divination. In the neighborhood of Labadi when I did research, people distinguished *tsofatsẹmei* (owners of medicine), *wulọmei* (priests), and *wọyei* (spirit mediums) as the major categories of practioners involved in what they referred to as traditional therapy.

Indigenous categories, then, are often differentiated by function. Many African societies make a distinction between those who are primarily ritual practitioners and those who may possess specialized medical knowledge.[2] In Ghana, the different categories of healers reflect not only variation of function but also the evolution of role specialization.

As we noted in chapter 1, archival and oral evidence indicate that the roles of priest, political leader, and healer were at one time fused in the head of the kinship group. This elder (tsę) had charge of the family gods. At the time I did research, most priests and some mediums continued to be associated with the dzemawǫdzii. The dzemawǫdzii are those family gods worshipped by the entire town, known as "gods of our fathers" or "gods of origin or creation" (*ade-bǫǫ*). Associated first with lineages, then adopted by the entire town, they are said to uphold the collectively-held values. During hǫmǫwǫ, a ritual that stretches over a six-month period, they are collectively worshiped by the town, with each lineage, represented by elders and priests, being assigned a specific role. Through priests, who were also elders, the kinship group continued to be linked to medical knowledge and practice. There is a plethora of other deities, referred to as *wǫdzii* (*s. wǫng*). For these gods, the ritual unit was based on the individual rather than the lineage. They were not associated with shared values and generally did not possess priests, although they often were associated with spirit mediums.

I interviewed five priests and ten spirit mediums, focusing on those of the major town gods. Most of the priests limited their involvement in healing to divination. While spirit mediums shared with priests the ability to contact gods as their main distinction, the mediums were often more involved in other aspects of healing. For example, mediums often had a working knowledge of herbs. The following example is taken from my field notes:

> D., a Labadi woman in her late fifties, is a spirit medium. When she was about thirty, a petty trader and a Christian, she began to have spells in which she would "feel dizzy, shake all over, and abuse people." Her family took her to a tsofatsę, who informed them that a god wanted her to become his medium. She trained with a medium in Labadi and she now teaches apprentices herself. She has built her own well-furnished house, with a shingle outside, proclaiming that she is a medium and open for business. Although she has some knowledge of herbs, she states that her power to cure is a result of her god (wǫng) informing her of each step.

Healing roles were differentiated by gender. The relative positions of medicine owners and priests, who are male, and spirit mediums, who are generally female, reflect the differentiation between men and women. Male and female roles appear to be somewhat complementary in traditional religion. Although the priests (men) were ultimately responsible for the care of the gods, the spirit mediums (women) were their mouthpieces, communicating the wishes of the gods. Despite what could be and often was, a powerful position, the mediums were perceived as somewhat subordinate. The medicine owners alleged that, although some mediums were competent healers, they were most effective when trained by medicine owners, and, even then, women were not likely ever to become as knowledgeable as men. Some medicine owners claimed that, although they, like the mediums, were possessed by gods, because of their greater strength they, unlike the mediums, manifested no outward signs of possession. "We do not give way. We train the spirit mediums." It is interesting to note here that members of the spiritualist church gave the same explanation as to why more women manifest signs of possession than men. "The men are above us so they can resist it and stand it; but women cannot stand it. It is as when a child cuts his finger, he will begin to shout, but a grown person will not need to do that."

Yet some women were able to obtain a degree of wealth and influence through becoming mediums in contemporary Labadi. The most extreme such case that I encountered was that of the spirit medium of the Akonnedi shrine at Larteh. Although she was born in Labadi, she was at that time the chief spirit medium of a non-Labadi shrine. I attended a "sherry party" to welcome her back from a successful tour of the United States, where she had been the guest of a group of Afro-Americans. Chiefs, lawyers, doctors, politicians, and other notable dignitaries attended the gathering; many greeted her in a way that accorded her more status than several of the chiefs. However, the Akonnedi medium is an unusual case in obtaining such prominence, wealth, and power. It appears that the situation of the average spirit medium is, in a sense, analogous to that of market women (Mullings 1976). Although such a role may offer a temporary avenue of upward mobility for a few women, because it is confined to the traditional sphere its potential for raising the status of women in a long-range sense is limited (see also Berger 1976).

A few priests and some mediums were not associated with the lineage and town gods, but with gods independent of the lineage relationships (wodzii). These gods, not directly linked to lineage groups, seem to be of relatively recent origin (see discussion in chapter 3). Tigari,[3] for example, became very popular in the early 1950s.

Membership, for which adherents paid a fee, was not based on kinship (Christensen 1954).

> C., is a Tigari priest and so is called by his name, with Tigari added as a suffix. He lives in a large three-sided compound decorated with symbols inscribed on one wall. He stated that Tigari, a famous "witch-finding" god that emerged in Ghana in the 1950's, originated in Ouagadougou, Upper Volta, where he journeyed to learn about it. Adherents must "drink medicine," take kola nuts and participate in prescribed ritual. He claims that the number of Tigari adherents declined between the 1950's and 1960's. He first learned to work with the supernatural from his father, who himself "possessed" two *wodzii* of his own. He has been practicing for twenty-five years.

The most efficacious healers were thought to be the tsofatsemei — owners of medicine, who possessed specialized knowledge of healing. That the role of medicine owner, though long-established, was a later and more specialized role than that of priest is supported by oral tradition in Labadi. Among medicine owners, the most respected were those who were members of the traditional society. As such, they had undergone recognized training and were linked with, and responsible to, the town and lineage gods. By the time Field did research in the 1930s, the members of the society of medicine owners constituted a court that tried all disputes involving affairs of the gods, but "they have not the power over priests" (Field 1937:42). These medicine owners, possessing both medical and ritual knowledge, conceptualized the two realms as inseparable for effective therapeutic practice. The tsofatsemei were very much involved with lineage therapy. In 1970 to 1972, there were twelve officially recognized tsofatsemei, who were members of the traditional society of medicine-owners. I interviewed ten of these (two were too old to be interviewed) and five part-time healers, inquiring particularly about causes of illness and treatment. The tsofatsemei ranged in age from forty to ninety years. The majority had no Western education, although three were educated through middle school. Tsofatse is a sex-linked role, only filled by males.

Although only one of the healers I interviewed claimed that he did not utilize the supernatural in healing (a Muslim healer — *maalam*), some healers combined biomedical and indigenous elements of medicine.

Mr. B., a forty-year-old Anglican, is a regional officer of the Ghana
Psychic and Traditional Healing Association and a traditional office-
holder in a suburban village, where he lives with his wife and ten children. He is employed full-time as a line machine worker at a printing
press and practices healing part-time. On my first visit, I was taken to
a clinic-like room. Bottled powdered medicines that he had processed
from herbs were stored around the room. He demonstrated apparatus
used to process an antipyretic herb. It worked by the principle of distil-
lation, with the herbs being heated in a can over the coal stove. Piping
from a lorry was attached, by a paste made of maize and water, to the
top of the can. The piping which was submerged in water extended
over a bottle where the distilled medicine was collected. He had attended elementary school and used Western anatomy and medical
books. He recorded symptoms and treatments of each case, in a notebook. On my second visit, he took me to the back of the compound
where the traditional healers' paraphernalia were in evidence: representations of the wọdzii and streamers of red, white, and black calico.
He had aspired to become a doctor, but his parents had been unable
to afford to educate him. He was taught about herbs by a malaam, in
exchange for information about ritual healing.[4]

The tsofatsẹmei were the most specialized of the traditional
practitioners. Specialists distinguish themselves by such features as
remuneration for services, formal training, and use of technical ter-
minology, monopoly and license. Thus, while the priests remained
bound by custom to accept only specific types of compensation
(drink, eggs, chickens) for consultation with the town gods, growing
commercialization characterized the practice of medicine owners
and spirit mediums, who were permitted to set fees and accept cash
as well as compensation in kind. For the medicine owners and the
mediums, however, a large percentage of their fees came only in return for success. They did not have the control over medical resources that allows for the prepayment, regardless of success (see
Unschuld 1975), that we find in biomedicine.

While priests fill ascriptive roles, medicine owners and spirit
mediums may be achieved roles. They control certain areas of
knowledge and may train apprentices for remuneration. Such training involves the transference of knowledge, including technical ter-
minology. The society of medicine owners (*agbaafoi*) functioned as
a body to control and legitimate medical-ritual practice.

During the Nkrumah government (1957-1966), autochthonous practitioners were recognized and legitimated in an attempt to reverse the setbacks suffered by traditional healing during the colonial period. The Ghana Psychic and Traditional Healing Association, formed to advance, regularize, and research traditional methods of healing, attempted to include all categories of people concerned with African healing. With 2,305 registered members in Greater Accra, the constitution required that all people calling themselves *wọngtsemei* (wọng owners), wulọmei (priests), and wọyei (spirit mediums) register with the association and made it illegal for those who were not members to practice. By the time I did research in 1970-1972, it had, like many of the organizations founded by Nkrumah, fallen into disrepute. Nevertheless, I met a number of the officers of the association who claimed that meetings were still being held. New efforts to legitimate and train traditional healers are presently underway (see Warren 1979; Twumasi 1979).

In the process of legitimization, diversification, and specialization, healing roles were becoming gradually alienated from direct control by the kinship group. While there were some traditional practitioners who were not aligned with the kinship structure, the recognized medicine owner (tsofatsẹ), particularly those who were members of the traditional society (*agbaafoi*), continued to practice a brand of medicine and ritual that had its base in the kinship structure.

SPIRITUALIST HEALING

Spiritualist healing further removes the healing process from the context and control of the kinship group. Such healing takes place in "independent" churches, which practice an African form of Christianity (see Bond, Johnson, and Walker 1979). The designation "spiritualist" (or "spiritist" or "spiritual") is a reference to the invocation of the Holy Spirit.

As we noted in chapter 1, Christianity was introduced into Ghana with the European presence and from the start was connected with health matters as missions imported medical officers to care for their personnel (Twumasi 1979:351).

The independent church movement came later to Ghana than to the rest of Africa. The visit of the Grebo prophet Harris initiated the first independent churches in 1914, but their spread was rather limited. The Church of the Twelve Apostles began with two people converted by Harris, and the Musama Disco Christo Church was founded in 1919. By 1955 a survey of Accra found only eleven independent churches, with membership being 2 percent of the population. The surge of independent churches that occurred in the rest of Africa in the 1950s came to Ghana in the late 1960s.[5] By 1970 Opoku (1970) estimated that there were 300 independent churches in Ghana. In Labadi alone, in 1970-1972 there were ten permanent independent churches.

All of the leaders of the spiritualist churches in Labadi engaged in healing. Although spiritualist churches come and go constantly, there were ten churches that had remained in existence for a period of a year and were housed in permanent structures. I interviewed all ten founders of the churches, as well as their assistants.

As one might expect, the spiritualist healers had more education by European standards than the traditional healers. Six of the ten were literate and had attended school to levels ranging between form two and higher education. For a few of them (like a few of the traditional healers), participation in the spiritualist church seemed to be an avenue taken when others were unavailable.

> Reverend B. is a twenty-one-year-old Fanti. However, his mother was born and raised in Labadi. He attended a Catholic school, but was not able to finish because of financial difficulties. After attending revival meetings he converted to the "apostolic" religion. He was a professional blacksmith before becoming a full-time pastor.
>
> The church, located on the main road of Labadi, consists of a large room housing several rows of benches. A small back room contains approximately sixty corked bottles of sacred water. In addition to the main church, started in Kumasi by an Ashanti, there are now six branches in Accra and three branches "out-station." He was assigned by the head office to start a branch in Labadi to "save lost souls who don't know how God loves them and how he can work miracles and heal the sick." The Labadi branch has been in existence for one year and eight months. He claims that the church presently has approximately five hundred members. All are from Labadi and all except fifty are women, mainly petty traders.

Two of the ten founders were female. Similar to spirit mediumship in traditional religion, leading a successful church can be an avenue to some financial success for women. However, the leaders of the major spiritualist churches in the La area at the time I did research were male. Women often participated in the leadership as visionaries, healers, and assistants, but relatively rarely as the central minister. Both of the female founders in Labadi were unable to read, as compared to only two of the eight male founders.

> Sister C. is a twenty-year-old unmarried woman from Accra. She has never attended school and claims to be illiterate but able to read the Bible. She became a Christian at the age of twelve, but "did not concentrate on Christ." For the last six years, she has "had the spirit," as manifested by her visions, healing, and speaking in tongues. For two years she had a church in central Accra, and then "the spirit pushed her to Labadi," where she has been for the past three years.
>
> The church consists of a makeshift building. She claims to have two hundred members, all Labadians, with women predominating. In addition to the Sunday meeting, there is another general meeting on Tuesday, and Thursday is reserved for healing. She is the main minister and has several male and female assistants who pray or preach when she is not available.

Nine of the ten claimed to have experienced a prophetic vision that resulted in the founding of the church.

> Reverend A. is the founder of a church outside the center of town. He is a fifty-eight-year-old Labadian, who is married and the father of ten children. Educated to form two, he was a carpenter before founding the church. He claims that, although he was a Christian since childhood, he only began to see visions thirty-one years ago when he was stricken with an illness. "Before I was healed, I saw a vision and angels told me to build a church in this place. When the sickness came, I would feel dizzy when I was working. My heart would start to burn within me." He did not consult a medical doctor about this illness; someone took him to a spiritualist church and he subsequently improved.
>
> The church has been in existence for six years. For five of those years, the congregation met in his house, which he occupies with his wife and children. One year ago the temple, consisting of a large, rectangular structure of corrugated iron, was built across the courtyard from his house. The large white cross standing in the middle of the courtyard is reminiscent of the *otutu* of the traditional healer. According to the Reverend A., the church membership hovers around fifty, most of whom are fishermen, market women, and unemployed people.

Women predominate. He has three male assistant pastors, all of whom see visions. General meetings are held on Sunday; Friday is reserved for healing and Tuesday for those who wish to conceive.

All spiritualist healers claimed that some diseases may have a natural cause, but all have a spiritual component. Most had no objection to patients receiving biomedical treatment while attending the church and some even approved of African treatment as long as it was confined to herbal and not supernatural ministrations. In fact, on one occasion a founder developed a sermon around the issue of biomedical versus African herbal medicine. He warned the congregation against the view that the sick cannot be healed unless they receive an injection from the hospital and urged them to use the herbs that God had created for their use, quoting verses from the Bible to support his point. He closed by reiterating that the people should turn back to these herbs but avoid traditional religion. Since spiritualist healers generally did not dispense pharmaceutical medicines, they did not object to the patient obtaining such treatment elsewhere. But they insisted on exclusive control of the "spiritual" realm. As we shall demonstrate, such control involves jurisdiction over a new ideological orientation and usurping the traditional authority of the kinship group.

Similar to traditional healing, spiritualist churches may be a means to achieve financial rewards. In many ways, the surge of spiritualist churches is analogous to the proliferation of small business in Labadi. Spiritualist churches often functioned as small businesses. Most founders seemed to have expectations that the church would become a fairly lucrative enterprise that would allow them a certain degree of upward mobility and prestige. Although the offering alone might not fulfill this expectation, there were additional sources of income. Founders who attained a reputation for success, particularly in healing, might achieve a measure of prestige, attracting influential church members. In this way the founders were often able to obtain sponsors who helped them to expand their enterprise and influence. Some were even able to go abroad and there obtain contacts with U.S. based Pentecostal groups that were in a position to render concrete moral and financial support. Such a relationship also increased the prestige of the founder in Ghana, which could, in turn, bring him more wealthy and influential clients. This aspect has been described in other parts of Ghana:

clearheaded people primarily interested in making money establish churches the way others set up businesses. Ostensibly, the sects and separatist churches are there to show votaries the true way to the "everlasting kingdom" and salvation . . . however, as a few skeptics admit, they are a major source of income and power for the founders. (Owusu 1970:109-110)

Most successful healers, then, had the potential for the accumulation of some wealth. But as important, as we shall demonstrate, is the function of the healer in mediating a new ideology.

BIOMEDICAL HEALING

Although biomedical facilities are not part of this study, the utilization of ritual therapies can only be fully understood in the context of their relationships to biomedicine. As early as 1844, British medical officers were posted to what was then the Gold Coast to care for the health needs of the senior colonial administrative officers. Although over time the use of biomedical facilities was extended to those elements of the local population who were working for the administration, the colonial health service remained largely a medical service for officers and their families. The missions, however, did set up some dispensaries and infirmaries to administer drugs to the local population under their influence. Needless to say, medical care was tied to the other activities of the mission. Some public health measures that benefited the entire population were instituted in Accra. The installation of pipeborne water, for example, reduced the incidence of amoebic and bacillary dysentery, diarrhea, typhoid fever, guinea worm, and other waterborne diseases (Patterson 1979:254). It was not until 1924, however, that a general health plan directed toward the general population was enacted, establishing Korle Bu Hospial in Accra.

Thus, there was a basis for arguing, as some Africans did, that the colonial public health policy "protects the few and abandons the many" (cited in Patterson 1979:256). The approach toward control of mosquitoborne diseases, which included residential segregation of Europeans (along with inspection of African domestic water supplies and measures to prevent breeding in ponds and lagoons), understandably raised the ire of Africans. It is not surprising that we find differences in the assessment of the performance of the colonial government in the field of health. Patterson (1979:257) suggests that, "While the colonial government might have done more to improve its capital . . . reasonable public health progress was made." Twumasi, a Ghanaian, concludes that the moderate attempts made by the colonial government "were too few and belated to meet the overall health needs of the country in this period" (1972:64).

After independence, the Nkrumah government in 1957 established health centers throughout the country. By 1971, Ghana had 12,390 persons per physician; in 1972, there were 780 persons per hospital bed (United Nations Department of International Economic and Social Affairs, 1980).

Despite impressive postindependence achievements in health, political independence has not succeeded in eliminating the glaring disparities in the distribution of health care or in revising the essential character of the health system. Geographic and class disparities are pervasive and the orientation of the health system has continued to be curative. In 1969, while there were 5.5 doctors per 100,000 people, this limited number of doctors was concentrated in a few towns and regions. For example, there were 29.5 doctors per 100,000 in Accra, but only 1.3 doctors per 100,000 in the Upper Region (Sharpston 1972:206). In 1973 the situation remained about the same. Of 951 physicians, 82 percent of those in public services worked in towns and cities with a population of 20,000 or more, covering only 18 percent of the population. Thus, the National Health Planning Unit notes that at least 70 percent of the population is without easy access to the formal health care system (Warren 1979:11).

The emphasis on curative rather than preventive services has not been substantially changed. In Ghana 88 percent of funds allocated to health are used for curative programs, as opposed to 12 percent for preventive efforts. Twumasi notes:

> Besides the effect of economic incentives, there is an additional Western influence which can be seen as having a negative effect upon health care in the country. In most of the Western countries there has been and still is a strong influence toward curative medicine. . . . Treating directly the infectious diseases and other organic disorders is of high priority in any developing country; but the tendency to emphasize the curative at the expense of the preventive can be considered serious. (1972:70)

The institutionalization of Western psychiatry has not been considered to be a health priority, and facilities continue to be limited (Twumasi 1979:352). With the exception of a brief period in 1929, there were no psychiatrists in Ghana prior to 1951. In 1888 the High Court in Accra was converted to a lunatic asylum for custodial segregation of the mentally ill. In 1970 there were two psychiatric hospitals in the country, with a total bed capacity of 687 (Twumasi 1972:68): Ankarful near Cape Coast receives patients from the Central and Western regions; the Accra Mental Hospital, still popularly known as "the asylum," receives patients from the remaining regions. Care has been primarily custodial, with limited drug treatment.

Biomedical facilities, then, continue to be based on the Euro-American model of curative, institutional-centered activities. As such, this system goes farthest in removing medical resources and decisions from the patient and family, and places such responsibilities with a specialized group that has no formal ties to the patient and family. This is particularly striking in the case of psychiatric services (see Higginbotham 1979:16). As we pointed out in the introduction, the National Health Planning Unit has criticized this model and noted its limitations. One feature of the attempt to transform the health system was the decision to involve traditional practitioners in health care.

CHOICE OF THERAPY

Patients and their kin devise treatment regimens that make selections from among the many possibilities. In general, the frequency of utilization of biomedical facilities is high, but often seems to occur in combination with other forms of treatment. Citing figures for patients treated at Korle Bu Hospital in Accra, Twumasi (1975:101 ff.) claims that in 1967 the majority of people in Accra availed themselves of biomedicine. Although numerical data on utilization of traditional and spiritualist healers are not available, the evidence seems to indicate that they are patronized in conjunction with other forms of treatment. Jahoda's (1961) study of traditional healers, spiritualist churches, and the mental hospital in Accra demonstrated that indigenous healers handled many of the physical and mental ailments of the general population. The majority of traditional and spiritualist healers I interviewed did not object to their patients consulting a biomedical practitioner or utilizing such a practitioner concomitantly, and, in my sample, the majority of patients participated, often serially, in all of these systems.

It is not surprising, then, that despite significant differences between categories of treatment alternatives, we do not find distinct categories of patients associated with one or the other modality of healing. Acquah's (1958) survey of 501 persons in Accra indicates that both educated and uneducated make use of Western medicine. Jahoda's (1961:256) sample of 315 adult patients who patronized traditional healers was generally congruent, in terms of literacy and occupation, with the Accra population at large. Warren's (1978) study of 4,266 Techiman-Bono in Ghana, categorized by subgroups according to religion, age, and education, concluded that Western-educated Bono students go to indigenous priests for treatment, that monolingual Bono of the older generation attend the mission hospital, and found a striking similarity of response in all four subgroups. My patient sample, drawn from traditional and spiritualist healers, included all but the highest strata.

Choice of therapy is determined by a complex interaction of variables. While accessibility is related to extent of utilization, it does not seem to be the determining variable in Labadi, where biomedical facilities—hospitals, clinics of private doctors, midwives, and druggists—are available. In addition to variables such as rural-urban living, extent of formal education, availability of clinic or relevant medical technology, age, and sex, Twumasi (1975:104) cites extent of kinship influence and type of therapy. Recently, Janzen (1978) has documented the role of the kinship group in therapy management in Zaire. In Labadi some segment of the kinship unit is usually involved in decision making, and the way in which the illness is perceived, both by the patient and the kin group, seems to influence the choice of therapy.

A major variable, cutting across educational differences, seems to be the nature of the illness. Making choices among medical systems according to their perceived efficacy for types of disorders is a general practice in Africa (and elsewhere). In Zaire, patients distinguish between "diseases of god," which can be treated by biomedical facilities, and "diseases of man," for which only traditional practitioners are effective (Janzen 1978). The Akamba of Kenya distinguish between *kikamba* illnesses and hospital illnesses (Mburu 1977:

167). Among the Yoruba, traditional healers are considered most appropriate for treatment of smallpox, madness, and diseases of the reproductive system (MacLean 1976:306). The Hehe of Tanzania consult European-trained medical workers for "natural" diseases, and traditional doctors for "other than natural" diseases (Edgerton 1971:260). Among the Zulu of South Africa, *umkhulane* illnesses (illnesses that "just happen") are believed to be understood by the Western-trained doctor and respond readily to his treatments, while *ukufa kwabantu* (diseases of the people) can only be understood and treated by Africans (Ngubane 1976:322-323).

In Labadi, as in other areas of Africa, people distinguished between natural illnesses and spiritual illnesses. In general, it was thought that natural illnesses may be treated by all categories of practitioners, with biomedical practitioners often being most effective. Spiritual illnesses, in contrast, were not amenable to biomedical techniques and must be treated by practitioners who deal in the spiritual realm. As is true in most of the world, people considered accessibility and evidence of efficacy in choosing among treatment alternatives. For most illnesses that were thought to fall within the category of natural illnesses, patients first consulted a biomedical practitioner, but where the cure was not rapidly forthcoming, or when the patient or patient's family perceived a spiritual aspect to the illness, a healer who took cognizance of the spiritual became necessary. Where Western medicine was deemed effective, particularly in treating infectious diseases, patients, including traditional healers, took advantage of it. Where illnesses remained essentially uncontrollable and unpredictable within the biomedical paradigm, patients sought other alternatives: the traditional or spiritualist healer remained the treatment of choice. Thus, people made selections based on their perception of the efficacy of treatment alternatives.

As with chronic illnesses, mental disorders are not effectively treated by biomedicine. For most parts of Africa, the literature reports that mental illness is deemed unsuitable for biomedical care (MacLean 1976; Twumasi 1975:102). It is generally agreed that in Ghana the majority of psychiatric problems are treated by indigenous healers (see Jahoda 1961; Twumasi 1975; Twumasi 1979; Field 1960), despite high utilization of biomedical facilities (Forster 1972). Most telling is the comment by Dr. E. F. B. Forster, Director of the Accra Mental Hospital:

Owing to the typically asylum character of the hospitals, the traditional medical practitioners flourish and are often consulted and give some form of treatment before any patients are removed to scientific medical institutions, irrespective of the illness. Except in the case of the destitute insane, no patient went direct to mental hospital for treatment. The traditional medical practitioners are regarded as able physicians who possess skills unequalled by those of the scientific medical practitioners, particularly where the treatment of psychosomatic disorder is concerned. (cited in Twumasi 1972:68-69)

Jahoda (1961:268) likewise notes, "Were it not for this extensive preliminary screening [by traditional healers and healing churches] . . . mental hospitals would be overwhelmed by a flood of cases with whom they could not possibly deal."

The fact that the great majority of mental disorders were treated by autochthonous and spiritualist therapists was not simply a reflection of unavailability of medical facilities. It was also an acceptance of the type of treatment that involves the examination of the social matrix of the patient. In the next section we will examine the premises and techniques of healing in the settings in which the majority of mental therapy occurs — the traditional healer and the spiritualist healer.

PART II

THE ETHNOGRAPHY OF HEALING

Introductory Note

BECAUSE the modalities most frequently utilized for mental healing appeared to be the traditional healer and the spiritualist church, I focused on these two therapeutic settings. Thus I selected one traditional and one spiritualist healer for intensive study, although I administered structured interviews to a sample of traditional healers and to all spiritualist healers as discussed in the previous chapter. Given the limitations of time and the fact that care in the Accra Mental Hospital is primarily custodial, I limited my work in this setting to a few observations and interviews.

The problem of the extent to which the two healers are representative is a complex one. A primary consideration in selecting the two therapists was their impact on the town, specifically the relative frequency with which their facilities were utilized. In this respect, the two healers selected were unambiguous choices. The autochthonous healer was generally recognized by all strata of the town as the most competent tsofatse and the only specialist in mental disorders. The spiritualist healer was the founder of the spiritualist church with the largest membership in Labadi. If the size of membership is any indication of importance, the spiritualist church I selected far outstripped the other churches, with a membership of one thousand compared to claims of between fifty and a few hundred typical of the other churches. Structured interviews were administered to ten of the twelve recognized tsofatsemei; in all other spiritualist churches the founders were interviewed and a few meetings were observed. The tsofatse selected was typical in terms of age, training, place of brith, and status as a ritual specialist. He was somewhat atypical in that he was literate.

The founder of the spiritualist church where intensive study was undertaken was not atypical in terms of age or literacy. Although several of the founders were not born in Labadi, it at first appeared that the fact that he was born in Accra might have some bearing on his healing techniques. Comparison with other spiritualist healers, however, demonstrated no significant differences in the general framework of illness and healing employed between those who had been born in Labadi and those born elsewhere. It soon became clear that through church members and other networks, the spiritualist healer had quite as much access to information about the interpersonal relationships as did the traditional healer, although he did not choose to utilize such data for the same purposes.

As in all medical systems, much of healing is art, involving the idiosyncratic. Although I have indicated where significant differences may exist between healers, interview and observational data suggest that both healers were typical of others in their category with reference to theories of etiology of illness and methods of treatment. As I will discuss in more detail, the general agreement is not surprising when we consider that one of the tasks of psychotherapy is that of transmitting a specific version of the social order.

In both settings the patients were, in general, congruent with the general population, with exceptions that I will discuss below. During two selected periods of one month each, I kept records on all patients I observed at the traditional healers and the spiritualist healers, systematically varying the time of the visit,[1] giving me a sample population for each institution in two random months. At the traditional healers, I have included only those patients that I encountered,[2] for a total of twenty-seven. At the church, I limited the sample to church members (as opposed to including other visitors) who consulted the healer individually or in meetings for illness-related problems. The total number of patients was twenty-four.

With the exception of the elite group of university graduates, all strata of the general population were represented. Women tended to make greater use of both forms of healing than did men. While the 1960 census of Labadi listed the population at 50.7 percent male and 49.3 percent female, of a total sample population of 51, males constituted 39.2 percent (20) and females 60.8 percent (31). If we remove children under fifteen, the gender differences become more marked, with males being 30.8 percent (12) and females 69.2 percent (27). The gender discrepancy is more pronounced in the spiritualist church, where 29.2 percent (7) of the patients were males and 70.8 percent (17) of the patients were females, than at the traditional healer, where 35.3 percent (6) of the patients were male and 64.7 percent (11) were female.

Several factors might have a bearing on the fact that women seemed to make proportionately greater use of the healers in both settings than men. Concern with reproductive functions or a greater degree of traditional orientation have been suggested as relevant issues. In the absence of figures concerning the usage of biomedical facilities, these variables are difficult to evaluate. It is of interest, however, that the figures on admission of women into the Accra Mental Hospital from 1959 to 1971 are significantly lower than those for men (Forster 1972). A related line of studies has associated increased participation of women in cults with their low status in society (see Lewis 1971; Messing 1958), with cult membership increasing their prestige. While participation in this form of traditional healing does not result in an organized cult relationship, in the case of spiritualist healing people do become church members and participate in the activities of the church. Except in the instance of a very few, however, it is rare that such participation becomes a vehicle for mobility.

It is the case, however, that women are disproportionately represented among the small-scale self-employed or protoproletariat. In Labadi, the vast majority of women work in marketing, and certainly the majority of women patients are in petty marketing. As we shall see in the case studies, it is here that life is most uncertain and that personalistic explanations for misfortune abound. Men are also involved in fields that leave room for witchcraft and sorcery as explanations of success and failure, but they are more evenly distributed across the occupational spectrum than women, who are concentrated in the informal sector.

Examining the patient population over six years of age, we find slightly greater rates of those who have never attended school: 42.9 percent (6) of males and 73.1 percent (19) of females, as compared to 30.1 percent of the general male population in Labadi and 60.4 percent of the female population according to the 1960 census.[3] In both forms of healing, the highest numbers of patients who had never attended school were found among females, although the spiritualist church had a higher proportion of illiterate males as compared with the traditional healer, where a higher proportion of females who had never attended church was found. In the spiritualist church, 57.1 percent (four of seven males over age six) had never attended school, while the rate for women was 66.7 percent (10 out of 15). The patient population also included three people with commercial and technical training. At the traditional healer's compound, 28.6 percent, or two of the seven males over six, and 81.8 percent, or nine of the eleven women over fifteen, had never attended school. Yet the patient population included six patients with middle, secondary, teachers', and commercial training. It is, thus, difficult to generalize except to note that at neither institution did we encounter patients (although there were clients and church members) with university educations.

Overall, it appears that the patient population is not significantly discrepant from the general population in terms of education and literacy. Although it is difficult to draw conclusions from such small numbers, other studies support this point of view. Jahoda's study of 302 adult patients of five healers in Accra noted that "the healers' clients did not differ markedly, in terms of literacy and occupation, from the Accra population at large" (1961:99). Although Jahoda suggested that churches seem to be utilized by literates, of the eight longitudinal cases I will present, five of the patients (63 percent) had, at some point in their illness careers utilized both traditional and spiritualist therapy, suggesting that the lines of distinction cannot be so clearly drawn. (Five of the eight had also utilized biomedical facilities.)

Thus, although I have focused on the patient at the traditional healer's compound or at the spiritualist church, in reality the majority of patients move back and forth between treatment modalities. Such behavior is perhaps particularly characteristic of an urban population. As residents of Accra, the capital city, people live in close proximity to a range of treatment modalities and make use of them.

I concentrated, then, on two treatment facilities with the goal of explicating the framework for the treatment of mental illness. To this end I utilized structured and unstructured interviews with healers, patients, relatives, and a sample of residents of Labadi that varied according to age, sex, occupation, and education; some componential analysis where feasible; content analysis of sermons, prayers, and so forth; observations of ritual events within and outside of the therapeutic setting; and observation of patients and others in therapy and in normal life pursuits.

In order to understand the way in which therapy operates in each setting, I utilized case studies. In the study of traditional therapy, I relied primarily on the case studies to demonstrate the ways in which ideas about illness are translated into actions. I have presented, in detail, all cases that were diagnosed as mental illness by the healer and that were thought to be serious enough to be remanded to residential custody. I have not presented those cases that were already in residence before observation began.[4]

In the spiritualist setting, the major healing rituals took place within the context of meetings. Patients did not receive the individualized attention that was the case in traditional healing and were generally left to themselves to carry out basically similar healing rituals. Thus, I have focused on analysis of the meetings and sermons, which were the main vehicles of learning for the patients. For comparative purposes, I have presented some cases to illustrate the way in which ideas about healing are operationalized. The cases presented were those that were in residence during one selected month of the observation period. It was not possible to present all the patients who were in residence during the period of the study: patients came and went with frequency, without the knowledge of the healer, in a less structured situation than what pertained at the traditional healer's compound.

The emphasis on case studies has the disadvantage of more limited numbers than a survey approach might produce, but it permits a richness of contextual data not found in more quantitative approaches. Long-term, longitudinal studies allow us to follow the patient through different phases of illness and treatment, unwrapping the layers that envelop illness behavior—the various diagnoses and perceptions both through time and according to the vantage point of the observer. Thus, it becomes possible to evaluate what people say in the light of actual behaviors over time. For both sets of cases, then, patients were studied in one or the other type of treatment facility (although, as we have noted, patients often went back and forth between both). Patients were observed almost daily during the period in which they were followed; they and as many members of their family as possible were interviewed; major rituals and therapeutic episodes were observed; and gross changes in affect were observed and recorded.[5]

With respect to this last point, I resisted the temptation to attempt to affix biomedical disease labels to specific conditions. The reader will, no doubt, note similarities of symptom complexes and frankly organic symptoms. Interesting though an exploration of this area might be, comparison of Ga and biomedical disease categories is beyond the scope of this volume. Thus, I relied on the healer's diagnoses that a disorder involved mental illness at some level, and confined myself to descriptions of affect and to reporting symptoms described by the patient and family. For an overview of the epidemiology of mental disorders in Africa from the perspective of biomedical nosological categories, the reader is referred to Corin and Murphy (1979).

The cases I have recounted, although typical for their category, were thought to be atypically serious cases. As is true in most parts of the world, the majority of illnesses are not treated on the scale of the cases we will describe. By focusing on mental illness, I a priori selected cases with an unusual degree of complexity. Because we know so little about the dynamics of mental illness and psychiatric healing, and with a concern for the variety of purposes for which the data may be utilized, I have presented the case studies in as much ethnographic detail as possible.

As the reader follows the case studies, it will become evident that the problems patients bring to the traditional and the spiritualist healers are remarkably similar. Further, concepts of witchcraft and sorcery seem to be utilized by both sets of patients to express a link between social experiences and incidents of illness. This raises the issue of the connection between social relations and illness. As I noted in chapter 1, several scholars have posited a direct link between social relations and signs and symptoms based on impressionistic evidence, as well as controlled epidemiological studies (e.g., Beiser and Collomb 1981; Inkeles and Smith 1970; see also Corin and Murphy 1979:159 ff.). While it seems clear that significant relationships exist, conclusively demonstrating this to be the case requires epidemiological and historical studies beyond the scope of this work. Thus, although it is difficult to make conclusive etiological statements about sociocultural factors as ultimate causes of disorders, it is important to note that people believe in a relationship between what we might call "social stress" and illness, and that concepts of witchcraft and sorcery become idioms for expressing such relationships.

The use of these categories of explanation transcends ethnic boundaries. These urban patients come from a variety of ethnic backgrounds. Their presenting problems and the way in which they interpret them seem to have more relevance to common economic and mobility problems than to an ethnically-bounded belief system.

In examining people working out life-threatening problems of illness, caution and tact must be employed by the ethnographer. It was not always possible, or desirable, to pursue sensitive lines of questioning. Accusations of witchcraft and sorcery have legal ramifications (see Appendix 4). In discussion of the case studies, I have modified minor details where they do not affect the accuracy of the account to protect the identity of those concerned. As discussed in chapter 1, first and last names in Labadi accurately and definitively identify individuals. Thus, I have assigned "day names" to those who used African names and English names to those who employed European names. The use of first names in the text, then, is an attempt to avoid identification, and no disrespect is intended.

We now turn to a detailed examination of these medical systems. While we do not have conclusive evidence that the incidence and underlying pathology of illness changes with time (although we suspect it does), we do know for certain that therapies change. We will find that therapies are a response to illness, but also pattern illness and recovery.

Traditional Healing

THE MEANING OF ILLNESS

Tsofa is the Ga word that connotes medicine. As in many West African societies, this word is a complex symbol, encompassing two poles of meanings, denoting both the cause and cure of the disorder. The tsofatse is the father, owner, or controller of medicine that may kill or cure. Though the tsofatse possessed a specialized knowledge of the disease theory system of the society, there seemed to be agreement within the general population on the principles of disease etiology, labeling, and treatment. This observation is supported by Warren's survey of several thousand Bono of central Ghana, in which he found that "the relationships expressed in this system by one priest are held quite consistently by other healers and by students and hospital workers" (1979:42).

My analysis of the disease theory system, then, is based on intensive discussions with one medicine owner, but is also informed by a year of observation and interviews with other healers, patients, farmers, small manufacturers, craftspeople, market women, clerks, and ritual experts. There was no significant disagreement about the general principles of disease. There are, however, levels of knowledge that are mastered by ritual experts and not by others. In addition, as we shall note in the case studies, there is much contention and debate about etiological considerations in specific cases, based on different interpretations of the nature of the social relationships surrounding the case.

While I was primarily interested in what people did and how they rationalized it, rather than in the formal structure of meanings, some explication of the disease theory system is necessary for understanding behavior. That disease categories interdigitate with, reflect, and reinforce other areas of culture and society is no longer in dispute. Since Zborowski's (1952) studies of subcultural patterning of the experience of pain and Frake's (1961) classic study of Subanum disease categories, we know that culture not only mediates the experience of symptoms — the internally perceived signs of the disease — but also determines the symbolic representation of these as patterned symptoms in the disease classification system. Although we have abundant evidence of cultural determination of disease in other societies, studies demonstrating this signification in our own society are relatively rare. Yet it is becoming increasingly evident that the diagnostic ideas underlying Western biomedicine are far from clear-cut and are very much dependent upon the social relations and symbol systems of society at a given time.

To some extent, the diagnostic system and disease categories reflect the state of science at a given historical point. We see this most strikingly as discovery of cells and the development of bacteriology became basic to the notion of cause. The early attempts of the modern period to classify disease, perhaps most systematically delineated by Linnaeus in 1735, relied on distinguishing pathognomonic signs as an underlying diagnostic principle. While this principle continues to be basic to diagnosis in modern medicine, Janzen points out that only 55 percent of the entries in the World Health Organization's International Classification of Diseases are "scientifically diagnosable," reducible to a single sign-symptom complex. The remaining entries are classified somewhat arbitrarily, with independently varying signs and symptoms. "In other words, cultural assumptions, rather than laboratory experiments, pervade much of the ICD" (1978:192).

We find, then, a great variation in interpretation of symptoms and preferred treatment. Most particularly, where "scientific facts" are inadequately specified, there is room for the proliferation of diversity based on culture — values, ideologies, and idiosyncrasies. These latent concepts underlying the biomedical disease classification system have not been specified.

Recognizing these and other problems, more recent formulations of diagnostic principles have attempted to limit reliance on sign-symptom complexes in favor of emphasizing analysis based on anatomical, physiological, and pathological deviations from a norm. While this approach is certainly more dynamic, as Fabrega (1974) points out, it continues to be culture-bound, not only in its organismic emphasis but in reliance on norms (from which deviations are measured) that are those of a particular, and perhaps atypical, population — Western, urbanized man. Cross-cultural studies of hypertension support this critique. They suggest that what we consider to be normal parameters of hypertension are derived from measurement of a population that can, in light of the cross-cultural evidence, be considered hypertensive (see Eyer 1975).

Similarly, the way in which the Ga classify disease involves several types of data — those gained from empirical trial and error observation as well as those associated with a cosmological belief system. Disease labels change, evolve, and develop as new knowledge is integrated into the medical system through discovery or cultural contact.

Ga disease names are classified according to a taxonomic structure differentiating diseases by several variables: susceptible population, anatomical location, symptomatology and process, and etiology. The same illness may be given different labels as it is described according to different sets of criteria. As in Western biomedicine, the initial classification is often tentative, subject to being modified as new knowledge is integrated into the therapeutic situation.

On a general level, the disease label may reflect the focus of a disorder; an illness may be named for its target population or anatomical focus. For example, the disease term *yei ahe hela* (sickness of women) may be used to refer to what biomedicine terms spontaneous abortion: "When you conceive, your abdomen becomes painful, then you abort." However, this disease has several labels. It can also be referred to as *adidai* and *owede,* medicines that are thought to be used by a sorcerer to cause the illnesses. Disease labels may reflect the anatomical location of the illness: *sẹ hela* (throat illness) or *wui amli hela* (sickness within the bones).

Illness labels may reflect the symptomatology, signs, or perceived process of the disease. For example, *gbligbli* (said to be onomatopoeic for the shivering motions of muscle tremors) refers to the complex of symptoms matching the Western disease term epilepsy; *hela tsuru* (red sickness) describes a type of dermatitis that spreads on the body with a red color; *hẹkpee* (waist bind) refers to a disorder characterized by the inability to bend from the waist; *yitso gbamo dengdeng* (head broken severe) refers to a severe headache; *kuumọ hela* (broken sickness) refers to various forms of crippling; *kladowa* (lock) or *blotshi* (the Ada word for block) is used to describe the inability to expel the child during childbirth; *fuumọ hela* (swelling sickness) refers to diseases characterized by edema; *wọlọmọ hela* (coughing sickness) refers to an illness where coughing is a major symptom.

A perceived similarity of symptoms to a nonmedical phenomenon may give the disease its name. For example, a disease called *akatangwia* (umbrella) is described as follows: "five men cannot hold you, you become stiff as a tree; in three minutes it [the sickness] loosens you, and then you become stiff again. We call it umbrella because the person jumps up in the same way as when an umbrella is pressed." *Ngwei hela* (sky sickness), a complex of symptoms matching the biomedical description of tetany, is thought to be associated with thunder.

Symptoms may be differentiated and labeled according to severity or stages requiring specific treatments. Ngwei hela, most frequently found in children, is thought to have a male and a female type. The male type is said to be violent and easier to cure than the female type, which is "more sedate and makes the patient dull and difficult to get up." The disease *asra atridii* (yellow fever), apparently adapted from the biomedical disease name, is observed to progress through different stages. The first stage, referred to as *atridii* (fever), is characterized by the person becoming "foolish." A different medicine is used for that stage than for later stages.

The Ga classificatory system, then, like that of biomedicine, labels illnesses according to associated complexes of signs and symptoms that have been recognized over time. These labels are known to the experienced healer and, to a lesser extent, to the general population. The classificatory system describes the illness and, by doing so, prescribes the treatment. While many illnesses are given one or more labels based on the descriptive categories outlined above, some diseases will not fit a recognized pattern and therefore will not have a descriptive disease label. All diseases, however, will be assigned an etiological label that points to the cause of the disorder and therefore to its cure. The label reflecting causation evokes the most general interest; it is this aspect of diagnosis that indicates the prognosis of the patient and is most directly related to treatment. It is this level of analysis that links the illness most directly to social relationships.

On the most general level, disorders are differentiated with respect to whether they are thought to be common or simple sicknesses (*hela flo* or *hela keke*) or spiritual sickness (*hela mumo*, literally "breath"). These terms are used contrastively to distinguish between those disorders that are thought to have a supernatural origin and those that are not. Such a distinction is common in Africa, as well as in other parts of the world. Among the Ga, common diseases are referred to as creation (adeboo) diseases, connoting that they are thought to have existed since "creation," thus antedating "spiritually" caused diseases. Labadians say that adeboo diseases do not kill. A farmer stated, "Every person has an adeboo in him. For example, if you are not feeling well, you just take a purgative and wash this disease out. It [the disease] is called *aboa* [animal—apparently adapted from Twi]. There is no person that doesn't have this aboa in him." Some diseases, then, such as malaria, are usually considered to be adeboo or straightforward diseases, and are not diagnosed as having a supernatural cause. Naturalistic explanations of the cause of illness include old age, diet, and climate.[1]

A disease may have the appearance of a straightforward or common disease, but may be fomented by witches and thereby be, in reality, a spiritual disease. While common diseases are latent in every person, the use of supernatural forces can cause them to become manifest. The disease label *kookoo* presents an example of the potential relationship between common and spiritual factors in disease. The *lexeme* kookoo, matched with the English term "piles" by traditional practitioners, appears to refer to a small swelling. It is considered to be a creation disease in that everyone is said to be born with seven such swellings. However, supernatural intervention may cause them to emit heat or vapor (*lamo*), resulting in a variety of diseases such as mental disorders and blindness.

Disorders that are in any way "unnatural" (chronic, resistant to treatment, occurring in young people, etc.) are immediately diagnosed as having supernatural causation. Common diseases, then, are generally those that are known, understood, and to some extent controllable. Spiritual diseases are those that are unknown (in the sense of understanding) and therefore less controllable. Even diseases that are usually thought to be common may reach a stage where they are not easily cured, and it will then be assumed that some supernatural agency has become involved. Therefore, in almost all cases there is a possibility of supernatural powers entering the picture. What this in fact means, as we shall see, is that a diagnosis of social relationships may become relevant to almost any illness.

The attempt to name a disease, then, is the first step toward treating it. Diagnosis based on etiology is first made on the level contrasting natural and spiritual diseases (level I, see figure 1). If the disease is diagnosed as natural, the appropriate treatment is given. This will usually include medication, taken with a libation —,a drink poured for the gods and the ancestors with the prayer that the illness will be easily cured and will not become spiritual.

If the disease is diagnosed as spiritual, the next concern is to ascertain its agent (level II): whether it is a curse sickness (*loomọ hela*), ancestral shade sickness (*sisa hela*), witchcraft sickness (*ayẹ hela*), or sorcery sickness (*suu hela*). These categories are not mutually exclusive. A disease may be caused by a combination of agents. Often *abonsam hela*[2] (demon sickness) is used as a general term when the healer is unable or unwilling to specify the agents of the disease. While theoretically illness may be caused by any of these agents, as we shall discuss, the interesting question is what agents are, in fact, thought to cause illness at a given historical point in time.

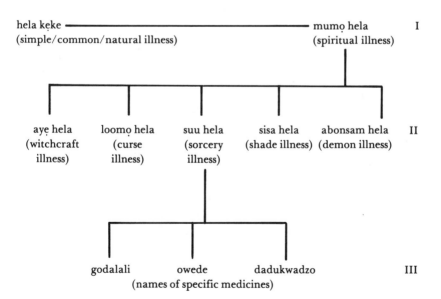

FIGURE 1

LEVELS OF CONTRAST OF ETIOLOGY OF ILLNESS

ETIOLOGICAL CATEGORIES AND SOCIAL CHANGE

Sisa hela (shade sickness) refers here to illness thought to be caused by ghosts of the dead, most often ancestors. The notion of ancestral shade sickness is premised on the generally held belief in the power of dead ancestors to act, as intermediaries or in their own right, on behalf of their descendants. Upon death, the *susuma* (soul) is thought to become a *sisa* (shade). For the individual who does not die a natural death, the sisa may become an *otofo*, a wandering dissatisfied spirit.

Ancestors are fed and ritually commemorated at homowo, the major public ritual, but they are also remembered and addressed in the course of ordinary misfortunes. Throughout healing rituals, ancestors are implored to bless the proceedings. Most libations begin by referring to the day of the week as grandmother's Saturday, grandfather's Monday, and so forth, commemorating the ancestors. When I recount the case of Abla, we shall see that in her distress she asks her deceased father to intervene to send her susuma (soul)[3] back to her and keep death at bay:

> My father's ancestral shade, you must help me from afar because you know that I do not have anyone except my mother.... My father, I know that you are standing outside hearing everything that I say. I know that you were with me as I came to this place, so try to drive my susuma away [from the place of the dead] so it will stay with me.

While belief in the power of ancestral shades to bless or smite their descendants is generally acknowledged, I came across only one case (in the sample and during the entire time I observed the traditional healer) where ancestral shades were diagnosed as the cause of illness. This was the case of an elder who had allegedly misused lineage funds and had suffered from a stroke (cerebrovascular infarction) that had left some facial paralysis on one side, producing a grimaced appearance. It was said that the ancestors had "slapped his face" in warning, and if he did not mend his ways, next time he would be killed.

Loomo hela, which translates literally as "curse illness," refers to illness that results from a judgment against the affected in a case put before the town gods (dzemawodzii). The consequence of a negative judgment may be the capture of one's susuma by the town gods, leading to illness and death. In order to understand the premises underlying judgment by the town gods, we must examine the characteristics of the dzemawǫdzii.[4]

Ga traditional religion presents the observer with a multitude of deities, leading Field to comment: "In each town are dozens of gods. At first sight they present a seemingly hopeless chaos . . ." (1937:5). She seeks to bring order by categorizing the various gods according to cult type — *kpele, akong, obutu,* and *me* — distinguished by alleged origin of the deity as reflected in language and specific customs. While this set of distinctions illuminates certain features of Ga religion, I found that the distinction between the categories of *dzemawǫng* (pl. dzemawǫdzii) and *wǫng* (pl. wǫdzii) seemed to be rooted in historical relationships between social units, and most salient in explicating behavior.[5]

Labadians refer to *hewale,* most accurately translated as "power" or "force," an attribute of beings and some inanimate objects. At the highest level, this power is manifested in the supreme being, referred to as *Ataa Naa Nyǫngmǫ* (Ataa and Naa are terms of address for venerated males and females, respectively). In all healing rituals, the cup of libation is first lifted to the sky, and invocations begin by calling on the supreme being. All gods are characterized by this "enabling force";[6] the same attribute gives medicines their power, and perhaps influences the destiny of individuals through their susuma (soul).

While wǫng is the general term for supernatural beings, the people of Labadi distinguish types of supernatural beings, modifying the term by contrasting wǫng to dzemawǫng. Dzemawǫdzii (pl.) are described as follows:

> Dzemawǫdzii are the ones from the beginning of the world, that our ancestors brought from the place where they were. *Dze* means world. Nobody knows the time when they were brought and nobody can make them now. We can only cleanse them and sacrifice to them, but we cannot make them. But the wǫng, when you want one, you can go and see someone and he will build it for you. But the dzemawǫng, they cannot build.

In Labadi, the dzemawǫdzii are worshiped by the entire town and are thus sometimes referred to as "town gods," "gods of our fathers," or "gods of origin or creation" (abebǫǫ).[7] They possess sacred groves. Most of them have priests and some have spirit mediums. As such, they are associated with a defined value structure in that they are thought to uphold "what is right." I was told by a medicine owner:

> If you see a wongtse [spirit medium] who claims to be possessed by them [the town gods] and is doing evil, you know that he has another wong. . . . When the dzemawodzii see him doing this they will harm him. They may not do anything at the time, but the man will die a horrible death. The dzemawodzii will not tolerate evil-doing.

Wodzii, on the other hand, are associated with individuals or groups of individuals, rather than corporate lineages or towns (federations of lineages), and act purely according to the interests of the individual as long as he or she adheres to the set of taboos associated with them. These interests may be antithetical to the collectively defined system of values. Wodzii are not associated with "sacred groves," but rather, unlike the town gods, have a physical representation, referred to as *woku* (pl. *wokui*).[8]

In contrast to the town gods, which are said to be "from creation," the individual gods are said to be made by man. Anyone may "obtain" this god, set up a shrine, and accept petitioners. Describing the fact that such gods are removed from the traditional centers of power in that possession is not confined to traditional authorities, Ranger (1972:11) refers to them as "democratic" spirit possession cults. These petitioners often constitute a loosely knit cult group that cuts across lineage, ethnic, and sometimes national lines. These cult groups, however, unlike the lineages which constitute the group of worshippers for town and family gods, are temporary. The difference between these "individual" gods and those bound to a permanent kinship or national group was recognized by the government of Ghana: individual gods were required to be licensed, while those attached to permanent groups were not.

Because individual gods are loosely tied to social groups, they tend to wax and wane within relatively short periods of time. Some die with their owners, others may take on a less ephemeral character. Tigari and Blekete, for example, were medicine cults whose fame spread beyond the borders of Ghana before receding into anonymity. A few individual gods become family gods and then town gods, depending upon power relationships.

Thus, a god that is recognized and collectively worshiped by the entire town is always a dzemawǫng. Lineage segment gods are generally considered to be wǫdzii, but may be transformed into dzemawǫdzii. Individual personal gods are always considered to be wǫdzii. The tsofa (medicine), as the term is now used, often denotes a lower level of wǫng that functions under very well-defined conditions. It is reversible in that it can be used for good or for evil.

Basic to the distinction, then, is the issue of whether the deity is associated with a corporate group and therefore proscriptions and sanctions related to the maintenance of that community are enforceable by the group, or whether the deity is associated with individuals thought to be beyond the ritually codified standards of behavior.

As Fustel de Coulanges (1901) demonstrated long ago in his account of Roman and Greek religion, and as Robert Adams more recently indicated in his description of Mesopotamia (1966:129), these categories are never fixed, but are modified and transformed by changing power relationships. Thus, family gods of powerful families become town gods (dzemawǫdzii); as we noted in chapter 1, most of the current town gods are those that were brought to the town by those lineage groups that founded the town or were associated with the autochthonous groups, or were later added by more recent immigrants (although these seem to have somewhat lesser status). Both Field (1937:63) and I observed lineage gods in Labadi being transformed into town gods. Similar processes are documented by Kimambo and Omari (1972) among the Pare of northeastern Tanzania, and among the Padhola of eastern Uganda (Ogot 1972). Powerful medicine owners referred to their individual gods or medicines as dzemawǫdzii and attempted to persuade their adherents to agree to this classification, and chiefs attempted to raise their lineage gods to the status of dzemawǫdzii.

The town gods are collectively worshiped by the entire town during the annual public ritual, homǫwǫ, which stretches out over a six-month period. The seven lineages are represented as corporate groups, performing various ritual acts to assure that all will go right with the town. The rituals express the basic concerns of a village community mode of production (a small-scale farming community, organized through corporate kinship groups, based on egalitarianism and respect for elders): prosperity in agriculture, fertility, and victory in war. Some of these concerns are reflected in the following song, repeated over and over again throughout homǫwǫ:

God, God, God;
God;
God, the congregation calls for abundant rain.
God;
God, the congregation calls for abundant rain.
God, water.
God;
God, water.
Water, water;
Water, water;
Water, water;
Millet, millet;
Peace, peace;
Abundant food.
(Translation from Kilson 1971:117)

While both individual gods and town gods may be the instruments of illness, only town gods are thought to "judge the case" according to collectively enforced standards of behavior. While the town gods were appealed to and implored to bless the proceedings in every healing ritual I witnessed, in only two cases was a curse by the town gods diagnosed to be the direct cause of the illness. In both of those cases, one of which we will recount in detail farther on, the town gods acted true to form, holding the kinship group as a whole responsible for the individual. When Field wrote of medicine and religion among the Ga in 1937, she recounted numerous cases of illness caused by the curse of the town gods. This difference cannot, I think, be attributable only to differences in the fieldworker, but seems to indicate that changing conditions have transformed emphases on causes of illness.

If the ancestors and town gods seem to be less active in regulating affairs through causing illness, individual gods, medicines, and witches seem to be more active. Individual gods and medicines are often used by individuals to work harm on others, but are, as well, used as protection against witchcraft and sorcery. The individual gods, then, figure prominently in the etiological categories of witchcraft (*aye*) and sorcery (*suu*),[9] personal powers employed by individuals against others. Aye does not necessarily connote an evil influence, but is rather a special type of inherent power that may be used for good or for evil. Suu, on the other hand, is thought to be manmade and always to be used for evil purposes. Individual gods (wǫdzii) and medicines (tsofa) are utilized by the healer to combat the effects of bad ayẹ and suu.

Witchcraft, then, is not an inherently evil power, but is considered to be a wondrous spirit (*naakpẹẹ mumǫ*). Good witchcraft (*ayẹ kpakpa*) may be used by someone who possesses it to help herself or protect her family. There were numerous examples of the power of witchcraft being used for good: of mothers who were able to protect their children, and people who could forsee the future and change events. The power of witchcraft was used to explain otherwise inexplicable coincidence. I was told that if two people had the same qualifications and one got promoted and the other did not, this was because the person who was promoted possessed witchcraft.

Most ayẹ are thought to be conscious of possessing these powers. However, it can be surreptitiously transmitted to a relative through her food. Labadians say that in these days, although there are some good witches who use their powers to help people, most people use ayẹ for evil purposes — bad witchcraft (*ayẹ fong*), working its harm by injuring, weakening, or killing the victim's susuma.

Sorcerers (*tsulǫ*), however, are "created wicked and evil." Unlike witchcraft, which may be an unseen, general power, a sorcerer is thought to utilize a palpable object to tap power. That was expressed to me as follows: "The ayẹ walk in the air, but a tsulǫ traps people on the earth," or, "ayẹ can go straight to your susuma but tsulǫ must utilize a medicine to bind you." People say that today witches and sorcerers frequently work together. The witch will capture a victim's susuma, and the sorcerer will then use medicines to "bind it."

Labadians, then, like other people, distinguish between the categories of witchcraft and sorcery. Witchcraft is inherent, non-empirical, occasionally involuntary, sometimes morally neutral. Sorcery is comprehensible, empirical, and generally evil. The sorcerer does not possess power himself. He uses medicines, which may be used for good or evil purposes. It is the sorcerer himself who is immoral. Sorcery, then, is comprehensible, mundane, and easily understood. Witchcraft is mysterious and uncontrollable.

This level of classification is of great interest to the healer, patient, and family, and will be generally known and freely discussed. What is, of course, most interesting is the specific individual or individuals involved in activating or employing the instruments of illness. The diagnostic statement specifying causation on this level of classification may have legal ramifications. Where litigation is assigned to the traditional courts, accusations of witchcraft and sorcery may be placed before a traditional healer to mediate. If both parties agree to such a procedure, the decision will be legally binding (see Appendix 4 for an example of such a case). This intermeshing of the legal and medical systems is reminiscent of our own society, where a medical diagnosis may have serious ramifications in a court case, and, further, where diagnostic labeling may constrain an individual's civil and legal rights.

If an illness is diagnosed as being caused by sorcery, the concern of the healer is then to determine the medicine that caused it, which will also be used to cure it. The name of this medicine may be in any of the languages of Ghana, and sometimes from beyond the borders of Ghana. On this level, then, hela and tsofa are sometimes used interchangeably. An illness may be called (name of medicine) hela or (name of medicine) tsofa. Unlike levels I and II, which will be generally known and discussed freely by the patient, family, healer, and others, level III is highly specialized knowledge and may only be known to the tsofatse. While Labadians insist that both witchcraft and sorcery have increased in recent times, they distinguish between the two, saying that whereas sorcery existed "since creation," the proliferation of witchcraft is of recent origin. In support of this, they point out that whereas the word for sorcery (suu) is a Ga word, the word for witchcraft (aye) was borrowed from Fanti.

The reasons people give for this phenomenon are basically similar: "The difference is that these are modern times. More people want to destroy than want to help. Within your own family, someone will envy you; they will go to a sorcerer and do something to destroy you. For example, because you are studying, someone in your family will envy you and destroy you." The increase in witchcraft and sorcery is seen as a phenomenon that is symptomatic of changing times. It is said that children are not trained in the old ways. Without this training, "young people easily decide that they hate someone and then get some medicine to kill them."

The most prevalent explanation concerned personal gain. I was told that, "People love money too much. A woman goes to a witch to learn devious ways of making money and then before she knows it, she has turned into a witch. Bad witchcraft and sorcery have grown because people have a love of money and want to make it fast without having to work for it." There is a general notion that people first purchase medicine in order to improve their status, with no evil intent. Once they become involved in dealings with these powers, however, they may inadvertently be forced to utilize them for evil purposes. It was explained as follows: "If someone helps you on your farm one day, then you must go and help him the next day when he cultivates his farm. In the same way, if one person requests help [supernatural] of someone one day, he cannot then refuse to aid him when he needs this type of help." These illicit dealings with these powers are often thought to involve the agreement to sacrifice members of the kinship group.

While assurances that individual gods, sorcery, and especially witchcraft have increased must be treated with caution, they cannot be entirely discounted. Much of the anthropological literature, as well as other accounts, points to an upsurge in individual gods and witchcraft following World War II (see Ward 1956; Field 1960). Field, whose sojourn in Ghana as a teacher, ethnographer, and psychiatrist spanned over twenty years, remarks on the emergence of privately-owned shrines, particularly after World War II, and suggests that in Tema, where the town gods continued to flourish, witchcraft was virtually unknown (1937:135n). Although Goody (1957) discounts the recent origin of these shrines, much of the evidence from other parts of Africa seems to support the contention that the "individual" cults (in the sense of not being connected with a social group) are of relatively recent origin (see Ranger 1972:13; Sangree 1966; Schoffleers 1972).

Perhaps the important issue is not so much that of fixing the time of the origin of individual gods, shrines, or witch-finding cults, but rather that of delineating the conditions that favor the emphasis of collective or individual forces as active agents in the regulation of everyday life, including the cause of illness. While it seems that individual gods and medicines, in the form of hunting medicines, war medicines, and so forth, have been in existence for some time (see Field 1940:73), they seem to have become more active agents in everyday life. Field noted:

> If centralized disciplined faith is weaker, vagrant credulity is stronger. If the priestly revenues have dwindled and ancient ethics decayed, the coffers of private practitioners of all kinds are in a fair way to become inordinately swollen. (1937:133)

Today in Labadi we find that in the realm of traditional healing the town gods and ancestors continue to be revered, but seem to have lost some of their power to regulate behavior through causing illness. The blessings of the town gods, the lineage gods, and ancestors were sought for agricultural plenty, victory in war, fertility, and freedom from starvation. As Labadians have increased their control over the environment with a higher level of technology—tractors, fertilizer, etc.—the threat of crop failure, famine, and starvation has somewhat subsided. As farmers become wage workers, store-bought food replaces food from the earth, which may or may not be forthcoming. As fishing on larger vessels with outboard motors replaces fishing in canoes, fishing is not quite so dangerous or tenuous, and Naie, the god of the Sea, not quite so important. As the corporate nature of lineages declines, lineage gods and ancestors no longer have the same power over the activities of their lineage members and descendants, as "everyone paddles his own canoe."

What becomes much more important, and to some extent capricious, incomprehensible, and uncontrollable, is paddling that canoe—individual success in employment, promotion, education, and business. The increasing emphasis on individual gods, medicines, and individual powers, then, underlines the transformations in social relationships to contract labor and individual business enterprises; it reflects the undulating margin of success particularly characteristic of small-scale self-employment. Thus the retreat of the town gods and ancestors in favor of individual gods and powers.

Within traditional healing, it seems that the emphasis on agents of illness has shifted. Although Field does not give precise statistics, her accounts give numerous cases of illness caused by ancestors and dzemawọdzii (1937:116-118). In addition, she refers to several cases of people being sued in the native court for calling upon dzemawọdzii to harm others (116). In contrast, I came across only two cases of illness attributed to the wrath of the town gods, and only one diagnosed as being caused by the ancestors. The vast majority of spiritual illnesses were attributed to witchcraft and sorcery, with witchcraft being the most frequent. At the same time, the ancestors and town gods continued to be essential to successful treatment.

MENTAL ILLNESS

The complex of symptoms associated with *sẹkẹ* is roughly congruent with the biomedical category of mental illness and is equally indeterminate. This disease label illustrates the way in which various areas of knowledge are organized into disease terms. The term sẹkẹ reflects what is considered to be a most significant symptom of the disorder. Sẹkẹ is short for *sẹẹ kẹ,* meaning "keeps long"; mental illness, then, is *hela sẹẹ kẹ,* illness that is of a long duration. This term subsumes a variety of forms of mental disorder. There are also a number of nicknames that are generally used with common understanding: people may refer to someone who is considered to have a mental disorder by saying "ame ye fa" (they are many). People who are so afflicted are recognized by their symptoms: there is general agreement about the type of behavior that is considered to be disordered. Mental disorders, then, are inferred from the affective behavior of the patient who may "shout, speak, or laugh inappropriately, not understand, may jump up and run into the bush or the ocean."

Several stages and types of sẹkẹ are recognized. These are distinguished by the different affective behavior patterns of the patients. Early stages of mental disorder are referred to as *eyitso nkalẹ* (something touching the head) or *yitso fitemo* (head spoiled); it may also be called *ying kamọ* (*ying* meaning inside the head, *kamọ* to stop). These behavior forms are, however, distinguished from those of retardation. Instead, these terms are usually used to describe someone who was previously considered normal, but has recently manifested symptoms of early mental disorder, such as inappropriate singing and abuse of others. This, then, is a stage of sẹkẹ that is usually transient, in that the patient will either be cured or become more seriously ill.

Sẹkẹ dwen represents both a type and a stage of sẹkẹ. Dwen is the Twi word for "think." While the patient may move toward normality or toward "full sẹkẹ" from this stage, it may itself constitute a particular form of mental disorder. This label describes a person who appears to be normal, but who on closer contact is found to be abnormal, the abnormality being demonstrated in sudden, uncharacteristic behavior. Sẹkẹ dwen was described as follows by a healer:

You will see a mad person, who likes to talk sense. But while the person is talking and talking, you will find that the person is mad. The person with sẹkẹ dwen will sit down here. You may have a patient coming. You will then go outside for a few minutes to restrain this patient and send him to a herbalist. Then when you come back inside, the person with sẹkẹ dwen will say to you, "Oh, you're coming to tie me up, are you not?" If she has a child, she can hold and feed the child, but if you don't watch her, she may at some point take a rag and tie the child up.

A layman described it as follows: "The man will eat from his plate and then he will wash it. After washing the plate, all of a sudden, he will pick it up and break it. He would have been washing it very well and then this thing comes on him and he does this."

The final stage is referred to as *sẹkẹ dientse* (true sẹkẹ) or *sẹkẹ yelọ* (full sẹkẹ). Full sẹkẹ is characterized by the most extreme symptoms. The essential variable appears to be the patient's inability to communicate appropriately with the outside world ("The person does not answer and mixes his talking.") Although someone may begin at the first stage and go through sẹkẹ dwen and then go to sẹkẹ yelo, the patient may also immediately develop a case of full sẹkẹ. This is thought to be a definite indication of supernatural causation of the disorder.

Classification of sẹkẹ by etiological categories includes the full range of causation. Natural causation includes a blow to the head, high fever, yellow fever, "piles," and thinking "too hard" or too much (said to cause sẹkẹ dwen, specifically). If there is no supernatural intervention, a rapid cure is expected.

While naturalistic causation for sẹkẹ is recognized, it is most frequently diagnosed as having a supernatural etiology, witchcraft and sorcery being the main agents. Specific medicines cause particular forms of disorder. *Sokposali* (an Ewe term), a medicine which lends its name to a disorder, is usually employed by men against women who have refused them sexual favors. The symptoms include inappropriate singing and dancing; severe stages may result in a woman throwing herself into the ocean or running into the bush. It was described by a healer as follows:

Sokposali acts like this: when it comes to you, you will sing and dance. When other people are dancing, you will jump up and down without knowing what you are doing. Sometimes, you may just get up, go to the sea, and throw yourself in without knowing what you are doing. When a bird makes a noise, you answer. You also shout. When someone speaks, you think he is speaking to you. When children are playing, you start dancing.

Gbesa is sometimes used interchangeably for sokposali or may refer to a disorder characterized by the inappropriate desire to fight with others. It is episodic in nature; cure is effected by nasal installation of medicine and by pouring cold water on the body.

Because diagnoses were constantly modified and often indefinite, it is difficult to draw conclusions about the frequency of mental illness. Jahoda (1961), who examined 315 adult cases handled by his five healer informants, found that in addition to physical problems, 12 percent of the cases were classified as "mental," 18 percent as "jobs, love and marriage," and 16 percent as "protection and ritual." As Landy (1974:111) points out, a significant proportion of cases in the latter two categories might be looked upon as emotional disturbances by biomedically-trained psychiatrists.

THE TRADITIONAL THERAPIST

The explanations of disease categories become meaningful in actual incidents of illness. We will now examine cases that demonstrate the ways in which these ideas are actualized and reworked in practice. The cases that I will recount will be those of the traditional healer described in the Introductory Note, whom I will refer to as Ataa (a respect term for an elder).

It was generally agreed that Ataa was the most competent tsofatse in Labadi, renowned for his command of spiritual forces as well as for his knowledge of herbs. He specialized in the treatment of mental disorders. As a member of the agbaafoi, the society of medicine owners, he also had responsibilities for overseeing the spiritual welfare of the town.

This role often brought him into conflict with the chief of Labadi. The chief, who in 1971 was thirty-five years old, had been taken from school in 1955 to be enstooled, but had subsequently completed the four-year course in public administration at the University of Ghana at Legon. The right of the chief's lineage to the office of chieftaincy was disputed by one faction of the town, including Ataa. The struggle over the office, which continued to have significant influence in such issues as land distribution, often manifested itself in the realm of ritual. In these incidents, the chief was usually in the position of attempting to make changes, "modernizing" ritual practices. Ataa was often in sharp disagreement with him, insisting that things must be done according to "custom and tradition," in which he was considered to be one of the experts.

In 1971, Ataa was eighty-four years old. Before he had begun to practice healing in 1926, he worked as a "fitter" and a blacksmith. He was literate, knew a little English, and had been educated to the level of middle school. He learned medicine by taking a seven-year apprenticeship with his mother's father. He considered his training to have been thorough and systematic, in the course of which he compiled a notebook of disease names and treatments. He himself was now training an assistant, who was his mother's brother's son.

Patients came to consult the healer at his compound. Ataa resided in a private (rather than lineage) house away from the center of town with his three resident wives and eighteen of their children. The compound consisted of several cement structures: in one were housed representations of the gods, including pots of sacred water used for healing; other rooms were used for sleeping; another room contained a well-furnished, though little used, parlor displaying personal acquisitions, including several cabinets of perfumes, liquor, china, ceramics, and other gifts from patients.

The value and number of these acquisitions were evidence of Ataa's success and renown as a healer. He was able to live quite comfortably on his fees and invested them in other enterprises, such as the purchase of cattle. Yet Ataa's fees did not appear to be exorbitant and he often used a sliding scale approach. Further, payment was tied to the success of the treatment. A patient's family would pay an initial fee when the patient entered treatment, which could be as low as a few cedis and as high as thirty, and the costs of the initial medicines and animals to be sacrificed. Throughout the treatment, the patient's family would be expected to provide goats or chickens for sacrifices (as well as the patient's food) and might give occasional gifts to the healer, but a major payment would not take place again until treatment was deemed successful. Ataa and the patient's family would then negotiate the fee for successful treatment in a special ritual, which we will describe later in the chapter.

Fees ranged from twenty to one hundred cedis, depending on the seriousness of the illness and the family's ability to pay.

Most activities, as is the case everywhere in Labadi, took place in open courtyards. Red, white, and dark cloth streamers used in previous treatments hung from the buildings, and herbs in various states of desiccation littered the courtyard. There the wives cooked, groomed, and cared for their children. It was there, also, that the patients and families resided (as many as seven patients and their families have been in residence at one time), and that therapeutic treatment took place.

DIAGNOSIS OF ILLNESS

The diagnostic process is a long one, and conclusions are modified as findings change. The etiological statement is rarely fixed. Its flexibility allows for an exchange of opinions, the airing of grievances and, as well, provides a potential point of pressure for bringing recalcitrant kin into line. While it is the healer's prerogative to carry out the diagnostic procedures that indicate the cause of illness, various individuals, in different structural positions, will continue to hold their own views about the cause of illness.

In the case of Aba, a young woman schooled to standard four, I shall highlight the diagnostic procedures and the way in which social facts provide the information for classification of illness. This case also illustrates an incident where presenting problems focused around kinship and marriage obligations. Relevant to the particular sharpness that these universal problems take on are both the transformation in mode of production, resulting in contradictory obligations and expectations, and the high rate of unemployment characteristic of a neocolonial society.

In 1971, Aba was twenty-two years old. According to her mother, Aba had contracted the usual childhood diseases, including measles and fevers, but had never suffered from convulsions, headaches, or unusual illnesses. As the price of books and uniforms began to rise, her parents no longer found it possible to keep her in school beyond standard four. After leaving school, Aba went to stay with her mother, father, and their five other children, of whom she was the oldest, in one of the Labadi farming villages founded by her father's lineage. We have noted earlier that much of the farming in

Labadi takes place in villages settled by a lineage group, and that, for the majority, farming may be an economically precarious occupation. Aba's family farmed a small piece of lineage land, subject to the form of inheritance described in chapter 1: property was divided among two generations of patrilineal relatives. In conditions of land scarcity, the portions that pass to inheriting individuals decrease with each successive generation. This was particularly the case where the land was not maintained *in toto* as lineage property to which members had access, but rather became private, individual plots. It seemed that, although Aba's father's father held a relatively large portion of land, after it was divided among the father's generation her father's portion was relatively small.

Approximately four years prior to her illness, Aba's father died. As was the custom, a member of the lineage was selected to "marry" Aba's mother in the sense of taking responsibility for raising the children. Since the father's full brothers were dead, his brother's son was selected by the lineage. The father's brother's son, however, did not contribute to the support of the children. Aba's mother's interpretation was that he was unable to withstand the objections of his wife whenever he was asked for aid for the children and therefore contributed nothing to their upkeep. While she felt that it was reasonable for him to choose not to marry her, she had expected him to assume responsibility for the children, fulfilling his lineage obligation. Aba's mother, then, was receiving no aid from the patrilineage in caring for the children.

This type of situation was not unusual in Labadi at this time. We noted earlier the shifting focus of responsibility from the lineage to the individual. While most Labadians expressed the belief that the lineage should be responsible for its members, in actual practice this was often not the case. Common and expected as this may be, it often left people floundering. Aba's mother had to support the five children by farming a small piece of land with help only from Aba.

The contradictory pulls of collective versus individual responsibility and ownership were manifested somewhat differently in an additional problem. As land became a commodity — something that could be bought and sold — confusion, and subsequently conflict, about whether land was lineage land or privately owned land often emerged at the time of death and inheritance. In this particular case, there was a question as to whether Aba's father's land was lineage land, which should therefore automatically revert to the lineage, or whether it was his privately owned land, which could more easily be inherited directly by his children. One segment of the family thought Aba's mother should be allowed to keep the land so that she could support the children, and the other segment maintained that it should revert to the lineage. This issue remained unresolved, although Aba's mother, and Aba before her illness, continued to farm the land.

Shortly before her father died, Aba married a schoolteacher and had a child by him. Soon afterward he lost his job and was still unemployed at the time of Aba's illness. For a period of time, he lived with Aba's mother and siblings in the village, but he was expelled from the house by Aba's mother because she felt he had become argumentative and recalcitrant. Aba, however, maintained a relationship with him and continued to visit him, as she would tell her mother, to talk to him about support for their child. To the consternation of her mother, she had another child by him, who was a little more than a month old at the onset of her illness.

Aba's illness began five weeks after the delivery of her last child.[10] Her mother described the onset of the illness as follows:

> Five weeks after she had given birth to her child, on that Sunday, she was sleeping in the room that both of us occupy. She woke up in the night. She called me, saying, "mother, I cannot sleep." I told her that I could not do anything about what was wrong with her. I told her that she would soon sleep and that things were sometimes like that. I also told her that "thinking" (*dzwengmo*) can make a person become sleepless. So if she could not sleep today, she would sleep tomorrow. That morning she started talking and continued until the following morning, without sleeping. She has been baptized and has been to school. Our church is in another town. So she asked me to go and call the pastor to come and give her some prayers. I went and called him and he came and prayed for her. That Tuesday evening after that man had prayed for her, some members of another spiritualist church in our town came and prayed for her. We also went to yet another pastor who prayed for her. All that night she was not able to sleep. Wednesday at dawn, the talking continued; it had not improved. So I went to see my sister. She asked me when the sickness had come, and I told her that Aba had had a good delivery. When she was pregnant, I sent her to the hospital. Even when I did not have any money, I would borrow

some to send her to the hospital. So I did not know what this is. My sister told me that I should bring her to this place. So this is how it came about.

As Aba's mother has recounted, her initial move was to call members of a spiritualist church to pray. Her final decision to bring Aba to the traditional healer was conditioned, however, by her relationship with her sister. Because the patrilineage had not participated in caring for the children, Aba's mother had borne most of the support expenses herself. She received some help from her elder sister, who happened to be the healer's senior wife. Since it was her sister who had shared some of the responsibility of rearing the children, she thought it prudent to bring Aba to this healer as her sister advised, rather than to the mental hospital or to a spiritualist church. Janzen (1978) has amply demonstrated that the kinship group constitutes a therapy-managing group, deciding on the road to therapy. Here we see that not only is this true but also that the question of which segment of the group prevails very much reflects the exigencies of a given situation and may vary as conditions change. In this case the patrilineage had not assumed responsibility for the family and no longer had the prerogative of giving advice about the course of therapy. As the responsibility of others increased, their advice prevailed, supported by their ability to contribute to the therapy.

Early one morning in the beginning of October, Aba arrived at the healer's compound accompanied by her mother and her mother's sister's daughter. She was slightly disheveled and hyperexcited in her motions and speech. She talked incessantly from the time she arrived until she left three hours later, with the exception of brief periods when she was persuaded to sit quietly for the sake of the ritual. Most of the time she was extremely agitated, constantly moving her legs back and forth or jumping from a sitting to a standing position.

The three women, the healer, and his eldest wife (Aba's mother's sister) entered the inner room of the compound for the divination procedure. Needless to say, the social facts of the case were well known to the healer through his wife. First, the healer wrote their family names and day names on a piece of paper in which he wrapped two cedis in silver coins. He placed this package under an old broken mirror, to which was attached a bone.

Aba directed her soliloquy to the healer:

You must try for me. You must try to heal me. I am very sad. In a short time, all of my body has gone away from me. See how I am now. My father's shade [sisa], you must help me from afar because you know that I do not have anyone except my mother. I am sad, I do not have anyone to help me. So you, my father, I leave it to you, unless you want to disgrace yourself. And so, my susuma, you must come and stay in me, come and stay in me. You must put everything on the fowls because we have a proverb that says, "We breed fowls or animals because of human beings." They say when something is going to happen to a person, that thing rather goes to the animals. You know I do not have any money, but anywhere you go to borrow money for me, I will serve that person when I am healed. Mother, you should be patient and not worry. Pray that your susuma stands firm. You care for me. You suffered and borrowed food and so many things to feed me. So pray that I do not die. For three days I have not been able to sleep. I have been walking around as though I were mentally sick. God [*Naa Nyongmo*] help me, so that anything they do for me will make me well. My father, I know that you are standing outside hearing anything that I am saying. I know that you were with me all the way to this place, so try to drive my susuma away from the place of the dead so that it will stay with me. Help me because I am your first child. So, stand there and shout to my susuma, "Hey, what are you doing here!" Mother, be patient, I tell you I will be well, As I am standing here talking now, I do not see my ancestral shades. My father will be able to drive away my susuma. Susuma come, susuma come. Come and stay with me. Drive my susuma to come back to me so that anything they do for me will make me feel well. Naa Nyongmo, you created everything on earth. You created stones and trees so that when someone is sick, herbs can be used to cure the person. And so you created me. Any herb that is used for my healing, you must help so that it will make me feel better because this is not how I am . . . . You should let me talk to you because you are my mother. I should bury you rather than you burying me. You know that caring for a child is very difficult, but you struggled through and provided for all my needs, and now you are taking care of my children also. I have two children, but I cannot take care of them properly. I should be able to do something for you. Let me talk. If it were not for this talking, I would probably have been dead since yesterday. You do not want me to talk. Why? Let me talk. Do not be worried when I am talking. I'm not mad [seke]. There is a proverb that says, "If you put yam on the fire, your hands will be black." But I have not toasted any yam, so my hands are not going to be black [referring to the fact that she has not done anything wrong]. I do not feel that I am a human being, but since I could eat and drink, I know that I will be healed. . . . Nyongmo, call back my susuma from wherever it has gone to. My father's shade, I know that you are standing there listening to what I am saying. You must stand there and drive back my susuma. Try to frighten my susuma so that it will come back to me. . . .

Revealed in Aba's monologue was genuine distress. As we shall see, Aba, like the healer, phrased the link between external events and inner states in terms of the susuma. Clearly Aba, the layman, understood the susuma to be an inherent component of herself, the permanent abdication of which would cause her death. As is also evident in her monologue, she adhered to the view that serious illness may be a result of wrongdoing.

The healer than poured schnapps over the mirror and the various representations of the gods (wokui). Lighting a candle, he passed it over the mirror with a circular motion seven times. He threw six cowrie shells onto the back of the mirror, observing the pattern in which they fell. After pouring a libation for the gods housed separately in a smaller room, he threw the cowrie shells a second time. In reaction to the healer shaking his head and kissing his teeth after a second glimpse into the mirror, Aba began to talk compulsively again:

Since you have shaken your head, you here made me afraid. I do not see any ancestral shades. If I were to say that, I would be lying. All these stones and trees here, you must help me. Nyongmo, help me. You must pour water into the air for me [a sign of efficacy]. You must help me because this morning some people came and sat around me. You all came and sat around me [referring to people who do not wish her well]. Nyongmo, forgive me all my sins. You, my susuma, Aba [Thursday], you brought me into this world. You must come and stay with me so that I will not be worried. The man that I married, people say that he is not good. A friend of my mother's insulted me by saying that I have married a corpse. Even if he is bad, I am still with him, but I have never even spent his threepence, because he is unemployed. I beg you to help me to feel better so that in the future I may be able to spend his money. Because I have suffered with him, I should be able to have a part. All these stones and trees here, go with my dzema-wodzii to help me to feel better.

Although Aba was a practicing Christian, she called on the spirits of the healer's medicines, the town gods, ancestral shades, as well as Nyǫngmǫ, to help her. Everyone in the room became very solemn. The healer stated that the cause of the illness was three women and two men who had been following Aba, and had now succeeded in trapping her susuma. The healer continued to gaze into the mirror. Aba again began to talk:

> You must go and borrow some money so that the things that are needed can be done. I beg you to save my life. My susuma, come back from the bush. Come and stay with me. [Aba sang "Guide me O thou great lord" in English.] God, you are my saviour. You must kill those two men and three women with an arrow. Susuma, I know that you are alone, struggling with these five people. Try to defend yourself and come back to me. . . . My father, beat these people with sticks so that they leave me alone. I have not taken anything from these people [referring to the fact that she has never engaged in sorcery or witchcraft that would bring gain to her and require an exchange].

The healer continued to gaze into the mirror, while everyone strained to hear his words. In a low and saddened voice, Ataa stated that the woman who was instigating the incident was a member of the family. Aba asked the person's name, which the healer refused to disclose. She received no response to her query as to whether the person was a member of her father's lineage. Evidently interpreting the evasion as a positive response, her mother remarked that she did not understand why anyone in the father's lineage should do such a thing. "What have we taken from these people? Since her father died, I have been suffering to care for her." The healer reiterated that the person who was engaged in this should not be, because she is a member of the family. All participants shook their heads in dismayed agreement.

Continuing to gaze into the mirror, the healer began to compile a list of things to bring when they came the next day to begin treatment, adding that he would not charge anything for himself, but that it might be necessary to "beg" the spirits that were causing harm to Aba. He instructed them to bring: one bottle of palm oil, a pure black fowl, seventy-seven red kola nuts, one bottle of schnapps, nine eggs ("the good ones, not the ones that come from the poultry farm"), one box of powder, twelve yards of white calico, twelve yards of dark blue calico, one packet of candles, seven crabs, one cigarette tin full of small red peppers, one bunch of small onions, one cigarette tin of salt, and one large bowl for mashing the small peppers. He admonished Aba's mother to bring the things as soon as possible so that they could start treatment before it was too late, and to watch Aba carefully so that she would not walk out of the house and fall into the sea or a lagoon.

After throwing the cowrie shells one more time, he placed white clay on the mirror, poured a libation to the wo̧dzii, and brandished a ceremonial knife (*tshi*), which he explained was an instrument of the gods. In conclusion, he set flame to some gunpowder, which exploded with a bang, frightening all of us present. The three women then left for home.

By this time in the treatment process, the healer had made a general diagnostic statement: he had confirmed the generally held opinion that this was, indeed, a spiritual illness. At this point, the healer said, he could not give the illness a specific name, but it was an illness caused by witchcraft and sorcery and may be the initial stages of mental illness (sȩkȩ). He was considering several possible motives for the use of witchcraft. These included land dispute and the chance that Aba had contravened some norms and therefore insulted someone. While he claimed to know the names of the agents involved, he declined to reveal them to the family because of the danger of their anger and in consideration for the confines of the law. The generality of the diagnosis, of course, led the patient and family to examine a range of relationships.

Aba's mother alone remained doubtful of the diagnosis. She continued to suggest that the cause of Aba's disorder was "too much thinking" caused by the anniversary of her father's death and that Aba and her children had been dependent on her for three years, pointing to the content of Aba's discourse to support this view. Although Aba's mother thus expressed some skepticism, she nevertheless declared her confidence in the healer and his diagnosis.

The next evening, Aba returned with her mother, mother's sister's daughter, and four male members of her matrilineage. Various rituals, including ritual bathing, the sacrifice of a goat, and the ceremonial cutting of strips of red, black, and white cloth binding the patient (to be described later), were performed. Medicine was rubbed into small incisions in her skin and given to her to drink. All these were accompanied by libations to the high god, the town gods,

Aba's ancestors and lineage gods, and the healer's personal gods.

In the morning, Aba's hyperexcitability had vanished. She appeared somewhat tired and spent the day talking to her mother and caring for her small child. Her matrilineal kin and their children stayed with her, setting up shop in the courtyard with cooking implements and toilet articles. Like all patients whose relatives stay for a period of time, they became integrated into the family of the healer, often sharing cooking, household tasks, and childcare. This behavior was explicitly encouraged by the healer, who frequently stated, "When someone in the family is in trouble, it is necessary to see her through that trouble." He expected all family members to visit patients and show their support, materially if possible, but at least by visiting—that is, if they wish the patient well.

The diagnostic procedures, then, are a crucial phase in the healing process for healer, patient, and family. These are often seen as the first phase of treatment, initiating the curing process by identifying the cause. For traditional healers, the initial diagnostic steps are accomplished through divination. Divination often involves several phases. Usually the patient and family make preliminary visits to the healer, explaining the problem. If it is a straightforward disorder with no supernatural involvement, the healer may make an examination and prescribe treatment. If, however, supernatural involvement is suspected, the healer will ask the patient to return in a few days for a reading of his or her susuma. In the interim, the healer may procure information concerning the patient's essential social relationships and potential points of disruption, having ample opportunities to make inquiries that will illuminate the context of the occurrence of this disorder.

Divination is often accomplished by reading the susuma of the patient. This is based on the assumption that, although the patient may not consciously comprehend the problem, her susuma represents another level of awareness and knowledge that can be acquired by the healer. The susuma may be read in a variety of ways, including peering into a mixture of herbs and water in a calabash (*tsęsę*) or gazing into a mirror. Because this reading is an essential part of the treatment process, the particular method selected will be determined by the way in which the healer perceives the needs of the patient. It is the beginning of the revelation of the problems of social relationships. As I noted above, the susuma is seen as the link between external events and inner disorganization. In certain circumstances, the susuma may be the agent of inner disturbance. As in other West African societies, such as the Tallensi (Fortes 1959), a dissatisfied susuma may cause illness, but is more likely to cause stealing, unemployment, barrenness, and sterility. Here again, however, the susuma, like the ego, is reacting to external events. When sorcery, witchcraft, and ancestral shades are the instrumental causes of death or illness, they act by injuring the susuma. The ultimate cause of injury or weakening of the susuma is to be found in the patient's relationship to others.

Divination may also be achieved through direct mediation of the gods. The usual method for this is the throwing of cowrie shells. The "reading" is accomplished through a variety of interpretive means: the position in which the shells fall, the pattern they make, or the side upon which they fall.

In divination, then, two sorts of processes are at work. First, an arena is created in which certain information may come to light. Second, these revelations are structured into an episode of dramatic significance. Throughout the ritual sequence, Aba discoursed at length about the manifest focuses of her anxiety: the death of her father, the unemployment of her husband, and the resulting problems for herself, her mother, and her children. The healer was also able to gather other pieces of data: views of other members of the family, the nature of Aba's relationships with others, and the general situation of the family. These data were structured into a dramatic sequence that enhanced their significance. An atmosphere of tension mounted as the disturbance of the patient increased and the healer sought to divine the cause of her disorder. As the cause of the illness was revealed, a focus was provided for the anxiety. The identification of the illness was the first step toward the cure, bringing at least temporary relief and optimism, somewhat dramatically climaxed by the explosion of the gunpowder—a demonstration of the power and ability of the healer and perhaps, as we shall discuss later, a type of shock therapy.

Thus, identification of disease depended here on several types of data: medical history, description of behavior, and, most important, social history. As these became known, they could be organized into disease names that denote symptomatology, process, etiology, and, eventually, therapy. As we shall see, the process of identifying and treating the disease occurred over a period of time. As new facts came to light and circumstances changed, the diagnosis was adjusted. The initial diagnosis, then, is often tentative. For the traditional healer, diagnosis is often a dialectical process; disease names are not arbitrarily or immutably assigned. Process and change are observed and lead to modification of diagnosis, treatment, and introduction of new methods.

By mid-October, Aba was wearing ankle chains because she had become *basa-basa* (rough) and attempted to run away. She was plagued by nightmares and frequently talked in her sleep. The healer explained that her illness was not yet seke and was, at this stage, constantly changing. The treatments determined by reading the susuma consisted of various rituals designed to drive out the malevolent spirits, and the administration of medicine. During one treatment, which included sacrificing a fowl that had been rubbed over the patient, the gods of Aba's mother's and father's family, as well as the healer's own personal gods, were requested to find the cause of the illness and assist in the treatment. According to the healer, the overall treatment involved two aspects: driving out the evil spirits and caring for the injuries caused by them. "If a tree falls on you, even if it is taken off, you still have to be cared for. If it is lifted immediately, your injuries will be able to be treated more quickly. If it stays on you for some time, it will take a longer time to cure your injuries."

By the end of October, Aba appeared to be much improved, spending the day caring for her children. She seemed slightly depressed, but behaved normally, communicating with others in the household with no sign of her former hyperexcitability. The healer claimed that he had dealt with the cause of her symptoms, but was not yet quite satisfied with her. "If you are hit by a stick, you must not only stop the stick, but cure the place where the sore is or else the stick will hit you again."

By mid-November, Aba seemed depressed, although not withdrawn. She communicated when necessary, but in a very subdued manner, remaining quietly in the courtyard. The healer shaved her head and rubbed medicine into it. This was thought to be a critical stage in the illness: she was now said to be at a stage of seke, referred to as yitso fitemo (head spoiled), that could progress to seke yelo (full mental illness). Her present stage was defined by her behavior, which was initially normal and then periodically became abnormal — intermittent verbal abuse, along with inappropriate singing and dancing.

The instillation of nasal medication, in this case an extremely uncomfortable procedure, precipitated an episode of shouting and fighting. This was expected by the healer, who claimed that the purpose of the procedure was to "see if there is any sickness left and to bring it out." He predicted that symptoms would appear after the medication, subside, and would appear again as he continued to give the medication. When she no longer manifested symptoms upon taking the medication, the illness would be considered entirely cured.

The prediction proved to be correct: a week later Aba was again constantly moving her limbs, singing, and crying. Her steady stream of conversation was inappropriate, often including nonsense syllables. She spent much of the day standing in one spot, talking, crying, and singing. She was now unable to care for herself or her children, although she ate if food was given to her. After an incident in which the healer's wife scolded Aba for shouting, the healer admonished his wife, explaining that the talking was a symptom of the illness and that "it must come out."

The healer continued to focus his analysis and treatment on the different phases of the illness, emphasizing the importance of distinguishing between quiescent phases or remissions and complete cures. At this point in Aba's illness, the healer diagnosed the condition as full sẹkẹ and attributed its severity to Aba's family not having brought her for treatment immediately.

By the end of November, Aba was again very depressed, crying, and talking incoherently. Discussions between the healer, Aba, and other members of the family continued. According to the healer, it is necessary to talk to the patient in order to understand the illness. Medications, baths, sacrifices, and special rituals continued.

A week later, Aba was again in the manic stage. The healer continued to maintain that this state represented the release of the "hidden" illness and that she would soon be well. Discussion in the compound centered around censure of Aba's husband, who now visited for the first time and had only contributed two cedis. All relatives who wish the patient recovery were expected to visit frequently and bring small tokens of appreciation for the healer. The husband was held in general contempt for his lack of support of Aba and the two children, all of whom had been dependent on Aba's mother. Aba's relatives were opposed to the marriage and continued to urge Aba to leave the husband. At this point, Aba's youngest child became ill and was a source of constant anxiety to everyone. The deteriorating circumstances led to renewed discussion of the agents of illness.

The healer confided to me that Aba was being bewitched by her mother's sister and her father's brother's son, who had refused to assume the responsibility for Aba's mother and her children. The evidence of the mother's sister's complicity rested on her visit, where she had allegedly refused to enter the room where the healer keeps his gods. It was not entirely clear why these people wished her harm, and the possibility that she had insulted someone by not maintaining the traditions of politeness remained open. The healer frequently discussed Aba's behavior with her, admonishing her to show more respect for people. If she had been disrespectful, the illness was a warning to mend her ways.

A week later, the most tragic dimension entered the case when Aba's baby died. Aba was not told for fear that the news would aggravate her condition. When the husband came to visit a week later, he adamantly insisted that Aba never exhibited any symptoms until two months ago. He was of the opinion that the cause of the disorder lay in the machinations of her father's lineage; because she is the oldest child of her father, she should have some input into the discussion about how the land left by the father and now in dispute should be used and distributed. He concluded that her father's father's brother's son was employing sorcery in order to turn her mind away from her husband, so that he could dispose of the land as he wished.

Through the last week of December, Aba continued to be lethargic, spending most of her time sleeping on her mat. Her participation in conversation was limited but entirely appropriate. The healer felt that she was now improved, in that she was now able to sleep at night and accepted her medicine willingly. Her mother continued to live at the compound with her, taking care of her, cooking, washing, and fixing her daily medicine, while making occasional visits home. Other relatives spent shorter periods of time living at the compound.

By mid-January Aba was sitting up, talking compulsively but not inappropriately. Despite the fact that no one was listening, she continued to talk, gesticulating elaborately. When she was able to get someone to listen, she talked directly to that person. The healer engaged her in conversation frequently, reminding her that she had insulted her mother during her illness and that this was improper.

She agreed and indicated that this type of behavior was entirely unacceptable. The healer claimed that she would soon be well.

In traditional therapy, then, the diagnostic procedures seek out those relationships in which the rules of the village community may have been breached, which have implications for illness. Aba's mother attempted to utilize the illness episode to mobilize support among relatives and pressure them to revise their relationship with Aba, her mother, and brothers and sisters. Although this action was generally deemed to be appropriate, her success in obtaining large-scale aid was limited.

TREATMENT: PROCEDURES

The administration of medicine is a central procedure in healing, having both symbolic and physiological ramifications. As I pointed out earlier, tsofa is the Ga word that connotes medicine. Although the literal meaning of tsofa is tree roots, the usage of tsofa has extended to include a much wider range of meanings. Sacred and mundane power are not dichotomized concepts; herbs effect their cure through the physical properties of the leaves (every mother boils tsofa for the common cold), but also through being a medium for "extra-natural" power, both of which work to restore the susuma of the sick individual. Tsofa may be used to cure illness, but also to cause illness. Tsofa connotes both the cause and cure of the affliction. Illnesses may be labeled for the medicine that caused them, which will also be used to cure them: "You look for the medicine from the cause of the disease." Thus, someone may "cut tsofa to turn you into a madman" or may procure gbligbli tsofa to cure or cause gbligbli. An inability to expel a child will be known as *fomo* tsofa and will be cured by medicine of the same name.

While tsofa can be translated as medicine, its usage has been extended. Writing in the 1930s, Field noted that tsofa was used to designate a variety of substances, including "machine-oil, paint, baking powder, petrol, whitewash, gum, perfume, boot polish, etc." (1937:127). Today its usage extends into areas of concern in social interaction. Someone may procure *saneyeli* (dispute, litigation) tsofa to win a litigation, *shika* (money) tsofa to increase one's success at the market, or tsofa for special protection (see Appendix 5). Tsofa, then, is most commonly used for curing illness, but also may be used to cause illness, for protection, or to bring about a desired result. Tsofa is most often visible and palpable (*afole* tsofa; see Appendix 6), but may also act without being seen (*asule* tsofa).

Several different tsofa — utilizing different herbs (*badzii*) — are commonly employed in the treatment of complex illnesses. Often the experimental method is practiced, with the recognition that individuals react idiosyncratically to different medicines. Medicines are prepared by various methods; most often, herbs are ground, sometimes they are cooked, until they become a powder that may in turn be mixed with something else. For many medicines, the preparation is fairly straightforward and may be done by the family of the patient. The preparation of other medicines, particularly those used for witchcraft and sorcery, requires esoteric knowledge and rituals known only to the healer (see Appendix 7).

Medicines are administered in a variety of ways: orally, through the nose, in bath water, or rubbed into small incisions on the body (see Appendix 8). Some healers incorporated aspects of aseptic principles by cleaning lesions and applying lemon juice (an astringent) to the lesions before dispensing medicine. In cases of serious illness, particularly spiritual illnesses, medicine is rarely used alone; it is always dispensed in a ritual context, with libations and invocations to the ancestors, lineage and town gods, and the high god, imploring them to work with the medicine to cure the illness.

In serious illnesses, then, medicine is always administered along with ritual procedures. The case of John was fairly typical in that respect. The fact that the illness episode was of relatively short duration and the patient was declared definitively cured within the time of observation made the case particularly interesting. As in the case of Aba, both the healer and patient associated the etiology of illness with strains in social relationships.

In 1971, John was a thirty-eight-year-old Fanti married man, and the father of three children. Although he was originally from Cape Coast, he had lived in Labadi for thirty years. The fact that his father was a well-known civil servant with a position in second-level administration allowed him relatively unusual options in his choice of occupation. He worked as a buyer for the Volta River Authority for several years, eventually saving enough money to go into the business of buying and managing a number of lorries. It was soon after his venture into business that the first signs of illness appeared, three and half years before my observations. The symptoms, which he described as consisting of headaches, "feeling something moving in my head," and intestinal problems causing flatulence, resulted in his inability to continue his business activities and in the eventual sale of the lorries.

As indicated in chapter 1, the urban areas of Ghana are characterized by the proliferation of small businesses, many of which are doomed, by the nature of the economic system, to failure. The hazards are recognized, and expressed, as pointed out earlier, in the inscriptions that appear on the sides of the lorries. Failure, however, is not blamed on the vagaries of the capitalist market, but is attributed to personalistic forces in the form of envy and subsequent witchcraft and sorcery. Yet, the idioms of witchcraft and sorcery express the belief that the gain of one person is at the expense of another, that individual success in business is contradictory to the principles of corporate ownership of the kinship group.

After the onset of the illness, John consulted several biomedical doctors. Some found nothing wrong, others prescribed medicine. None were effective, and having decided the etiology of the illness was spiritual, he tried two spiritualist churches, where he was treated with prayers and the burning of candles. The illness continued, sometimes subsiding, but returning again after a few weeks. Two weeks after he attempted to attack his wife with a machete, he decided to consult Ataa, of whom he had heard from friends. He explained this decision to me as follows: "When the trouble has a spiritual cause, you may go to hospitals but they cannot help you. You must go to an African medicine man, who can treat the illness properly. He will charge you money, but will take this money and implore the spirits that are causing your illness." He arrived, accompanied by his wife and members of his wife's family, who were summoned by the healer to help shed light on the relationship between the spouses.

At the first meeting with the healer, his quick, nervous movements and speech patterns communicated his anxiety. He described his symptoms as follows: "itching in the head"; "feels as though my head is going around and around"; "when it comes on me, sometimes I am forced to jump up and run around." In addition, he complained of a feeling of abdominal fullness. After diagnostic procedures similar in form to those described in Aba's case, John and the healer agreed that this illness was not one with a specific descriptive label, but that it was abonsam deng hela (sickness from devils).

John and the healer agreed that the illness was caused by witchcraft. John's half-sister, his mother's daughter by a previous marriage, was alleged to be engaged in witchcraft because she was envious of his success in business. The healer later supported this analysis with the evidence that the children of John's half-sister had not visited John, although all of them lived in Labadi. Although the half-sister attempted to visit John on one occasion, the healer surreptitiously prevented her from seeing him. That the sister's children had not visited aggravated suspicion of the mother. Given the traditional matrilineal system of the Fanti, John's half-sister became a logical candidate for this accusation. As lineage membership is derived through the mother, John and his half-sister belong to the same lineage. With the emergence of privately-owned wealth, tensions arise between the principle of matrilineality and relationships between fathers and children. In this case, where certain advantages accrued to John through his association with his father, and not to siblings by other fathers, this tension might be exacerbated.

During the month of November, John was treated with daily administrations of medicine—orally, nasally, rubbed into his head, and through small incisions in the skin. Some of the medicines were directed toward specific symptoms such as flatulence, while the effects of others were said to be more generalized.

Medicine was given in conjunction with occasional ritual procedures. This included a ritual that was performed for several patients, said to be one of a series of treatments directed against witchcraft and sorcery (referred to as *musu*). John was taken to the bathing area early in the morning. Strips of dark cloth were tied around his head and used to fasten together his elbows, wrists, thumbs, knees, ankles, and big toes, so that he was completely bound. The healer then cut each cloth with a knife, repeating this procedure first with red cloth and then with white cloth. John was then bathed in sacred water, after which the healer poured a libation with the following invocation:

Ataa Naa Nyongmo [high god] you have created the earth and said everything was good. You are the person we have to beg for help, so that you come and bless us. Nii Tettey Lakpa, all the dzemawodzii, come and have some drink that what we do may be successful. Naa Sakumu [god of the lagoon], Naa Kpeshi [another lagoon], come and have some drink. From north to south, from east to west, and from Accra to Ada, I call all of you without leaving out any. I call all of the fathers [ancestors] to join me in the feast. I call all of our mothers to make this successful. [A detailed discussion of John's history followed.]

Within a few weeks John began to exhibit interest in his surroundings. Occasional episodes of violence, depression, and anxiety were met with increased intensity in conversation with the healer and apprentice. After a few weeks at the compound of the healer, John's behavior was generally appropriate by the standards of the healer, myself, and John, and he spent long periods of time casually conversing with the healer, other patients, and relatives who visited him. His wife visited daily, bringing food.

By December, the healer declared his case cured, but John said he did not yet feel fully well. In addition to the treatments mentioned above, John periodically slept in the room where the representatives of the gods were housed. Here, he said, he was able to dream of his enemies, to see the identities of those who were causing him to be ill, and to draw power from the gods to fight them. He regularly discussed his dreams with the healer. By January he agreed with the healer that he was indeed cured. All trace of depression and anxiety had disappeared—he was outgoing, interesting, and involved in his surroundings. Although he was confident that the illness would not return, he decided to stay for three more weeks before going home. At the end of this period, he went home.

TREATMENT: THE DRAMATIC HEALING RITUAL

It has been suggested that "symbolic bombardment" is an important aspect of non-Western therapy (Kennedy 1973:1171). Certainly symbolism is pervasive, and ritual is a major component of therapy. Ritual events and symbols correspond to those utilized in traditional religion. Much of the symbolism is utilized and explicated in the dramatic healing ritual, where the various components of therapy come together. In the next case, I will highlight the dramatic and symbolic character of traditional treatment procedures and their correspondence to ritual and symbolism in traditional religion.

Mensah was born in Labadi twenty years before I first encountered him at the compound of the traditional healer in May 1971. Although his father had once worked as a mechanic ("fitter") on the railroads in the north, he was working only intermittently at the time. Mensah's mother did not work outside the home. The household was a nuclear one including Mensah, his father, mother, a son from the father's previous marriage, and the younger children of the present marriage. Their residence was a house in Labadi, half of which was owned by Mensah's father. The other half, owned by Mensah's father's brother, was rented out.

Mensah had completed elementary school and commercial school and, before his illness, had been working as a typist in a government office. Both parents associated the onset of his illness with his work. They reconstructed the following history. Mensah had a fairly normal childhood. Although he had once suffered from convulsions associated with a high fever, he had been given medication by a traditional healer, and had not been sick since that time. His father had encouraged him to go to school and had paid his school fees. The father apparently had been very anxious that Mensah study. His mother seemed to think that this had some bearing on the present illness, recalling an incident where his father had found Mensah playing checkers and had insisted that he get back to his studies, to which Mensah had replied that not even Europeans study all the time.

After completing commercial school, Mensah suffered from a period of protracted unemployment until a man from the Ewe area (to the west), who was renting a room in their house, gave him the information that there was an opening for a clerk in the government office in which he worked. Mensah's father took him to apply for the position, and he was selected after passing the civil service examination. According to the parents, at the time when Mensah received his first paycheck, the man who had given him the information about the vacancy "was not available to be thanked properly." Two weeks after receiving his first paycheck, the first episode of illness occurred. Fellow office workers told the parents that Mensah had been typing quietly when suddenly the typewriter was pushed off the table onto the ground. Shouting that the Ewe was using sorcery to harm him, Mensah began to chase him. He was restrained from attacking the man by other employees who, thinking that he was having an attack of yellow fever, took him to the police station and from there to the mental hospital. Although the man denied any knowledge of Mensah's problem (and understandably took offense and insisted on moving from Mensah's father's house after being thus accused), Mensah's parents remained convinced that this incident was the cause of the illness. While the parents generally referred to this incident in discussing the onset of the illness, they also expressed the feeling that Mensah was especially vulnerable to the "envy" of others because he had attained some level of education.

While Mensah never directly expressed an opinion about the cause of his illness, it became clear that much of his anxiety focused around the possibility of obtaining further education abroad and thereby raising his status. In conversation with me, he constantly alluded to traveling, passports, borders, and the possibility of studying abroad. Being a clerk with limited training placed him in that intermediate stratum which was discussed in chapter 1, with the possibility of unemployment ever present, but also the potential for advancement with further education.

After a three-month stay at the mental hospital yielded no improvement, Mensah's parents took him to one of the "modern" indigenous healers living on the outskirts of Labadi. The healer, who was also a part-time small businessman, administered medication without improvement. Mensah returned to the mental hospital and from there attended a spiritualist church, where he was given prayers and candles. He subsequently returned to the mental hospital for a third time. In this case, as in the previous cases, though the patients and families were nominally Christians, there was great flexibility of treatment modalities. A major concern was the extent to which success was detected. Mensah's father was a member of a spiritualist church, and his mother was a Jehovah's Witness. Because the Jehovah's Witnesses did not involve themselves in earthly healing, they advised her to take Mensah to a traditional healer.

After five years of pursuing various types of treatments, in fact all that were available to the general population, his parents decided to bring him to Ataa, who had been recommended by a friend. Mensah was immediately diagnosed as full sẹkẹ (sẹkẹ yelo), which would require months to cure. While the healer knew the parents' account of the onset of the illness, throughout the treatment process he maintained that the cause of the illness must lie within the family. After Mensah had been residing at the compound for some months, the healer concluded that the perfidy of Mensah's father was the cause of the illness. Mensah's father's brother had purchased some property in Labadi and built a house on it. Purchased property is privately owned, with proceeds belonging only to the individual. The healer alleged that when Mensah's father returned to Labadi from the north, he had purchased sorcery medicine to kill his brother, thereby allowing him to inherit the property. According to the healer, Mensah's father had admitted that this was the case. Thus, while the immediate cause of Mensah's illness, as diagnosed by the healer, was the fact that the father had not kept the taboos that are said to be associated with this dangerous and disreputable individual medicine, the ultimate cause of the illness was the father's wrongdoing in engaging in these measures for private gain. The retribution was visited on the son. The healer's advice to the father was that he dispose of the sorcery medicine as soon as possible and not engage in such things again.

Mensah arrived at the compound of the traditional healer, accompanied by his mother, father, two sisters, and two brothers, early one morning in May. The family brought with them a goat, firewood, and several large burlap bags of medicines, which would be used in the course of the treatment. Mensah, who was confined by ankle shackles to prevent him from running away, exhibited no physical symptoms, such as convulsions or tremors, but occasionally laughed or discoursed inappropriately. For example, although he seemed oriented according to time, place, and person, he insisted that he was going to his office. This was judged to be inappropriate by the healer and family. He was lucid enough, however, to translate my rather halting Ga into English and to discuss with me, at length, the necessity of studying abroad and the difficulty of organizing it.

The three bags of herbs brought by the family were lined up against the wall of the compound. Calabashes and grinding stones to prepare them stood ready. On a goatskin in the middle of the courtyard were four long leaves, approximately two feet in diameter, painted on both sides with seven lines of white and seven of red; ten smaller leaves, also painted with red and white lines; an old calabash approximately one and one-half feet in diameter; a garland of herbs; a small hand broom such as the priests use in the traditional religion rituals to whisk away impurities; four varieties of herbs; *ayilọ* (white clay) and *tung* (red clay).

As everyone sat around the courtyard conversing and observing, the assistant began the preparations. After scraping the ayilọ into a bowl and moistening it with water, he proceeded to apply it to the outside of the small bowl and the calabash. The reminder of it was rubbed on the broom. Using the second and third fingers of his right hand, he mixed the red tung and painted seven sets of two short lines around the mouth of the bowl and the calabash. The remainder of the red clay was then speckled onto the broom by flicking four fingers on the thumb. The bowl was then put aside, and the calabash was placed on the wreath of herbs, which remained on the goatskin. Ataa came to supervise the placing of the herbs in the calabash. First, the long leaves were placed crosswise, the short leaves were arranged around the bottom, and then the other herbs were added. After pouring water into the calabash from five different bottles, representing the dzemawọdzii, the healer chewed the small seeds, one of the medicines brought by the family, and spit them into the small bowl, whispering an invocation as he did so. (Spitting, in this context, is thought to be a method of invoking the powers.) After raising an acorn cup of schnapps to the sky for the blessing of the high god. Ataa spit the schnapps into the calabash. The calabash, the broom, and the small bowl were then placed in the bathing area, to be used for Mensah's daily bath.

As in most societies, water is a dominant and efficacious symbol. The god of the town, the Lakpa, is associated with rain, and in a drought villagers will send an emissary to the Lapka priest for a small pot of sacred water, which is thought to bring rain. In fact, all gods possess a small pot (kulo) of this kind through which they are invoked. Rain is a mediating substance between the world of men and the world of divinity (Kilson 1971:69). The necessity and benefits of water in an agricultural society are elegantly described in the homọwọ song recorded on page 72. All large bodies of water are the abodes of gods—the ocean, the lagoons, the lakes, and the rivers of Ghana. Collecting water from these sources with the proper ritual procedure (usually including an invocation and throwing in tremma shells) harnesses sacred power. Such water is used extensively in healing procedures. Ritual bathing, for example, is a significant element in traditional religion and healing.

Mensah's younger brother assisted the apprentice in stacking the firewood against a wall. Small pieces of shavings were placed inside a black calabash in which two white lines had been drawn from rim to rim, crossing at the bottom, to keep away evil.

The healer summoned Mensah's mother and father to an inner room to discuss the cost of treatment. Clearly, the family did not have much money and had recently incurred heavy expenses. To the obvious dismay and disapproval of Mensah's mother, the immediate family had been forced to bear much of the cost of Mensah's illness themselves, with only limited help from one of the father's brothers. They had spent approximately twenty cedis at the mental hospital, ten cedis more at the spiritualist churches, and additional change to buy candles and to give pennies to the poor.

Mensah's mother expressed great disappointment with the father's lineage, where, she said, they only help if they are specifically asked for money, as compared to her lineage, where it is customary to help members in trouble. The father complained that, in addition to the expenses of Mensah's illness, he had just spent forty cedis on his own bout with illness. The healer replied that, under ordinary circumstances, he would charge twenty-four cedis to commence the treatment but, because they did not have much money, he would take less. He insisted, however, that they put down some money to initiate treatment: "It is necessary that the spirits have something to stand on, so that they will do their work." He distinguished his approach to payment from that of biomedical practitioners, in that he does not charge his patients "20 pounds [40 cedis] and more, every month for medicine, as Western doctors and the mental hospitals do," but rather charges them an initial fee to begin the treatment. If the treatment is successful, a ceremony called *awroke hamo̱* (to be described later) is performed, where the entire family is invited to contribute, according to their conscience, toward the cure. He claimed that on two recent occasions he had received fifty-eight cedis and fifty-four cedis. In addition to the payments at the beginning and end, the family must also bear the expenses of the initial medicine, the goat for sacrifice (which may cost as much as fourteen cedis), and other small items necessary to initiate treatment.

The father replied that, although he did not have much money, since he was Mensah's father, he wanted to do something for him. Before leaving to try to raise some money, he poured a libation and delivered a long, moving invocation, in which he implored the gods to intercede for the success of the treatment. Several hours later, he returned with ten cedis, raised from relatives. Mensah, his mother, the healer, the assistant, and I retired to the inner room. The healer and his assistant donned long, wide robes of broad strips of red, navy blue, and white cloth. The healer, the assistant, and Mensah knelt in the center of the room, among the wǫkui. After the healer poured individual libations to them, Mensah's mother and I again poured libations, requesting his return to health.

One of the brothers assisted in bringing in the goat, which was held by its hooves and raised toward the sky, to the high god, three times. After the apprentice slit its jugular vein with a sharp knife, it was carried around the room so that blood could be applied to all the wǫdzii. During this procedure, the healer continued to make invocations, alternately appealing and admonishing. The remainder of the blood was placed in a bowl, mixed with schnapps, and again distributed to the wǫdzii. In the bathing area, a chicken was sacrificed amid libations and invocations. The fact that it died chest up was judged to be auspicious for treatment.

Aspects of treatment such as sacrifice, libations, invocations, ritual bathing, reflect, on the individual level, rituals performed by and on behalf of the entire town, represented by lineages, during the central public ritual of homǫwǫ. The first phase of the public ritual consisted of a few months of ritual episodes, in which each of the town gods charged to specific lineages was "purified." Upon arrival at the dwelling of the god being purified that day, representatives of the seven lineages first ritually washed their hands and faces in a large basin of sacred water and herbs. The spirit medium of the god then applied the set of red and white clay markings to the wrists and faces of the participants. During the sacrifice of a sheep or goat, in which the jugular vein was slashed, it was held up to the high god by its hooves and carried around the compound, blood sprinkling on the feet of the participants. Each of the participants poured a libation to the deity being addressed, asking blessings for the entire town. The person pouring the libation began with:

> Tswa, tswa, tswa amanye aba
> Tswa, tswa, tswa amanye aba
> let there be blessings.

(With each "strike," the priest of the Lakpa made a swatting motion with his ritual broom of palm leaves, which was approximately one foot in length, with a handle decorated with red clay.) The other participants responded with:

> Yao: We agree [rising slightly from their seats]

The pourer of the libation then continued:

> Our broom should have a big head
> [Death should stay away so that we will be many]
> I bless the chief and the royal household
> I bless the *dzranoyei*
> I bless the *amrakui*
> I bless the mediums
> I bless you in the name of Sakumo
> I bless the fishermen and the farmers
> Let there be fish and let there be millet
> I ask that we should bring forth twins
> If we fall into the river, let us not drown
> [In trouble let us conquer]
> If someone stands and says "Look what the
> Boni people are doing," let that trouble go back to him
> Let there be blessings
> *Yao.*

When used in healing, a ritual such as sacrifice has meanings associated with its role in traditional religious ritual with which all participants are generally familiar. In all major illnesses, the initial treatment always includes a sacrifice, which might be repeated at any time deemed necessary during the treatment process. The healers say that the purpose of sacrifice is to "beg the spirits" to use their powers to aid the patient. On this general level of explanation of function, there is little discrepancy between the explanations of the specialist and the patients. Aba, for example, gave a similar explanation of the significance of sacrifice. "You must put everything on the fowls, because we have a proverb that says, 'We breed fowls and animals because of human beings.' They say that when something is going to happen to a person, that thing goes instead to the animals."

This explanation is remarkably similar to that given by investigators as the function of sacrifice in healing systems. Prince (1979; 1964) describes the anxiety-reducing effects of sacrifice in Yoruba psychotherapy. Among the Ndembu and elsewhere, sacrifice is restorative and regenerative, emphasizing, but atoning for, the guilt of the victim (Turner 1967:276; see also Kiev 1972).

The healer's assistant then began to grind a root. This was a time-consuming process, but after it had been accomplished the ground root was mixed with water, producing a thick, viscous liquid, which was inserted into the patient's nose by means of a bulbous syringe. Mensah became extremely uncomfortable, crying, shouting, blowing his nose, and holding his head. The signs of discomfort and consequent hostility and disorientation continued for approximately an hour and a half. The healer's explanation of the procedure was that the patient was plagued with the presence of evil spirits in his head, and the medicine allowed him to expel them, as was evidenced by his frequent sneezing and blowing of his nose. Clearly, the procedure had a shock effect on the patient.

In the meantime, the mother and one of the sisters had been given the task of grinding more roots for medicine. Then Mensah's mother and the healer took Mensah to the bathing area, where he was stripped and bathed very thoroughly with the sacred water from the calabash by the healer, the apprentice, and the healer's senior wife. After throwing an egg that had been placed in the basin and pronouncing its landing auspicious, the healer rubbed Mensah's head (which had been shaved) with a paste made from the root the women had been grinding.

Mensah was then chained to the post in the courtyard. He was still, but extremely hostile, as he continued to abuse verbally all those who had assisted in his treatment. At this point, the healer assumed an authoritarian relationship to the patient, scolding him if he did something wrong and using physical force to move him when necessary. Everyone, including Mensah's family and that of the healer, laughed outright when he said something inappropriate, until Mensah himself began to laugh. At the same time, everyone was very sympathetic and made every attempt to comfort him and to make him comfortable.

At about 6 A.M. the next morning, the healers and patient proceeded again to the bathing area. Mensah was very reticent and, although not actively uncooperative, participated in the treatment unwillingly. His conversation was somewhat more disoriented than the day before; he spoke very slowly, slurring his words. This time, the small calabash and broom, prepared the day before, were used for bathing. A libation of schnapps was poured into the calabash. The assistant bathed Mensah with the broom, striking him firmly on the head and shoulders several times, in a manner similar to that used by the priests in their purificatory rites for homǫwǫ. Each time he dipped the broom into the calabash, he first spit on it, invoking power. (After this, the patient was bathed daily with water.)

Following the bath, the patient's entire body was rubbed with the paste from the brown herb, ground the day before. The healer explained that the purpose of the ritual bath was to "cool" him and to "make the vapor or heat [lamo] go out of him." The paste medicine was to kill the evil spirits that were in him.

The concepts of "heat" and "coolness," as used in medicine, extend the concepts of health and illness to social relations, and draw a link between illness and conflict. As in classic humoral theory, heat is associated with illness and coolness with health. Much of healing consists of measures to remove heat and restore coolness. This has a literal aspect, in the sense of reducing fever, but also functions as a metaphor that equates illness with conflict and health with peace. Coolness is said to be a condition of peace, which allows society to function. Thus, one of the names for the high god is the owner or father of coolness (Dzobo 1978).

In the next case, the gods are repeatedly asked to make the house, where there is a conflict and subsequent illness, cool, so that mushrooms may grow and health may prevail. Such illness, characterized by heat, the opposite of that state of coolness, is referred to as "sitting on a hot thing" (Dzobo 1978). These metaphors occur in other African societies. The Zulu speak of healing as *lungisa* (literally, cool), to put in order, to restore order "with reference to the position of people and their relations to other people, to the environment, to the ancestors and to the mystical forces which produce pollution" (Ngubane 1976:327).

Following these treatments, Mensah was given medicine to drink and food to eat. He sat in the courtyard, unchained, among the healer's wives, children, and the other patients, who exhibited only mild curiosity or amusement when he did something that was considered funny. He remained, however, the center of attention, with everyone concerned that he eat well and become strong. Another brother, who had not been present the day before, arrived to greet him, although Mensah appeared not to recognize him. Everyone joked with Mensah and teased him good-naturedly until he, himself, had to join in the general merriment.

During the next two weeks, Mensah's affect remained about the same; he conversed normally for the most part, although he tended to giggle inappropriately and often wandered from the subject of conversation. His answers to my questions were generally indirect. When I asked him whether he thought traditional treatments were effective, he replied: "Some people say that we must change our ways and adopt modern ways, but I disagree. I think some of our customs are good." Quite frequently he discussed the possibility of going abroad to study and seemed to be quite preoccupied with the question of borders, stating that he did not believe in borders or in passports. His mother remained with him, helping to care for him.

His treatments continued throughout the month of June, including the daily medicinal bath, administration of medications, and occasional special rituals and sacrifices. During the last two weeks of June, he became withdrawn, communicating minimally with others and complaining of feeling dizzy.

At the beginning of July, to the delight of everyone, Mensah's affect changed; he was no longer withdrawn and conversed at length with those in the household and with visitors. He requested books in English and read them. According to the healer, the appearance of different phases in his condition was owing to the fact that several different types of sorcery medicines were involved in producing his illness. As the healer drove them out, one at a time, each new one resulted in the manifestation of different symptoms. This analysis, similar to that given in Aba's case, is a clear example of the way in which the traditional healer, like the biomedical scientist, observes the regularity of a given phenomenon and seeks a theoretical explanation that will link as many of the data as possible.

At one point, when Mensah became more rambunctious, he was rechained. Mensah attempted to break the chain attached to his ankle shackles and run away. The healer responded by sending for his father to assist him in inserting medicine into Mensah's nostrils (obviously a painful procedure).

Throughout August, Mensah's condition improved, to the extent that he could hold long conversations without wandering from the subject as he had previously. This was noted by the healer, who stated that his "talking sense" was a sign of improvement. When his condition improved, his ankle shackles were removed. He often responded to this, however, by attempting to escape. At one point, he had rolled up his sleeping mat and slipped away from the compound when he was not being watched. When he was found sleeping on the road, he said that he had been attempting to visit his grandmother.

During September and October, Mensah's condition deteriorated. He was very withdrawn, accepting his medicines and meals, but spending most of his time sleeping. Occasionally he woke up and attempted to communicate, but was generally incoherent. The healer, undisturbed by the regression, stated that this was yet another stage of the illness. It was during this period that the healer, annoyed by the fact that Mensah's father had not visited as often as expected, elaborated the explanation of Mensah's illness that placed the blame on the father's purchase of medicines to bring him an inheritance by causing the death of his brother. When the illness did not respond to treatment, the healer sought new explanations. The explanation of etiology, however, rarely involved the individual patient's responsibility for illness, but rather allowed for shared retribution among kin—in this case, the sins of the father were visited on the son.

It is also interesting that the father was singled out at a time when he was not fulfilling his obligations as expected by the healer. All kin, although to different degrees, are expected to involve themselves in assisting in the treatment process to demonstrate their concern for the well-being of the patient. I have described the way in which members of the family were responsible for various aspects of the treatment, including procuring the medicines, assisting with their preparation and administration, pouring libations, and asking blessings. Mensah's mother and sister remained with him throughout his stay at the compound. He was frequently visited by members of the family. These days, it is often the case that many of the initial expenses are borne by the immediate family. It is also true that close kin who do not attend the thanksgiving ritual held at the end of a successful treatment, or show their goodwill by contributing to the patient's care, are immediately suspect and, to some extent, ostracized.

In November, after months of withdrawal, Mensah began to take an interest in his surroundings. He conversed with the other patients and the family of the healer, all of whom were very interested in his progress. He was quite oriented to time and place and wished to have the shackles removed before Christmas. He developed an especially close relationship with the healer's assistant, with whom he sat for hours, talking or just holding his hand.

Mensah's progress continued through the end of January, when I left Labadi. At that time, he appeared entirely normal (by my standards and by those of the healer) for the first time since I had encountered him seven months earlier. He was up all day and conversing entirely appropriately. He recounted a dream in which he was being attacked by crabs. A large crab bit him on the ear. Although he could see the crab coming, he was unable to repulse it because he was chained. He finally threw his cloth at it and told the crab to take what it wanted. He claimed that this particular type of crab was the embodiment of a witch. The healer interpreted this dream as additional evidence that evil forces were involved in causing Mensah's illness, but also as indicative of their impending defeat. The healer stated that he was now much improved and expected the improvement to continue.

In Mensah's case, the immediate family was more successful than Aba's mother in mobilizing a more extended unit to share the burden of Mensah's illness. The initial fee was raised from relatives outside of the nuclear family, and several kin participated in his general care.

TREATMENT: GOALS OF THERAPY

Suggestion, a major mechanism of therapy, is facilitated by symbolism, but is also implemented by verbal directives. Goals of therapy are often explicitly expressed in the dialogue that is a major aspect of therapeutic rituals. Although this case differs from the previous cases in that it represents a short-term, less serious illness, it manifestly demonstrates the premises that underlie etiology and treatment in the preceding cases. In the last case, I highlighted the form of treatment; in this case, I will emphasize the content, giving particular attention to the dialogue through which the verbal directives of therapy are transmitted.

Adzoa, a twenty-two-year-old, unmarried market woman from Labadi, approached the healer with complaints of "not feeling well," "pains all over my body," and cases of illness and death in her matrilineage. The healer was familiar, for good reason, as we shall see, with the history of the case. Adzoa's mother's mother's sister's daughter's daughter, Afi, was also a market woman. As noted previously, in the traditional kinship system, residential rights are traced bilaterally, in that people have the right to live in a compound of the parent of the same sex. Thus, Adzoa and Afi were eligible to live in the same house and were more or less classificatory sisters, which is how the healer described their relationship throughout the treatment. Although lineages were, at one time, corporate groups with resources shared by lineage members, the concept of private property was by now well developed, with the consequent inequality among kin. Adzoa and Afi were a case in point: although they were both marketing, Adzoa had not been making much money. Afi, in contrast, had recently been quite successful and, with her profits, had purchased a few houses from which she collected rent, further increasing her wealth.

This disparity was not unusual among market women. Although there was a generally held view that marketing was a road to wealth and independence, as I discussed in chapter 1, the small-scale marketing in which most Labadi women participated was very precarious and usually marginal (see Mullings 1976). Women normally sold agricultural produce, cloth, and canned goods. They were generally confined to small-scale concerns not destined for expansion or, as in the cases of fish and cloth selling, in areas where trade conditions were becoming increasingly monopolistic, ensuring success for only a few (Robertson 1976:131). I found that most of the Labadi market women had a relatively insecure existence, with the selling price of items varying with season, supply, and demand. This view of market women is substantiated by the findings of other studies of Ga market women: "most of the traders only make enough to get by" (Robertson 1976:131); that profits of the average trader were not substantial enough to raise their standard of living (Sai 1971:9); half of the traders had a daily turnover of £2 or less (Nypan 1960:40).

Despite the evidence, expectations of money to be made from marketing run high, and most women harbor the hope of making a killing and becoming a "market princess." In the absence of an analysis of the vagaries of the market economy, people seek answers elsewhere for what appears to be random success and failure. Adzoa, disappointed at her lack of success in marketing, especially as compared to Afi, and at the same time concerned with the death of her mother's sister's daughter, Akua, consulted the founder of one of the spiritualist churches. He informed her that the death of Akua and her own symptoms of illness were due to the fact that a member of the family had made use of the medicine *akpaso*.

Akpaso was thought to be a potent medicine (tsofa) that turns the owner into a witch and draws wealth by sacrificing members of the family. It was explained to me as follows: "Akpaso is the worst of all medicines. It can kill a whole family . . . it kills for no cause, when it is hungry. It is used by people because when it starts to kill in their lineage (*wekumli*) it draws money." It kills only within the extended family, but might single out any individual among those eligible. Only by killing kin could the akpaso draw power to amass money. The purchaser of the medicine could not predict who would die — it might be his or her own child. Anyone who would procure such medicine, then, must have values antithetical to those considered to be normal. In the concept of akpaso, people expressed, rather vividly, their perception of the opposition between the interests of the corporate lineage and private individual profits — the individual becomes personally rich by killing members of the lineage. Akpaso was not esoteric knowledge; it was generally known and discussed and thought to be in widespread use "nowadays, because we use people to gain money."

Adzoa concluded that the person who had procured akpaso was Afi. She initiated rumors that Afi had wooed success through akpaso, sacrificing Akua, her "sister," to wealth. During homọwọ, in which songs were spontaneously composed by townspeople memorializing events of the year and censuring those who do wrong, Afi's alleged witchcraft activities were publicized in song throughout the town. At Akua's funeral, Afi and her mother were taunted with having been the cause of Akua's death.

It was under these circumstances that, five days before, Afi had come to the healer to pronounce a curse (loomọ). As we noted on page 68, this ritual involved presenting a case to the town gods, asking them to judge it, and to punish whoever was the wrongdoer. The healer explained it as follows (throughout this case, I will quote the original text at some length, using Ga terms, in order to demonstrate the way in which the healers and the clients use key concepts):

> This is what happened. She [Afi] came and reported to the town gods that they said this about her. And so if she is really the one who had gone for some akpaso and *ayẹ sika* (witchcraft money) to kill her sister, then they must find out for her. She said that if it was true that she had really done it, then those of her immediate family should die. They [the gods] should not leave any alive: they should kill her father's side and her mother's side. If she was not guilty, then her name and her soul [susuma] have been ruined. Then her accuser and her family must die, so that the whole world will know the truth. As we live in the world, Nyọngmọ's [the high god's] truth is the same as tsofa's truth,

because the tsofa are Nyọngmọ's first-born children. Only human beings can tell lies. But gods do everything that is righteous. And so this charge was given to them. They went to the family, taking the gods from Afi's mother's lineage and the gods from her father's lineage. They will go through everything, and if they really find out that it is true, then they will know. And so if it is the case that Afi was wrong, they they would kill her and her lineage. But then they will go to the other girl's family. If they do not take care of it early, the gods will kill all and their gates will be locked [if Adzoa's family does not take measures to lift the curse soon, the entire family will be wiped out]. This is how the gods are. The gods, when you report a case to them and they find that you are wrong, they will ignore you. But they would rather take from those at your back (your lineage). And so you who have reported the case, if they kill you first, what will be the profit. They will leave you to stay and then see and know what is happening because of your stealing or dirtiness. They will kill your relatives.

Soon after Afi executed the curse, Adzoa's mother died.

The one who was killed was Adoza's own mother. She was killed at once. If your child goes to do something wrong or says something wrong which is not good, would you not get up to stop her from doing that and to ask her what she is trying to do to your *shia* [house/household]? Both sides of the family should rise and do this.

The relatives of the mother's side and those of the father's side must attend the lifting of the curse. Those that did not come because of work must take ritual water in a bottle so that it can be sprinkled on everyone in the lineage. When you take a wife and your child gets trouble, will you sit down and observe the child without doing anything? And so, all of the *weku* will have to get up. And so the quarter [*akutsho*] in which Afi was born, her patrilineage, will have to come. The entire families of both girls will have to come. When Afi becomes rich, will she not give some to her father's brother or her father's brother's children? When you are rich you enjoy it with your lineage. So if something bad happens, will you refuse to do something about it? So when something bad happens, they have to come.

Here the healer was explicit about the collective nature of lineage responsibility, the submersion of the individual in the lineage. The collective liability of the lineage is implicit in the concept of the curse—harm first befalls the kin of the guilty party, not the guilty party herself. Clearly, the healer's standards for social relationships were based on the organization of the village community system of collective ownership.

After Adzoa had been in residence at the traditional healer's compound for several days, fifteen kin from the maternal and paternal lineages arrived to attend the performance of *daṇ mọ,* the lifting of the curse. The healer requested an initial fee of 150 pounds (300 cedis, equivalent to $300), which was reduced to 50 pounds after much stylized bargaining. When the family asked to have it decreased still further, the healer informed them that this was impossible because of the nature of the offense. According to him, the payment is "claimed for the gods so that they will work"; if he were to lower the price, the gods would be angry and not lift the curse. After dispatching a few people to attempt to raise more money, the clients decided to postpone the ritual until the next morning in order to spend the day accumulating contributions from kin.

The clients returned the next day to begin the proceedings. Twelve people attended, including six young men, all of whom were "descendants of the same great-grandmother." We arranged ourselves around the courtyard, with the family on one side, the healer perpendicular to them, and the assistant, the linguist, and myself opposite the family and to the right of the healer. After an extended discussion between the healer and the family, in which the family was chastised for their lateness, the dialogue began, with the healer speaking through a linguist.

> HEALER: Afi, bring a stool and come with the one you have trouble with. [Afi and Adzoa, looking very sulky, brought their stools close to him.] You have burned a yam [referring to the proverb that if you put a yam in the fire your hands become burned; see p. 96].
> AFI'S MOTHER: [plaintively] It is burning me, I am feeling the pains so I am kneeling and begging.
> HEALER: Ask the copper-colored woman [Adzoa] who caused us to come and sit here.
> ADZOA: We are here because of me.
> HEALER: Let the woman know that our sitting here needs patience, and so when I ask her any questions she must try to answer with patience, because we are now going to sit in judgment. Ask her if she can remember what I asked her when they first came.
> ADZOA: Yes.

HEALER: And so our sitting here today, does it mean that you have come to settle the matter so that there will be peace in your house?
ADZOA: Yes.
HEALER: Good, this is what we want. Afi, for whose sake are we here today?
AFI: That woman caused us to be here.
HEALER: Good. Ask Afi if she has come here with her whole heart so that we may settle this matter, to maintain peace and the growth of mushrooms [when a place is cool, mushrooms can grow; see p. 107], or has she been persuaded by someone to agree? Have you come here so that we settle the matter or have you come here because someone has deceived you to agree? Or did you come with your whole heart?
AFI: I came here with my whole heart.
HEALER: Since this trouble occurred, has someone come from the family to say that you have caused damage in the house? Adzoa, is your father standing with you? Let Adzoa's father know that they will compensate [literally, bathe — *he dzuu*] Afi with one sheep and one bottle of drink, one bottle of Schnapps and forty cedis, and seven eggs. What do Adzoa's people say?
SPOKESMAN FOR ADZOA'S FAMILY: Let the old man know that we have heard all that he has said. We want to beg [to ask to have the price reduced].
HEALER: Let Adzoa's father also know what I have said. [Ataa skillfully insisted that all parties concerned agree to the premises of the proceedings at each critical point in the analysis.]
ADZOA'S FATHER: We thank the old man for what he has said and we have accepted it. But I would like to ask for something. We all beg that you reduce it a bit.
HEALER: Let them know that so far as custom [*kusum*] is concerned, we must go according to custom. This is a case judged by the gods. We are trying to judge here so that when you go back, nothing must come out again. And so if you leave here and you begin to argue about it among yourselves, it will lie with the one who raised it. We do not danmọ [lift the curse] and then leave the people just like that. In the end, people will ask what I did about it. Tell them that I know they are all sisters but as I have said last time, two children have trouble with each other and one said something against the other and the relatives of the one do not do anything about it. Then it means that they have believed that what their daughter said was true: that Adzoa has said that Afi is able to buy these buildings because she is a witch. She is still young and has been able to have some buildings. Nowadays because we use people to gain money, you assume that is why she has had the buildings.

Again the healer reiterated the premise that, within the lineage, guilt is collective; by not taking responsibility for the actions of an individual member, the entire lineage implicated itself. He voiced a common belief often stated by people in different walks of life: "nowadays . . . we use people to gain money." The healer continued:

> And so since the beginning, we Africans know that when someone falsely accuses you, we solve the problem in this way. If the kin [*weku-mei*] had not accepted it, events would not have come about like this. Because, so far as they knew, they live as brothers and sisters. So if there will be trouble, or not, it will come from the family relationship [*weku le mli*]. The one who accused and the one who is accused are all from one weku. The relationship makes it possible that they could all stay in one house. So if something happens, it lies upon the same weku. But if the case is such that when one abuses her neighbor, then the family of the one that makes the accusation must immediately try to settle the matter with the other weku. But instead they did not say anything about it. That is how these people act; they do not like to settle matters, they just like to beat drums and spread the news. . . . One's grandmother is second after the other's grandmother.

After the healer's discourse, emphasizing collective responsibility, the family dispersed to discuss the situation. When the group reconstituted, Afi's mother discussed her reaction to the accusation, stressing her own identification with the accusations against her daughter.

> AFI'S MOTHER: Let it reach the healer that what has been said is true. If we had gone to another place about Afi's case, the person would say, before anything else, that he will charge two or three hundred pounds. But because Afi wants to know the truth in the family, that they will all know that she was not the one who killed her sister [*nyẹbi le*] for the money, she came and said with her mouth that they must find out for her. If it falls on her, then it must come on her father, her mother, her brothers and sisters. So it was true that Afi came here to settle the matter because they are all from one family. When we heard about the case we were riding in a lorry. Adzoa spread the news around so that all the seven quarters knew about this case. And I cannot say that because Afi was right she should drop the case; because if you do not placate the susuma you will die. When I myself heard the case, my susuma left me [she was shocked]. If it were not for my father I would have died [her father soothed her]. I could not eat, I could not drink. Peo-

ple who came to greet me and comfort me made me feel as though Afi was dead. And so I know that if this case was to be somewhere else, they would charge more than this to bathe [compensate] Afi. But now it has come on our own neck. And so, we have seen the truth and the weku knows that it was not Afi who killed Akua for money; all those from Adzoa's father's family and all his sisters should know that it was not Afi who killed Akua for money. But they might know that Akua had her own death. The black cloth that I had for Akua's funeral, the family did not allow me to use it because they said that my daughter had killed Akua so that I am mourning for nothing . . . they were trying to tell me that we have killed Akua.

And so now that they all know that it was not Afi; now if I use the black cloth, I will be happy. Afi could not use her black cloth either. And so if they compensate Afi with some money, she will spend all and if she is compensated with cloth, she will wear it out. But what I want for Afi's susuma is the drink, ten cedis, and some eggs, to bathe her, just to comfort her susuma and to bring peace in the family. But we should think of our debts [think of money being expended, since they all come from the same kin group], so that we will be able to pay our debts. This is all that I have to say.

HEALER: Tell her that I thank her. I think they all came and that they have all heard. So ask her brother if he accepts what his sister said. Does everyone agree? [Everyone agrees.] Afi, this is what your parents have said. You must also say something. [Afi says that she has nothing to say.] The spokesman must thank the old woman, but she should claim two fowls instead of one — one cock and one hen — big ones, because the susuma is two — one male and one female — in addition to what she has claimed. [Everyone agrees.]

And so let them know again that everybody must be careful how he walks. If you go to say something, you must try to be careful of what you say. Somebody can do you some good, but not when you go you say bad things of them. . . . [The healer then proceeded to mumble about the fact that the family had brought a thin goat.]

There are some things, when put to someone's susuma [soul], will kill the person. Thus, any person who says something about it will be someone who wants the death of Afi. This would be the only reason he would say something about it.

And so you must not speak evil. If any bad-speaking comes out, it should be against the one who gave out the message. Those churches in which the pastors try to do things for money, do bad things; this is one of them. If the founder says that he himself is a witch, he must try to be a good witch in his church [cynically]. If you say you are working for people, if you want to defend someone, then you must defend the person righteously. And so we will all see what will happen, where the truth lies. Whatever the case is, no one goes to a tsofa naa [dwelling of medicines], with ears to say something only with his mouth. Before you send someone, you have to implore that one. So that day, Afi spent seven pounds, one big bottle of schnapps, seven eggs, kola, and some perfume and palm oil. These are things that she used to raise their ears [the gods'] with tears on her face. Things happen that are greater than this, that heavy amounts are being charged, sometimes one hundred pounds, seventy pounds, eighty pounds. The gods will judge with the aid of the gods on the father's and mother's side. So all these things are things for the soul, but that money will go to where it is supposed to go. It will by all means vanish. So you must try to settle that part for her. You must refund the money [that she spent on executing the curse] so that she can place it where she got it.

The healer drew a white circle on the ground with crossed lines in the middle, into which was placed a white marble calabash. The red, white, and black calico brought by the family was torn into strips, and three strips of each color were attached to the roof and to an iron sword. After changing into their red, white, and black robes, the healer and his assistant poured a few drops of each drink brought by the clients first onto the ground three times, into the calabash containing herbs in water and an egg, and then onto the sword leaning against the calabash. During this process, the following invocation was intoned by the healer:

Ataa Nyongmo, Twedeampong Kwame and his wife Asaase Afia, Jehowa Nyongmo, today's Tuesday. It is a day from your hands. I think you created the world and you settled everything for us. And you said everything was good. There are some works that are done customarily. And so we are here to do something. We are standing here, imploring. If you want to destroy something that cannot be renewed, then you can do it. But if you say something can be renewed, then we renew it. We ask that as we are standing here you must pour blessings on us, so that there must be peace and victory, so that the house [shia] be cool to grow mushrooms. Hey, all town gods, come and enjoy some drink. Everybody must come and enjoy this drink. Ancestors, I am not calling you for anything wrong. One of the children has annoyed another of the children. And so you must settle it. Truly, when someone is slandered, it spread over the four corners of the world and we want to know the truth. They are all from one weku, one blood. We want to know the good path and the bad path so that we can keep peace in the house so that mushrooms may grow. And so, fathers, you must all come and enjoy this drink. Hey [long list of names of gods], let it reach our fathers and mothers and children and unborn children. I have a small story to tell you. Some time ago, Afi came here with tears and told me that one of her sisters had put shame on her susuma. That if I do not defend her, she cannot do anything. Kla [sometimes used synonomously with susuma] can kill a person in an hour. It can kill any time it wants. And so, if it were she who had the chance of killing her sister, Akua, by travelling to get some tsofa to make money, you must find out. When she becomes rich, she will share with those from her mother's family and those from her father's family. And so, go and destroy her mother's family and her father's family. This was what Afi said when she came. Destroy everything so that it will be known what she has done. And as you are fathers and we are human beings, what you see, we cannot see. And so the gods journeyed to find out. When they went, they saw the truth. When they went to another place, they also found the truth. They have been walking for five or six days. But I am begging you: Afi's mother is your daughter. When we examined the case, it was one blood, one old woman produced these grand-children. And so, if it happened to someone in your family, what would you do? You would do the same thing. So I am begging. When you speak frankly then you become free. The goat they brought was skinny, no intestines. So, I am imploring you not to bother about the goat. Rather, do your work. They have brought one bottle of schnapps, one bottle of whiskey, different types of drinks, corn wine, eggs, kola nuts that are used for working. They have brought all these things so that there may be peace in the house such that mushrooms may grow. The founder of the church who is in his house sleeping, has made people's children suffer and burn. And so, Ataa, kill for me; kill him for me. You must come and drink. From here to Lama, from Lama to Nyame, you must all come and enjoy this drink. You must all come and have some drink to maintain peace in the house. Here is a bottle of schnapps for you. Come and enjoy it, to maintain peace and the growth of mushrooms. Here is some orange drink, corn wine, wine, to maintain peace.

Additional libations and invocations were performed by all present, expressing their agreement with, and commitment to, the proceedings. After the ritual sacrifice of the chicken and goat, similar in form to that described in John's case, a final invocation was pronounced by the healer as he ritually flicked water over each side of the calabash three times, completing his part in the ritual by taking water from the calabash into his mouth and spitting it back in.

Everyone present was bathed with ritual water from the calabash. Afi and Adzoa were given the most complete treatment: after their heads, shoulders, and arms were rigorously bathed in the sacred water, the apprentice used white clay to make longitudinal lines on their right arms, between their breasts, and between their eyebrows. The other kin approached the calabash, one at a time, bathing their faces, arms, and feet after placing some change into the calabash. The bathing was followed by friendly celebration and drinking, after which the clients returned to their homes. Although I was not able to see Adzoa again, I was told that her symptoms had disappeared.

In recounting the circumstances leading to the necessity for the ritual, the healer referred not only to the explicit events but made manifest the underling cause of dissension — Afi's privately-held wealth. Again, he clearly indicated the path to acceptable behavior —the reciprocal relations of corporate kinship.

> When she [Afi] becomes rich, she will share with those from her mother's family and those from her father's family.

As Field (1937:216) aptly suggested, "life, health and prosperity are the reward of goodness and goodness is attention to family obligations and family ritual." In this case, the largest group of kin participated directly in the ritual and contributed to the expenses. Sacred water was taken in bottles to the lineage house so that those kin who had been unable to attend because of work obligations could use it for bathing.

TRADITIONAL HEALING: A SUMMARY

In this section I will summarize the main features of traditional healing, using a modified version of Kleinman's (1980) categories.

THE THERAPEUTIC ROLE

In traditional therapy, the role of healer generally involves specialization. While various categories of individuals may engage in what might be generally defined as healing practices, the role of tsofatse, the recognized traditional healer-ritual therapist, requires not only specialized training and apprenticeship but also the proper constellation of moral qualities that will constrain the healer to use his art for the general good. A tsofatse's status is considerably en-

hanced and solidified by being an elder and ritual specialist of traditional religion. In the 1970s the role of tsofatse differed from that of
elder in that he was a private practitioner. As a well-trained, successful healer and ritual therapist, Ataa was able to command considerable fees for his services, sometimes as high as one hundred
cedis, as in the case of Adzoa. Yet, he often treated patients for
almost nothing, depending on their ability to pay. It was also the
case that Ataa asked an initial fee at the onset of the treatment and,
excluding animals for sacrifices and drink for libations, the majority
of the fee was obtained during the final ritual, held at the end of a
successful treatment. Several investigators have suggested that in
some areas the fees of the traditional healer are more reasonable
than those of the biomedical facilities (see, for example, Onoge
1975).

THE UNIT OF TREATMENT

In all serious illnesses, the optimal unit of treatment is the lineage and extended family; most often several members, representing the lineage, participate. The role of the kin group is first appar-
ent in decision making about the course of therapy to be implemented. On the initial visit to the healer, patients are always accompanied by some kin. Thus Aba was first escorted by her mother and
mother's sister's daughter for the diagnostic visit; when she returned
the next day, she was accompanied by six lineage members, some of
whom remained with her throughout the treatment. Similarly, in
the cases of Mensah and Adzoa kin participated at all levels—in
decision making about the course of therapy, in helping with the
treatments, participating in the rituals, and in contributing the
remuneration. This obligation is formalized and dramatized in
awroke hamo, a ritual which takes place at the conclusion of a successful treatment. On this occasion, kin of the patient gather around
a calabash of sacred water. As each individual walks up to the calabash to make a contribution, a linguist calls out the name and
amount of the contribution. At the end of this ritual, the patient is
ceremoniously returned to her family. See Appendix 9 for an
account of an awroke hamo.

It is, of course, for contributions to the cost of treatment that
the most serious mobilization of kin occurs; kinsmen are approached
to help with illness and are expected to do so, although expectations
are not always fulfilled. Nevertheless, participation of kin was en-

couraged, and often required, by the healer. Collective responsibility for illness was directly evident in the etiological statements in all cases, where the actions of kin have implications for the occurrence of the illness. In the case of John, where kin did not participate extensively, this was taken as an indication of their responsibility for his illness. In the case of Adzoa, the words of both the healer and family emphasized acceptance of collective responsibility.

Evidence from other areas of Ghana suggests that the emphasis on the kinship group in traditional healing is widespread. Among the Ashanti, illness requires the legitimization by an elder of the extended family or kinship group:

> If he decides to treat the patient, after the diagnosis, the patient's relatives appoint an *okyigyinafo* (patient supporter) who will remain with the patient during the course of treatment at the medical shrine. Literally the supporter is the person who stands behind the sick man. . . . No family will ever fail to support a sick relative, for to do so would be a standing reproach to the whole extended family unit. (Twumasi 1979:238; see also Appiah-Kubi 1981; Twumasi 1972)

THERAPEUTIC INTERVENTIONS

The traditional healer employs therapeutic interventions on both the somatic and symbolic levels. In fact, as I shall discuss in chapter 5, it is difficult to make a firm distinction between somatic and symbolic intervention. Increasingly, the evidence suggests that symbolic stimuli may produce physiological changes. Further, as is now clear from the studies of placebo effect, changes that may initially appear to be the result of somatic intervention may result from symbolic stimuli. The traditional healer utilizes somatic interventions in the form of medicine, rest, and certain forms of shock treatment (such as the nasal administration of medicine). He makes use of such psychotherapeutic techniques as dream analysis and confession and, of course, the mechanism of suggestion is basic to therapy.

Communication, through which suggestion occurs, involves both the verbal and symbolic levels. Every medication is taken with libations poured to the ancestors and town gods and a prayer that they aid in healing the patient. Treatments such as sacrifice, the cutting of the calico, and bathing in sacred water contain strongly symbolic elements. In fact, the general setting in which healing takes place is consciously manipulated so as to intensify symbolic communication.

Victor Turner's work on symbolism remains one of the most provocative treatments of symbolism in healing. He suggests that all symbols have two poles of meaning: the ideological, which refers to principles of social organization, and the sensory, which refers to natural and physiological processes, where the meaning content is closely related to the outward form of the symbol. "At the sensory pole are concentrated those *significata* that may be expected to arouse desires and feelings; at the ideological pole one finds an arrangement of norms and values that guide and control persons as members of social groups and classes" (1967:28). In cases of illness involving physiological processes, it stands to reason that the sensory pole, representing the products of the human body whose emission, spilling, or production is associated with a heightening of emotion (1967:89), would have particular salience.

The most pervasive symbols in traditional healing are those that also appear in the rituals of traditional religion. The broom used for the patient's ritual bath is reminiscent of the brooms carried by the priests to whisk away misfortune during the annual series of rituals that cleanse the town of evil. It also brings to mind one line of the song chanted at every homowo ritual: "May our broom have a big head," meaning, may we be fertile. Water is associated with the town, lineage, and national gods, who are said to act through the medium of water. In fact, some patients are asked to gather water to be used in their treatment from the lagoons, lakes, and oceans where these spirits are said to reside. In all major rituals, the entire lineage must bathe in sacred water with herbs, which promotes "coolness in the house"; sacred water is taken in bottles to those lineage members who are unable to attend. Just as sacrifices are a part of every major ritual of homowo, so too every serious illness will involve one or more sacrifices.

Color symbolism, particularly the use of white, red, and dark, is pervasive in ritual in Labadi. In religious ritual, white and red are most frequently used. White clay (ayilo) is used for body markings and to whiten the brooms that whisk away the impurities of the previous year in all the homowo rituals. Markings of white clay are worn to signify victory in litigation. It is said of a woman who is getting married, "eye [she is] ayilo," meaning that she is successful or she has won (Azu 1974). On ritual occasions, priests wear white cloth; white cloth is worn at the death of an elder.

The use of red seems to be connected with warfare. Red predominates in rituals concerned with war gods and is associated with political officers, whose roles were associated with warfare. Thus red is worn for the death of chiefs, who were, prior to British "indirect rule," considered to be "war medicines." In traditional ritual, then, red and white clay are frequently used together for body markings and for the decoration of almost all ritual objects, particularly those to be used during the homowo rituals.

Throughout healing rituals we find the use of red and white markings on herbs, bowls, calabashes, medicine pots, and brooms but, in addition, we find the use of black. Thus the healers wear robes of red, white, and dark stripes "so that the gods will know us." The numerous streamers of white, red, and black (dark) cloth hanging from the roof of a healer's compound indicate that he is well frequented. The vessels containing medicines and sacred water are marked with red and white lines, "a sign of the spirits, to invoke them to come and do their work," or with white lines to "prevent the evil spirits from spoiling the medicine." White animals are usually requested for sacrifice; however, in especially serious cases, a white one and a black one may be required.

One of the most interesting expositions of the meaning of color symbolism in ritual is again found in the work of Victor Turner. Using his Ndembu data, he notes that white tends to have a positive connotation, red an ambivalent one, and black a negative one. Surveying some cross-cultural material, he suggests that the red/white/black color distinction is common to all societies because these colors represent products of the human body, basic human organic experiences, which are then conflated with and come to represent experiences of social relationships. While more recent work by Berlin and Kay (1969) suggests that any uniformity of color recognition is based on the level of technology, Turner is more concerned with what he perceives as a uniformity in meanings attributed to colors, based on the universality of organic experiences, than with actual color discrimination.

Based on Turner's distinctions, certain aspects of which have been supported by much of the cross-cultural evidence, Kilson (1971:77) posits the following set of associations in Ga ritual based on polar opposition between black and white:

white	black
light	dark

life	death
immortal beings	mortal beings
sky	earth
ritual objects	secular objects
order	disorder
success	failure
purity	impurity
superior	inferior

As in the case of many purported bipolar oppositions, such assertions bear closer analysis.

My observations of traditional ritual support the contention that white is associated with purity, health, victory, and blessings. Red, on one hand, is associated with danger; thus, the expression *ke etsu* (when it is red) means "when there is danger." Red is associated with gods and personages of warfare. When a powerful medicine said to cure all manner of illnesses was prepared (see Appendix 7), half of it —that which was to be taken by mouth—was tied with a white streamer; the other half, tied with a red streamer, was to be applied externally only and was said to cause death if taken by mouth. On the other hand, red is used with white for markings of almost all ritual objects used in both homọwọ and healing rituals. The combination of red and white was utilized to promote the efficacy of healing rituals.

The use of black does not appear in traditional religion. However, it is said that all black cats born in Labadi must be taken to the dwelling of the Lakpa, where they will become his messengers: "the Lakpa likes black animals." Black is used in healing, where it seems to connote both power and danger, or danger through power. Thus, the gowns of the healers and the streamers used in healing are of all three colors.

The discussion thus far has focused on our observations of the associations of particular symbols. The exegetical level, what people say about the meaning of symbols, is also a source of data. Ataa, a ritual specialist, gave an exposition of the connotations of white, red, and black in the course of an explanation of dwarfs (*adope*), who are thought to be tiny human beings who live in the bush. Since one of their primary attributes is knowledge of herbs, medical practitioners are expected to be especially familiar with them. The healer explained that there were three types of dwarfs: red, white, and black. In addition to having knowledge of herbs, dwarfs are also associated with magic (*nkunya*), a power that does not fall into the realm of the supernatural. White dwarfs, he said, are the fathers or owners of all the herbs; they can be "kept" at home and they will aid the healer in finding herbs and curing illnesses. Red dwarfs, in contrast, are not dependable: it is never entirely clear what they will do. It is not a good idea to keep a pot of herbs and water (kulo) possessing their spirit at home—it is best kept in the bush. However, if it must be "fixed" at home, then it should be separated from the other wọdzii. A black dwarf is very dangerous. If you keep it at home and you make a mistake, it can kill you. "It is like a sorcerer, who does not use his power to do harm, but likes to do everything well. However, if you continue to irritate him, he will show you what his powers are." While this explanation was given by the ritual expert, most patients seem to hold similar views about the connotation of colors. Thus, Mensah, although he did not take much of an interest in his surroundings during the initial rituals and was not particularly well-versed in the intricacies of traditional religious symbolism, frequently volunteered such statements as, "the red and the white streamers are all right, but one has to be careful of the black one."

The ambiguity of black, its association with power rather than inferiority, seems to occur in other cultures as well. Thus, Buckley (1976) reports that among the Yoruba red, white, and black are dominant colors in healing. While black connotes darkness and secrecy, only in black can red and white be mixed without danger. Similarly, Ngabane (1976:343) reports that the Zulu use black and red in opposition to white; black and red represent all that is bad, but strength and power as well. Black and red medicines, then, expel illness and strengthen the individual against future attacks. They are followed by white medicine, which reintroduces health. Turner, too, notes that black is ambivalent in Ndembu symbolism — black clay symbolizes fertility and marital love. Finding that black is auspicious in many societies, Turner suggests that it is especially so in regions where water is short and dark clouds connote fertility (1967).[11]

While it is interesting to speculate on the origins and universality of color symbolism, particularly as employed in healing, the more significant problem is that of the way in which such symbols are used. Thus, Turner reminds us that symbols are dynamic, that they are manipulated by individuals for their own ends. Most important, then, becomes an analysis of how they are used and by whom;

the way in which social categories become associated with the positive and negative evaluations of colors; in what way is such symbolism maintained, changed, or discarded within a given historical context.

For example, Turner asserts that the inferiority of black in a ritual context extends to skin color (1967:69). If this is, in fact, the case, one wonders at what historical point, perhaps in recent colonial history, the association arose. It does not seem to be the case in other areas of Africa. Ngubane tells us quite clearly that among the Zulu, "the symbolic meaning of black, red and white does not extend outside the ritual setting. For instance, it is not important whether people are dark or light in complexion" (1976:342 4n). Among the Ga, basic identification is phrased not in terms of skin color but by place of origin. People who are not African, therefore, may be termed *blǫfonyo* (European) whatever their skin color. Skin color may be used to describe an individual to differentiate him from others. Thus, a man who is of a light brown complexion may be called by his family name with -*etsuru* (red) attached in the same way the -*fio* (small, younger) or -*nkpa* (big, older) will be attached to identify older and younger brothers of the same family name, without positive or negative evaluation.

It seems more useful to examine the way in which symbols are manipulated and for what purposes, rather than searching for universal common origins or meanings. Under specific conditions, black loses its ambiguity, becomes associated with evil and sin, and, at the same time, is identified with skin color.

CLINICAL REALITY

Let us now turn to a brief examination of what Kleinman refers to as the clinical reality. Traditional healing clearly includes an organismic component — what may be called the treatment of disease or the physiological malfunction. It also addresses itself, however, to the treatment of illness — the meaning of the malfunction to the patient and those around her, and hence the structuring of social relationships. The treatment of both disease and illness takes place within an explanatory framework that holds a particular order of social relationships to be the natural one and seeks to perpetuate it. Thus, the explanatory framework of traditional healing is based on the collectivity and reciprocity of the lineages as part of the village community, an order rationalized by the gods and ancestors.

Twumasi notes the existence of a similar explanatory framework among the Akan, where the goal of treatment is the "maintenance of the group" and "re-establishing the harmony of social relations" (1972:32). Thus, explanations for many illnesses are found in some antisocial behavior on the part of the individual or family. "To cure such ills, therefore, requires the righting of some social wrong." In Labadi, this outlook is evident in the content of the prayers, the libations, and the verbal interventions we have presented, which make unambiguous reference to the ancestors and town gods, who, similar to "the ancestral gods and spirits" among the Ashanti, "are believed to punish their living descendants for sins both of commission and omission, because they are known by the people to be guardians of the society's morality and they are known to chastise those who fail in their duty" (Twumasi 1979:238), and to the framework of social relations that they symbolize as the basis for the success of treatment. This framework is more directly expressed in the intervention of the healer: Aba must show more respect for elders; Mensah's father must desist from the use of individual medicines that bring money at the expense of kin; and Afi will share her money with lineage members. These behavior modifications are seen to be prerequisites for successful treatment.

Such premises are expressed explicitly by the healer, but are also communicated more subtly by the manipulation of symbolism. The content of such communication is indicated by the ideological pole of the dominant symbols. The fact that the salience of the sensory pole becomes particularly acute in situations of illness and healing perhaps renders the patient more susceptible to the message being communicated at the ideological pole (see chapter 5). The ideological referents of symbols are perhaps best understood through consideration of what Turner has termed the "operational" meaning of symbols—what people do with them, as opposed to what they say about them (1967:51). Analysis of the use of symbols in the homowo rituals makes clear that, on one level, the structural referents of such symbols as water and the colors of red and white lie with the solidarity of the lineage and the town. The exegetical level emphasizes the solidarity and reciprocity of lineage members, respect for elders, and the harmonious relations among lineages, all of which will result in the much desired fertility, prosperity, and health. It is immediately obvious, however, that the homowo rituals also mask, more or less successfully, real conflicts among people competing for resources and power, who nevertheless find it necessary to unify on some level.

So, too, in healing the emphasis on relations of reciprocity must derive in part from tendencies toward nonreciprocity. These exist in any historical epoch: cleavages may be owing to different migration histories, individual differences, and the like. Certainly today, where communal relationships are not dominant, such symbolism attempts to negate and minimize this fact — after all, Afi's money will not become lineage property — and to impose a version of social relationships implicit and explicit in this form of healing. Such a framework is, of course, in the interests of the healer, who possesses a certain amount of power and status within such a society. But it is also often in the interests of the patient and the patient's kin, who attempt to utilize the explanatory framework put forward in this form of healing to mobilize the reciprocity of kin, so necessary for survival in difficult times.

Spiritualist Healing

> The dialectic of Jaweh's kingdom necessarily
> embraced the totality of human experience
> ...secular and sacred components were
> indivisible; "this-worldly" and otherworldly
> themes were inseparable. Politics, religion,
> and economics were fused; heaven and earth
> were confounded, nature was married to
> God. In the new universe, life would be com-
> pletely different; everything would be turned
> upside down. The Jews would rule and the
> Romans serve. The poor would be rich, the
> wicked would be punished, the sick would be
> healed, and the dead brought to life.
>
> — Messiahs
> Marvin Harris (1974:162-163)

THE CHURCH AND THE HEALER

The Church of the Messiah indeed promised a new heaven and
a new earth, despite the lack of clarity as to whether blessings were
to be gained here or in an afterlife. Located on one of the main
roads leading to the center of town, the Church of the Messiah was
the largest spiritualist church in Labadi, claiming a membership of
1,200. A wooden cross, painted white, guarded the entrance to the
building, a rectangular cement structure, roofed with corrugated
iron. Two sections of benches (men and women sat separately), seat-
ing approximately one thousand people, faced an altar crowned by
a picture of Jesus.

The founder of the church, who was thirty-one years old in
1971, was, like many of the church founders in Labadi, a relatively
young man who certainly would not be reckoned an elder by the tra-

ditional system. In fact, "Father," as he was called by the congregation, was not a native Labadian, but had been born in central Accra, although he now resided in Labadi with his wife, two children, three brothers, and his mother's brother, who was the assistant pastor. Before becoming a full-time minister, he had attended school for several years. After experiencing a vision, he began to attend "Bible College" and first practiced as a part-time lay preacher while working for the Department of Agriculture. He worked as a minister for another spiritualist church before leaving to found the church in Labadi, three years before my visit. Since the founding of the Church of the Messiah in Labadi, he had established three other branches in outlying areas.

The founder was assisted in ministering to the congregation by other members of the church hierarchy: an assistant pastor, "president," and the praying band. The assistant pastor, called "Uncle" by the congregation, was the founder's mother's brother. Unlike the founder, he had no formal theological training. (The founder was, at that time, training five new assistants, two of whom were his brothers.) The president of the church was the chairman of a Ghanaian loan association, specializing in small businesses. In contrast to most of the congregation, he was relatively wealthy, as indicated by his ownership of several large houses, a large new American car, and his ability to finance the studies of two young daughters in London and Germany. It was through the financial auspices of the president that the founder—who referred to the president as "father," although there was no biological relationship—made a tour of pentecostal churches in the United States. The eight members of the praying band, who took an active part in praying, communicating visions, and advising the congregation, occupied positions analogous to those of elders in traditional religion. The members of the praying band were clerks or fairly successful market women, supervised by a Fanti skilled worker in his forties, who was a carpentry foreman for the State Construction Corporation.

The congregation included all age groups and most occupational categories. Farmers, fishermen, market women, clerks, and unskilled wage workers predominated, with occasional foremen, skilled workers, successful businessmen, and professionals. The Church of the Messiah differed from other spiritualist churches in Labadi, in which women were found in much greater numbers, in that 40 percent of the membership was male.

Unlike traditional religion, where ritual participants are bound by kinship, kinship relations were not an explicit aspect of participation in the spiritualist church. While kinship was perhaps a factor in recruitment (members often recommended the church to relatives) and leadership (several leading members of the church were related to the founder), ritual and belief in no sense reinforced kinship ties. In fact quite the opposite was the case. Unlike traditional religion, central roles in worship were not determined by the complementary rotation of the lineage or by generational position.

The founder and other members of the church hierarchy occupied special positions by virtue of their control over the content of sermons, their interpretation of visions, and their prerogative in instructing the congregation about proper behavior patterns. Unlike the elder of traditional religion, however, whose status was based on a chronological age and generational position, the elder of the spiritualist church attained his position through achieved prestige. Both the members of the hierarchy and the congregation phrased the requirements for seniority in the church in terms of the individual's closeness to divinity as evidenced in the effectiveness of prayer, efficacy of prophecy, and purity of life. Upon examining the lifestyles of the senior church members, it appeared that the achievement of status and a degree of material prosperity was accepted as a significant indication of the individual's successful relationship with God and worthiness of respect — the president was a successful businessman, and the members of the praying band were skilled workers, clerks, or successful market women.

For the congregation, who were, in general, a good deal less prosperous than the officials, "healing" was the reason most frequently given for attendance at the church or consultation with the founder. An examination of the consultation record for a random week in three different months indicated that in each week at least two-thirds of the clients came in order to be healed. In one fairly typical week (January 17 to 22, 1972), the founder saw thirty people. Twenty of the thirty came to consult about problems of illness, with complaints of stomach and chest pain being the most frequent. While many of those who sought consultation were not formally members of the church, church membership was frequently based on episodes of illness and healing.

Diagnosis and treatment took place in the public meeting or in private consultation with the founder, assistant pastor, members of the prayer band, or church elders. In each context, the premises of diagnosis and treatment differed consistently from those of traditional healing.

DIAGNOSIS AND THE MEANING OF ILLNESS

Although a few of the spiritualist healers had some familiarity with Ga disease names and categories, in general, they were not informed of nor interested in the art of diagnosis based on delineating regularities of symptom complexes. They were exclusively concerned with level I (see page 67) etiological distinctions — a determination of whether the illness was natural or spiritual. Occasionally, the founder gave the illness a symptom-descriptive label, such as seke, but where the illness was thought to be spiritual in cause, it was usually referred to as hela abonsam, suggesting that it was a manifestation of the devil. However, spiritual and natural etiology were not mutually exclusive. Spiritualist healers often recommended that the patient seek biomedical treatment but continue to be seen at the church, so that the spiritual aspect, which fell within their domain, could be addressed.

It is not surprising that every case in the sample population was described by the founder as including a spiritual component. There was some variation in the attitudes of various spiritualist churches toward the use of other practitioners: 70 percent (7) permitted members of their congregation to utilize other facilities; 60 percent (6) even permitted patients to use indigenous herbalists, as long as the treatment was medicinal only and did not involve traffic with the supernatural. All founders of spiritualist churches forbade their congregations to utilize tsofatse and priests or to participate in the practice of traditional religion. While my observations indicated that such singularity was rarely practiced, like Jahweh's demand of Moses, hegemony over spiritual (read ideological) matters was clearly one of the explicit premises of the spiritualist churches. Traditional religion, which was thought to be incompatible with Christianity, was antithetical.

When asked how they distinguished between natural and spiritual illnesses, most spiritualist healers agreed that chronicity always indicated supernatural etiology. When I queried the wife of a founder of a spiritualist church about the reason for her decision to take her daughter to a hospital rather than to the church, she answered, "We go to the hospital for natural illnesses. It is only for supernatural illnesses that we pray. We know that an illness has a supernatural cause if it does not go away. For example, if you have a sore and it does not heal for months and months, you know that a witch has touched it." In addition to chronic illnesses, mental disorders are always thought to have a supernatural etiology.

An illness that was considered to be spiritual may have, as its instrumental cause, witchcraft, sorcery, or *susuma* (soul). Clearly, the attribution of causality to the ancestors, lineage or town gods would be antithetical to Christian assertions as to where power lay. Beliefs about witchcraft and sorcery, thought to be manifestations of the devil, were similar to those held by the society at large. Church members claimed that witches ate the flesh of human beings to extract their internal substance. Like other Labadians, church members cited jealousy and the desire to get ahead as the major motive for the use of witchcraft. Witchcraft, again used as a metaphor to describe contemporary social relations, was thought to be more prevalent today than previously. One founder described the situation as follows:

> I am old now. But when I came to meet my parents [when I was born] I could see that there was not much witchcraft. People just did not hate their neighbors. Nowadays, there is hatred and jealousy. At my age, I have tried my best to buy one cloth, or maybe two. But nowadays, a small boy, who is not of my age, will try to get what I have. He will try anything to be richer than I am. He will pass through all these ju-ju ways and then something will be given to him to make him become a witch.

For church members, as for the patients at the traditional healer, a major point of distinction between witchcraft and sorcery was the unpredictability of witchcraft. A member of the congregation of the Church of the Messiah described the difference as follows: "A sorcerer will harm you for a particular reason, perhaps because you make him angry. But a witch will just harm you for no reason." Witchcraft was most frequently diagnosed as the instrumental cause of spiritual illnesses. Although spiritualist healers rarely indicated specific agents of witchcraft, patients freely drew their own conclusions.

Elizabeth, a fifty-five-year-old market woman from Labadi suffering from a combination of physiological and psychological complaints, was waiting to be baptized in the Church of the Messiah when I met her. She resided in one of a group of dwellings that surrounds the church; the land on which the church stands is owned by her family. She was a stately woman, with evidence of past beauty on her now careworn face. Throughout the three months I talked with her, she appeared to be in bad health and in some pain because of a urinary tract disorder that she claimed to have suffered from for nine years. She readily recounted her history to me, speaking at length with no provocation. She spoke deliberately and sensibly, without signs of flight of fancy, but with great bitterness.

Elizabeth had not attended school and had been a market woman all her life. Her mother had been a farmer and her father a fisherman. She had not attended any church until five years ago, when she began to have trouble.

Her present complaints included pain and pressure in the abdominal region, associated with blood and pain with urination and more generalized complaints of discomfort. Some of the symptoms had appeared as early as nine years ago, but had been intermittent, appearing and disappearing. Six years ago, the symptoms became more serious and caused her to seek help from a variety of sources. After a stay of three weeks in Korle Bu Hospital, she went to Keneshie Clinic, where she has been treated with medication for three months. She had also been admitted on an emergency basis to Ashaiman Hospital. When I met her at the Church of the Messiah, she was still undergoing treatment at Keneshie Clinic.

Five years ago, when her symptoms worsened, she began seeking help at spiritualist churches, where she was told that the disorder was a spiritual one. She was convinced of this diagnosis and that the illness had been initiated by the sorcery of her ex-husband, the father of her two living children. She reminisced that her family was originally against her marriage to this husband, who drove lorries for a living, because they felt that he had used "medicine" to seduce her. When she married him, the rift with her family deepened to the extent that they did not visit her when her children were born. By the time of the birth of her last child, which died shortly thereafter, Elizabeth had decided to divorce her husband. She attributed the death of the infant to witchcraft activities on the part of her husband's mother. When she left him fifteen years ago, he did not accept the divorce and threatened her with bodily harm. The mangtse had to be called into the dispute to restrain him.

She attributed subsequent misfortunes to her husband's vindictive use of sorcery. She claimed that her ability to form a relationship and to remarry had been hampered by her husband. In one case, she claimed, a man had gone so far as to bring engagement gifts. When he was informed of her ex-husband's propensity to use sorcery, he broke the relationship, reclaiming the gifts. There had been many others, she recounted, who had broken relationships, through no fault of hers.

Approximately six years ago, in addition to the above described illness, she began experiencing other symptoms that she attributed to witchcraft in her matrilineage, instigated by her elder half sister with the participation of some of her mother's sisters. When asked why members of her matrilineage would practice witchcraft, she gave the usual answer:

> Some years ago, my relatives [shia bii] rose up against me because of my work. It was the spiritualist churches which saved me, because they [the relatives] had wanted to spoil my head. Previously, when someone was talking, I was not able to hear the person. Something moved in my head for awhile. Then it stopped and I came to my senses to ask what the person was saying. So I do not have any idea about these things. This happened for five years, until I was healed in a spiritual church.

She recounted the history of her marketing activities, which bears out our earlier discussion of the ups and downs of the average market woman. Her last husband, who was a shopkeeper, helped to set her up in cloth marketing. When she began doing well, her sister saw that her "walk had changed." Elizabeth claimed that her sister visited her to find out if she was truly making money from marketing:

> What money! When I came from my travels outside the town, I married this man, my husband. I stayed with him a little at a time. I sold rice and beans. I started saving some money. I stopped selling that and started selling cloth. With my last husband, a storekeeper, I humbled myself for him, and worked hard; he also helped me. And so when they [her sisters] saw that something had come to my house and that my walk had changed, early one morning, at 6 A.M., she [her sister] came to my house. She said, "I have come to visit you. I heard of you, they say you are rich. I have heard the stories." So I asked her who told her. She said she heard from Labadi women who came to sell here. "That is why I have come to visit you, to see where you have come to."

I said, "Here is a stool." She said, "I won't sit." Then she passed me and went to my room. She walked around and then nodded her head. I said, "Sister, here is a chair. I have sent someone to buy you some *kenkey*." My sister said, "I will not sit, I will not sit, I will not eat kenkey. I am leaving. What I want is what I have come to see." This was the situation. So after she had gone, if things were given to me for one hundred pounds to sell, previously I used to add an amount to the price of twelve yards to make my profit. Now, before I could finish selling I would fall into debt.

After the visit from her sister, presumably followed by witchcraft activities, she claimed that she was no longer able to market successfully and began to fall into debt. At that time, both traditional healers and church founders told her that this was a result of witchcraft rather than sorcery. Her run of misfortune became so serious that she was forced to stop selling cloth and to sell bread, which was less profitable but also less risky. She stated that her sister then turned her witchcraft activities toward disrupting Elizabeth's marriage. Her husband left her, telling her that there was too much witchcraft in her family. She became quite successful marketing corn, purchasing forty to fifty bags of corn a day in Krobo, transporting them to Accra, and selling them, often for a price a cedi above what she paid for them. After two years of selling corn, she had paid off her debts and made some money.

She married a clerk, but divorced him after discovering that he was primarily interested in her money. She attributed her recent successes in marketing to spiritualist churches, where she "received Christ as her personal Savior" and protection from the onslaught of witchcraft. At the time of our interview, she was selling drugs for Kingsway Chemists and was no longer in debt.

She continued to feel, however, that the danger of witchcraft in her matrilineage was ever present and that it was being practiced against her children: witchcraft prevented them from marrying well, from doing well in school, and from marketing successfully. It was witchcraft that made the sellers give them things that were "heavier" than they could bear—items that they could not sell at a profit and so fell into debt. She claimed her two daughters were in debt as a result of witchcraft, and consequently she had asked them to cease marketing.

When asked why witchcraft is practiced in the matrilineage, she stated:

This is because you stay with your mother. So they see you from morning to evening, your progress and your life, and your downfall, and your everything.

It is interesting to note here that sorcery was thought to be utilized in the dispute with her husband, while witchcraft was the medium for expression of envy due to individual achievement.

While she was being seen at Keneshie for the symptoms described above, she consulted her sisters, who suggested that she attend the Church of the Messiah. When she first arrived, the founder was away, and she was seen by Uncle. He told her that he would help her, but that they were very busy at the time. After three weeks, she obtained a consultation and was told that her sickness was a spiritual one. She undertook the usual treatments of burning candles, ritual baths, attending services, saying psalms and prayers. A month later, her symptoms had not changed and she was waiting to be baptized.

Spiritualist healers, then, rarely attempted to penetrate the mysteries of diagnosis. They were not concerned with eliciting symptoms, analyzing their regularity, and matching them with diagnoses, but rather with analysis and treatment of the spiritual component. To this extent, unlike traditional healing, which addressed itself to both the disease and the illness, spiritualist healing was primarily concerned with the illness.

Thus, diagnostic procedures were less meticulous in the spiritualist church than at the traditional healer and took place in both private and public settings. Patients arrived alone or occasionally with one relative, friend, or church member known to the patient, to consult the healer. Following the patient's account of the problem, the healer either made the diagnosis on the spot or told the patient to return in a few days, during which time the founder would discover the cause of illness through prayer, visions, or dreams. The cause of illness would then be revealed to the individual in a private consultation or in the course of a public meeting. While it might appear at first glance that the less rigorous diagnostic procedures of the spiritualist healer reflected an inability to procure information about the social relationships of the patients, this was not borne out by investigation. Knowledge of one another's affairs among church members at least equaled that found elsewhere in the town, and the founder would have had no difficulty in procuring information had he desired it. Indeed, in many cases it became evident that he possessed such data, but did not always choose to make use of it.

Most problems were diagnosed as ultimately resulting from the individual's failure to maintain adequate standards of behavior, whether or not witchcraft or sorcery was the instrumental agent. One fairly typical Wednesday night meeting (not specifically designated for healing) was opened by Uncle. Through constant admonition to "feel the spirit" and repetition of such phrases as "the spirit will heal you," an intensely hypnotic atmosphere was created, during which two women became possessed. The founder then took over the meeting, publicly expounding his visions about individual members of the church, much to the interest of the entire congregation. One young woman was called up and warned against "playing" with a certain young man, as pregnancy would disrupt her desired career in nursing; a man was warned against too much drinking and womanizing, which would cause illness. In these instances, as was generally the case in the spiritualist church, the individual was held to be ultimately responsible for his or her destiny.

The emphasis on individual responsibility in etiology distinguished spiritualist therapy from traditional therapy. Whether the cause of the illness was revealed to an individual privately in a consultation session or in a public meeting, diagnostic statements often emphasized the reason why the individual was open to the powers able to cause illness. Unlike the traditional healer, the spiritualist healer was not concerned with illness as a reflection of the disruption of structured lineage relationships. Diagnosis did not include an examination of the body politic and rarely identified specific relationships thought to be problematic. Rather, it revealed weaknesses in the individual's behavior that resulted in his or her susceptibility to malevolent powers. It follows, then, that treatment, too, was directed toward reinforcement and strengthening of the individual, rather than to attempting to repair group relationships.

TREATMENT

As in its diagnostic procedures, there was no attempt to match specific treatments with symptom complexes in the Church of the Messiah. Treatments were more or less the same for all illnesses. Patients were told to purchase candles and incense to burn, and sacred oil and water to be applied to the body. They were given prayers and psalms, the repetition of which was to increase their faith, and they were encouraged to request prayers from the praying band whenever necessary. While the use of invocations and ritual bathing are similar to treatments utilized in traditional therapy, the major difference lies in the fact that the patient undertakes these by himself, in private, without support or participation of the kinship group. In fact, treatment often included explicit separation from the kinship group, in the form of advice to take up residence outside the lineage house.

Daily treatments, then, consisted of activities designed to strengthen the individual — prayers, psalms, lighting of candles, and bathing in holy water. Treatment regimens were a great deal less structured than those of the traditional therapist, and much of the implementation remained at the discretion or initiative of the patient. Clients, however, continued to use the therapeutic arena to make analyses of their social relations and often availed themselves of the opportunity to disengage from various kin relationships and obligations.

Charlotte, a thirty-year-old La market woman with seven years of schooling, appeared at the spiritualist church complaining of dizziness, chills, and anxiety. Although Charlotte's symptoms were less severe than those of Aba, like Aba, her symptoms appeared shortly after the birth of her last child.

Approximately eight weeks after the delivery of her eighth child, Charlotte was waiting in one of the clinics in Labadi to be seen for an eye infection. She described the onset of her illness as follows:

> So when I went there [to the clinic] and got my card, I was asked to go upstairs to see the doctor. I found that I was walking very slowly and quietly, so I asked myself what may have caused this trouble. I was called in to join the line at the consultation room of the clinic. As I was sitting there waiting for my turn, I felt something under my feet. Something very cold, like an air-conditioner, coming up from under my feet. So I ran out. The doctor called me and asked me what was bothering me. So I told him about what had been worrying me. He said that I should come and sit down. I could not sit because I was shaking all over, so I ran out again. As I stood outside, I saw one of my sisters, who had come from Adabraka. She asked me what was wrong. She took my child from me. As I was speaking, I was crying. So the

doctor came and saw me outside. He called me in and treated me. He told me to go home. He gave me some penicillin ointment to use for my eye. My sister led me to the bus stop. Still the thing [air under her feet] continued to bother me. When I entered a bus, it continued to bother me, as it had when I was at the hospital. I left the bus and decided that I would not go to Labadi. As I was kneeling there, another lorry came and I took that one to Labadi. When I returned home, I was feeling unhappy.

That night, she discussed the episode with one of her sisters, with whom she resided in her lineage house. Her sister suggested to her that she request help from a spiritualist church in Labadi, the Wings of Bethany, of which the sister was a member. Charlotte followed her advice and consulted the founder of this church, who told her to return the next morning. She did not return, after three days her symptoms reappeared and, as she put it, "I began to shout that I would die."

In this state of mind, she went to another of the Labadi clinics and was seen by a pediatrician, who inquired about the date of her last delivery. The pediatrician informed her that her illness was caused by "thinking" (*dzwengmǫ*—literally, mind or thought) brought on by her recent delivery and suggested that she see a doctor who treats "head sickness." He wrote a note for her to take to the doctor at the Accra mental hospital and gave her some medication. After returning home from the pediatrician, she asked one of her sisters to accompany her to the Church of the Messiah.

In this case the patient sought help initially from biomedical facilities. She was one of the few people I encountered who unequivocally denied ever seeking help from a traditional healer. She stated: "Everyone in my house is a Christian. We do not know anything about tsofa [using "medicine" in its ritual sense]." Most members of her family attended conventional Christian churches, and a few attended spiritualist churches. She was, however, the first and only member of her family to attend the Church of the Messiah. Her decision to seek help from the Church of the Messiah seemed to have been triggered by her reluctance to follow the biomedical practitioner's advice to seek help at the mental hospital, and was not based on any consultation with the kin group.

On Charlotte's first visit to the Church of the Messiah, the founder was not available, so she consulted the assistant pastor, describing her symptoms. He listened, inquired about the day of her birth—which determines the day name of the soul (susuma)—and told her to return the following day. The next day Uncle, informed by prayers and visions, diagnosed her illness as resulting from soul (susuma). Her soul was said to be causing her illness because people who lived in her lineage house were speaking ill of her and because she was quarreling with her husband.

At the instruction of the assistant pastor, Charlotte purchased incense and packets of red and white candles for burning, and a bucket, sponges, a towel, and consecrated oil for ritual bathing. For several weeks she burned candles and incense, bathed in holy water, anointed herself with consecrated oil and water, attended church, and repeated prayers and psalms. A baptismal ritual was performed in which she was immersed in the sea and prayed for by the assistant pastor and the praying band. After participating in the baptism, Charlotte claimed that her symptoms had receded, but a few days later dizziness and chest pains reappeared. At this point, the assistant pastor informed her that without intense prayer she was in danger of death. She began coming to the church every night for prayer with the assistant pastor and the praying band. The assistant pastor further suggested that she reside in the church, because residence in her lineage house was not conducive to her recovery. "He told me that the house is not good, and that when I stay there the sickness would not get better."

Despite the fact that the healer made no accusations of specific individuals, Charlotte drew her own conclusions. She decided that one of her mother's sisters was employing witchcraft against her. "There is only one person in the family who does not eat with me," allegedly because she was offended by Charlotte's good fortune. Charlotte recounted how, after the delivery of her last child, her husband made her a present of some money, which she used to buy goods that produced a marketing profit. In addition, her husband cemented and repaired the room in which she resided in the lineage house. "So this woman always talks about it, saying that I have been able to build a room and she also says that I have been provided with my own room." As in the cases we encountered at the traditional healer's, there was the general belief that differentiation, where one individual did better than others, resulted in envy and the use of malevolent forces: "I think it is because of hatred."

Charlotte continued to sleep in the church for three months, partaking of prayers, saying psalms, burning incense, taking ritual baths, and attending church services. She had a great deal of contact with the members of the praying band, who were responsible for giving her daily prayers. Her younger children were often with her, but she was not accompanied by any other relatives. At the end of three months, she stated that her symptoms had improved—she occasionally felt dizzy when walking and occasionally trembled and felt "the cold under my feet," but she thought that she was much improved and would soon go home.

Although the healer did not point to specific individuals, suggesting instead that there was a general negative influence in the lineage house, Charlotte, like the patients at the traditional healer, took the occasion to analyze and reconstruct her social relationships. In this case, similar to traditional healing, trouble lay in the lineage; however, the treatment was not to analyze and restore these relationships, but to destroy them. The patient was removed from the offending relationships of the lineage house and told to sleep in the church. Kin were not formally involved in any aspect of treatment. Treatments were, for the most part, private and directed toward strengthening the individual, not reconstructing the lineage relationships.

TREATMENT: DRAMATIC HEALING RITUALS

Although treatment rituals were primarily individual, patients were encouraged to become members of the church and to attend church meetings. Thus, in addition to the individualized, more or less private, treatments described in the last two cases, the dramatic healing ritual might also be utilized in therapy. However, the participants differed from those of traditional religion, and, while the symbolic forms were often similar, the meanings and connotations had been altered.

The meeting was the major public ritual in the spiritualist churches. Meetings were held three times a week. Although Friday evenings were reserved specifically for healing, some form of healing occurred at nearly every meeting. The weekday meetings were usually one-half to two-thirds filled, as compared with the Sunday morning meetings, which were generally filled beyond capacity, with people standing in the aisles and outside the church. The Wednesday and Friday evening meetings often had a more intimate atmosphere, in which the members of the congregation received more individualized attention. Meetings were conducted by the founder, the assistant pastor or both, assisted by the church elders, and members of the praying band—all of whom constituted the church hierarchy. The founder usually spoke in English, with simultaneous translation into Ga and Twi, and occasionally gave a sermon in Ga. The assistant pastor always spoke Ga. Although meetings varied according to type, there was a general outline to which all meetings conformed which included the singing of hymns, prayers, possession, and a sermon. I have described this in detail elsewhere (Mullings 1979), but certain distinctions between ritual in the spiritualist church and in traditional religion are of importance for an understanding of healing as it took place in the spiritualist church.

In prayer, possession, and singing, the ritual units included the congregation (as a whole or as individuals), the leader of the meeting (the founder or assistant pastor), and, to varying extents, the members of the praying band and the elders. These ritual units represented a significant contrast with traditional religion, where the units of interaction were lineages, as represented by lineage priests and elders. In the spiritualist church, ritual was orchestrated by the church hierarchy—individuals who had achieved a leading role, not by age, wisdom, or lineage membership, but as a result of the achievement of a degree of material success. At the same time, the congregation took an active part in ritual—any individual could spontaneously begin a song, become possessed, or mutter a prayer. This contrasted with traditional religion, where such roles were ascribed and based on lineage membership and position. Yet, it was not the case that any member of the congregation could give a sermon, explicate visions, or heal. These functions, which most directly controlled and influenced the behavior of church members, were the prerogative of the church hierarchy.

The leaders of the church played a significant role in structuring diagnostic activities during the meeting. Members of the prayer band saw visions about members of the congregation; the founder and assistant pastor decided which members of the congregation should be singled out, expounding the nature of the problem and, most important, how to correct it. Ritual structuring, then, played a part in reinforcing the answers to such questions as who has the power to heal and who has the status to guide behavior.

The case of Raymond illustrates the private and public aspects of healing procedures. This case has marked similarities to that of

Mensah. Both were young men with some education, for whom anxiety focused around their inability to obtain additional education, particularly through study abroad.

I encountered Raymond at the Church of the Messiah, where he had come for prayer. In 1971 he was thirty years old, educated through Kumasi Technical College, and working as a skilled worker in Accra. Although he had been born in Cape Coast, he was presently living in Labadi. He appeared to be anxious, tense, and nervous, but readily discussed his illness and its history. His major complaint, at the moment, was the recurrence of nightmares, which had an adverse affect on his ability to function during the day. He attributed this situation to witchcraft:

> My trouble started three years ago. I was innocent about these spirits moving about, but it happened that I started seeing some unusual things and I had nightmares: some people coming and troubling me and all of a sudden I had to shout. I would see them in different places. They were troubling me and dragging me here and there and I was forced to shout all sorts of things. Later on I felt that I was flying in the air when I slept. At times they would be chasing me. I sometimes returned from business with severe catarrh, which I tried to cure through the hospitals.

In reflecting on his illness history, he began to wonder whether supernatural intervention had played a part in previous episodes of illness. He recalled that ten years previously he had been plagued with chronic severe colds, for which he consulted an ENT specialist, without success. Two years later, while attending a technical college, he continued to be treated at hospitals for chronic upper respiratory infections. He did not at that time attribute the illness to a supernatural etiology, but rather to the fact that he worked with sawdust.

It was five years later, however, when he started to make plans with a friend to complete his studies abroad, that he began to experience serious disturbances:

> At times I felt as though something was pressing me down. At times the thing would grip me through the ear and then I would lose consciousness for some time. And I have to struggle to be able to wake up. When I wake up with a start, I am perspiring and my heart is beating strongly.

He attributed to witchcraft the fact that, although his friend had successfully organized study abroad, he himself had been unable to do so.

The year before I met him his symptoms escalated significantly. He reported feeling pressure, the sensation of the bed shaking, and continued symptoms of upper respiratory infection. When he visited his hometown for the Christmas holidays, he recounted the situation to his parents, who assisted him in obtaining treatment from a traditional healer.

When he returned to Labadi after the holidays, the symptoms became worse. He consulted a herbalist, who informed him that a "witchcraft substance" had been placed in his body. It was at that point, he said, that he realized his illness had a "spiritual cause." "I do not know where they put it, but I feel some vibrations in my thigh. Until that thing is clear, things will not go right with me."

Once it became clear to him that his illness was spiritual in origin, he began to attend healing services at one of the spiritualist churches in Accra. He claimed to have experienced slight improvement after a healing service, indicated by a calmness and ability to sleep. At another spiritualist church in Labadi, he was given psalms and prayers to recite, with instructions to repeat them twice if plagued by insomnia. Although these prescriptions were occasionally effective, Raymond concluded that he was spending a great deal of money at the spiritualist churches, with little change in his condition.

It was then that he decided to attend the Church of the Messiah. He first consulted Uncle, who, after blessing a candle for Raymond to light before he went to sleep, told him to return the following day for diagnosis. That night he had a dream, which he recounted the next morning to Uncle and Father:

> I was in a plane traveling, and we arrived in a place like London. All of a sudden I saw many graveyards. And I saw some others, too, some friends who are in London. They were waving and I was waving back. We came to a place where there was a river, so we all swam. But part of the place where we were swimming was very muddy and other parts were clearer. I was swimming with a friend and I left the other cloudy place to swim in the clear place.

The healers interpreted the dream as revealing that Raymond had many troubled areas in his life. The graveyards indicated that he would not be able to travel abroad to study unless he was able to clear away the witchcraft that was causing these troubles. Here, of course, the healers identified the patient's major concern, going abroad to study, pointed to a specific cause for his inability to facilitate it, and suggested a solution.

A week later, Raymond participated in special prayers with Father and Uncle at the seaside. That night he dreamed of three light-skinned women (who he interpreted to be witches), but they were not able to touch him. A few nights later, when he again dreamed that the women were approaching him, he decided to sleep in the chapel on the advice of the founder.

The next night, the founder selected Raymond for special prayer during the healing meeting. As is customary, the meeting was opened with hymns and prayers. The sermon, given by the founder, concerned the temptation of Joseph by Pharaoh's wife. The congregation was admonished to resist temptation. Various sectors of the congregation, based on nuclear family roles, were singled out for special instructions. Husbands were scolded for drinking and not working sufficiently hard to support their families properly. "You give your wife sixpence to buy food and you expect food for six shillings and [then] there is trouble in the house." Wives were reproved for going out late with their husbands, leaving the children with their mothers, and coming home intoxicated. (While leaving children with grandmothers was a common and acceptable practice fostered by the matrilineal residence arrangements, the founder linked it with the negative behavior of going out late and coming home intoxicated.) Young women were warned against too great a love of money and going with men in order to get money to buy "fine things." Mothers were further cautioned against encouraging their daughters to engage in these practices so that they, the mothers, could borrow their finery. Young men were exhorted not to smoke, drink, hang about with undesirables, or "think thoughts not worth thinking." The final exhortation, for everyone, was against the use of "ju-ju and witchcraft."

Raymond was then called to the altar for special prayer. He appeared to be in great distress; he literally wrung his hands, his face wore a tense and anxious expression, and he spoke in a weak and trembling voice. The founder asked him to recount his dream and assured him that something would happen to him within six days. In a low and trembling voice, he related his dream to the founder, who repeated it for the benefit of the congregation. The dream, in which the three women appeared, had first occurred three years ago and then recurred frequently. The founder asked Raymond to describe the women. At the disclosure that they were of fair complexion with elongated teeth, the congregation gasped — these were clearly witches. Raymond was told to kneel. Placing his hand on Raymond's head, the founder explained to the congregation that these women (witches), in attempting to capture his essence, had already ruined one-half of his brain. But Jesus would restore his brain, make him well, and he would not have to go to the "asylum." As the founder began to pray in short staccato sentences — "Lord, cure him of this sẹkẹ; drive away evil; make him well" — the congregation individually prayed with him. The founder's prayers became more feverish; he perspired and stamped his feet for emphasis. At the same time, the murmurings of the congregation rose in pitch, producing an increasingly charged atmosphere and giving the impression that the entire congregation was concentrated on effecting a cure. When the sound of praying reached what seemed to be its culmination, two members of the congregation became possessed, falling to the floor from their seats. Raymond was then told to rise and that he would be cured.

Before the close of the meeting, other cases were brought for prayer, including a young man whose lineage house had been damaged in the recent storm. He was informed that this was for the best because three women in that house were practicing witchcraft against him.

The night of the meeting, Raymond's dream recurred. He claimed, however, that the three women were not able to come near him. Although the founder had said nothing about the identity of the women, Raymond was convinced that his matrilineal kin, particularly his mother's sister, were involved. (Like John at the traditional healer, Raymond was from a Fanti area where descent is traced matrilineally.) He felt sure that the attempt at witchcraft was a result of jealousy over his possible achievements and that witchcraft was responsible for what he perceived as failures.

> Actually, what happened was that in 1968 I intended to travel to the United States. I was going with a friend of mine, but he has gone. But I had some difficulties. And the people in the house feel jealous because they think that you are better off than they are. They have no way to stop you but through that way. So they try to visit you in spirit

and destroy you. I thought that they were jealous because of my travels. They know your future. . . . [He explained that witchcraft usually
originates in your family.] It is because if I do not know you and you
do not know me it is very difficult to get information about me. But if
you are in the family, I know your movement, I know this and that.
These spiritual people have their ways you see. Sometimes the fellow
will take a bit of your hair or a bit of this or that. So if he takes a part
of your attire, your garment or anything like that, he can read you. So
people who can get nearer to you can do this. So that is why those on
the family side know everything that you are doing. And if they see
that you are progressing and that you are working hard, they turn
against you.

Participation in the dramatic healing ritual, which utilized
physical manipulation by the healer of the patients and the creation
of an intense, hypnotic ambience, appeared to have had some effect
on Raymond. A week after public prayers, he claimed to feel much
improved. He no longer felt it necessary to reside at the church, but
he continued to attend meetings and to request special prayers when
necessary.

In the next case, that of a thirty-five-year-old market woman
from Labadi, we will see a thanksgiving ritual, similar in form to
that of traditional religion (described in Appendix 9), but differing
in content and participants.

When I first met Esther, she lived with matrilineal relatives and
those of her seven children who were eligible to stay with her in a lineage house in Labadi. Her complaints of malaise, weight loss, and
insomnia caused her to consult a biomedical practitioner. She had
previously attended a Presbyterian church in Labadi, but when she
became ill her sister, who attended the Church of the Messiah,
brought her to the church:

I was in my house some time ago and I found that I was growing thin, I
did not feel happy. When I went to bed, I could not sleep. It went on.
I was still growing lean and did not feel happy. Sometimes I would
think that I was going to die. I did not know when I was brought here.
When I came to my senses, I found that I was here.

She consulted the founder, who told her that a vision had revealed trouble in her house—he was not more specific. Esther followed his prescription to move out of her lineage house and to reside

at the church. She was told to attend meetings, to light candles, and to participate in prayers with the founder, assistant pastor, and members of the praying band, all actions which were expected to strengthen her and help her to withstand the effects of witchcraft. For the first few weeks, she continued to complain of intermittent "pains all over my body."

After a month of following the prescribed treatments, she declared that her symptoms had vanished and that she was well. She had indeed gained weight and no longer suffered from insomnia. At a Wednesday night service, she gave thanks for her cure in the customary fashion. Toward the end of the service, Esther, a brother, and three friends stood in a semicircle around the collection box. She testified that when she was first admitted to the church she thought she would never be cured, and now the Lord had cured her. She gave thanks, dropped some coins into the box, and vowed to continue to attend the church. Her testimony was followed by that of her brother, who stated that when his sister was brought to church he thought she was dead, but that now she was fully well. He also dropped some coins into the collection box. The three friends followed, with testimony and contribution, and they were followed by a few members of the congregation. This thanksgiving ritual is similar in form to the awroke hamo of traditional healing, where the kinsmen of a cured patient gather around a calabash of sacred water to contribute coins and express their pleasure that their kinsman has been healed, in the process absolving themselves of any guilt for not wishing the patient well. The significant difference is in the ritual participants. In the spiritualist church, the participants are not kinsmen, but primarily friends and members of the congregation. After discharge, Esther decided not to return to her lineage house. She and her children would live alone in a house that her husband procured for her.

GOALS OF THERAPY

As I mentioned previously, patients were encouraged to become members of the church and to attend church meetings as often as possible. Healing was thought to occur over time as the individual attended church and strengthened his faith. Church membership and attendance were seen as evidence of "faith," the prerequisite for successful healing. Through attendance at church, one learned to please God, who was the ultimate source of power necessary for healing. One sermon projected this explicitly:

> It is Jehovah that heals. If God does not heal, who would heal? If you go to see a doctor without God's hand being in it, will it be all right? It will never be all right unless God is in it, because the person who gives you an injection must pray to beg God to have mercy on him.

The sermons, being the central vehicle for the transmission of ideology, had a message that was even more direct: to be healed, you must "go and sin no more," and sin, of course, was defined by the premises of the new religion. Sermons, considered by the founder and the members of the congregation as the major source of information on proper and improper behavior, were created and delivered by the founder or assistant pastor. This did not preclude the active participation of the congregation, which demonstrated approval and agreement through applause and interjection. Over a one-month period, I recorded all twelve sermons given. Analysis revealed that the following major themes occurred in the sermons: (a) salvation (appeared in some form in every sermon); (b) the exhortation to abstain from traditional religious practices (eight sermons); (c) personal responsibility for behavior (eight sermons); (d) admonition to place "the law of God" above that of one's forefathers (six sermons); (e) exhortation not to envy the property of others, but to "trust God" or "lay up treasures in Heaven rather than on earth" (six sermons); (f) brotherly love for other Christians (five sermons); (g) the shame of not being bred in a Christian household (two sermons). My observations over the period of a year, during which I attended at least one, and as many as three, meetings per week and took detailed notes on the texts of the sermons, confirmed the predominance of these themes. The sermons, then, gave information about the nature of desirable behavior without which healing could not occur. Certain aspects of traditional relationships and all traditional ritual were presented as undesirable.

The overriding theme of most sermons was salvation, which meant different things to different people. For church members, salvation referred to a state of being that would bring blessings in the afterworld, but more important, would result in help with the problems of this world. In discussion, although church members occasionally alluded to otherworldly phenomena, most associated salvation with divine assistance in solving everyday problems of "un-beez" ("unbusiness" or unemployment), family relations, and health. This was not only my observation but also the founder's, who noted that, "here in spiritualist churches, most people come with the simple aim of acquiring something from the church—getting healed or getting their requests answered by the Lord."

To the congregation, then, the importance of salvation involved help with everyday problems. The sermons told the congregation how salvation, and hence help with problems, could be achieved. This was often expressed in such formulations as the precedence of the "law of God" or "drawing away from the things of this world." Such concepts were often projected in the form of parables about conflicting loyalties in a family or kinship group.

One such sermon took as its central text a story about a domestic group, all of whom, except the youngest son, worshiped a traditional god. The father went to a traditional religion practitioner to see what could be done about improving his fortune. He was told that his circumstances would improve if his entire family was faithful to the traditional gods. As a result of this divination, the father requested that the youngest son stop going to church. Confronted with the dilemma of whether to obey the precepts of the Christian God or his father and the gods of his father, the boy decided that "the law of God is greater than the law of your father" and refused to stop attending church. The father attempted to have the son killed by an old woman. She accidentally killed the compliant first-born son instead, the Christian son was saved, and the parents were punished. The conclusion was greeted with enthusiastic applause by the congregation. This sort of parable was particularly significant in that it directly confronted and opposed the strong orientation toward filial obedience of the village community.

Sermons often admonished church members to refrain from a variety of traditional relationships and practices. Foremost among these were those practices concerned with traditional religion, which were characterized as evil and dangerous. The Christian God was said to be the only source of protection.

> Jesus is the only one who can protect you from the witches, fetish priests, ju-ju men, men who put something down for you to walk on. All these things are all around you and only Jesus can protect you. In

these evil days, you may eat with someone and your hand crosses and she will have some medicine in her hand that will harm you. Do not take anything from anyone.

The warning not to take anything from anyone repudiated other tenets of traditional society—hospitality and reciprocal exchange relationships.

The doctrinal insistence on the exclusiveness of the Christian God has frequently been cited as one of the distinguishing features of the transition to Christianity (see Horton 1971). This contrasted with the attitude of practitioners of traditional religion, who historically have been very tolerant of other religions, often adding foreign powers to the pantheon and acknowledging the Christian God as the Supreme Being of traditional religion. Their attitude toward Christians was usually one of amused tolerance. Although Christians often solicited treatment from traditional practitioners, the exclusiveness of the Christian God is one of the basic tenets propounded in the spiritualist church.

The themes of rejection of traditional gods and exclusive participation in Christianity were often combined with emphasis on each individual's responsibility for his own salvation. The individual was often seen in opposition to society, and urged to place personal salvation above everything:

> So far as you have loved the world for some reason; then it is enmity with God.... But if you think of the world and say to yourself that I could neither leave this thing or that thing, this person or that ... leave everything and come to the Lord, so that victory will be yours.

Unemployment (or the desire to improve one's occupational category), cited by both the founder and the congregation as a major reason for church membership, was a frequent topic in sermons as well as in individual requests. The related subjects of employment, wealth, and prestige were often elaborated in contradictory motifs. The congregation was frequently charged to work hard and admonished not to be lazy (cf. Weber 1930): "If you do not have a job, will your younger sisters and brothers respect you?" At the same time, any founder who desired to keep his congregation was forced to recognize that the high level of unemployment in Ghana was not solely the fault of the individual. The unemployed and marginally employed members of the congregation were instructed to have faith and were comforted with the exhortation that the Christian way is not to love money or to be envious of the wealth or possessions of others, but to concern oneself with otherworldly rewards.

The use of these themes is illustrated in the following sermon (see Appendix 10 for the text of the sermon). The founder recounted the story of the laying on of hands and the descent of the Holy Spirit unto the Apostles, emphasizing the fact that the Spirit could not be purchased with money, which is "the source of all evil." The founder reiterated the theme of the sermon: "The Bible tells us that we must lay up our treasure in heaven . . . and not be jealous of the suit, the shoes, the cloth, the necklaces that others have and you do not, because these are worldly things and they will pass away."

He then recounted a story about a poor man who was employed by a rich man. While the poor man was farming the rich man's land, he discovered a locked box. Although the rich man had never seen the box before, he confiscated it, insisting that it was his property. (At this point the founder interjected in Ga, "*Anibre* [greediness, covetousness]!") When the poor man contested the ownership of the box, the chief decided that the box would belong to whoever could bring him a key that would open it. The rich man, who bribed the caretaker of the box and had a key made, claimed the box by virtue of the fact that he possessed the key. When the box was opened and found to contain the head of the chief's missing daughter, the rich man was punished with death. The congregation was warned to take this as a lesson — never be jealous of the property of others. The congregation actively participated, expressing disapproval of the tactics of the rich man, applauding his downfall, and expressing agreement with the opening and concluding remarks of the sermon.

A number of themes were skillfully interwoven in this sermon. Implicit in the formulation that money is the source of all evil was the recognition of the money-centered economy, unequal access to resources, and their destructive effect on traditional relationships. The reaction of the congregation as well as the interjection of the founder indicated some hostility toward the unequal relationship between the rich and the poor man and a recognition that property is often acquired by exploitation of the poor, bribery, and corruption. This was seen as a negative aspect of social relations. Yet private property was rationalized, and the conclusion of the sermon further vindicated the new unequal relations: "Do not be jealous of someone's property, because if you follow it you will surely die one day. Let us lay up our treasures in Heaven, but the rich man laid his on earth."

Brotherly love was a frequent motif. Brothers and sisters, however, were no longer the classificatory kin of the lineage, but brothers and sister in Christ. Church members were continually exhorted to help and love one another, placing associations of Christian fellowship above those of the lineage. Although the Church of the Messiah was predominantly Ga, members of other ethnic groups attended as well. An Easter morning sermon instructed the congregation that all people, regardless of their ethnic group, are brothers in Christ as long as they belong to the Christian community. "A Mossi is your brother. How many of you would sit down to supper with a Dagarti? He is your brother in Christ."

The inclusive social unit in the spiritualist church referred, then, to a wider community than the lineage or the federation of seven lineages that composed the town. In some areas of Africa, this feature allowed the churches to be instrumental in consolidating divergent groups, developing national, and to some extent class awareness, and in organizing resistance to colonialism. At the same time, however, that the unit of interaction is expanded, the individual responsibility is emphasized. This equivocality was evident in projects such as funerals. Although traditionally the responsibility for funeral practices rested with the major lineage, the Church of the Messiah had initiated church funerals. A member of the praying band explained that some members of the church did not have families to bury them: "We are their brothers and sisters." In order for a church member to be buried, however, it was necessary to invest forty pesewas the first month and thirty pesewas per month for six months. On one occasion, where a man had died but had not invested enough money for the church to bury him, the founder took the opportunity to warn the members of the congregation to keep up their payments. The church would bury its members, but each must have invested the price of the coffin.

SPIRITUALIST HEALING: A SUMMARY

THE THERAPEUTIC ROLE

Spiritualist therapy does not necessitate the same degree of knowledge and training as that required of the tsofatse. The role of the healer is not intertwined with the traditional hierarchical structure, in which the status of elder or ritual specialist is advantageous. Indeed, frequently spiritualist healers are young men who would possess little prestige or power within the village community structure. Thus, spiritualist healing often is an avenue by which young men may gain ritual power. Ritual power is not unrelated to secular power; spiritualist churches often functioned as small businesses (see Mullings 1979:80-81). In addition to the offering and the sale of candles, water, and oil, additional income might derive from wealthy sponsors, grateful clients, and the training of new practitioners. As well as providing increased revenues, wealthy and influential clients might provide a potential access to power, which itself might lead to additional wealth.

THE UNIT OF TREATMENT

The unit of treatment was, without ambiguity, the individual. Patients arrived to consult the spiritualist healer by themselves or they were sometimes escorted by a relative, but relatives never became a part of the therapeutic process. Family members were neither expected nor encouraged to participate. In fact, the founder often encouraged the discontinuity of these relationships as an aspect of the treatment, as in the cases of Charlotte and Esther. Residence at the church is often seen as a way of removing oneself from the evil influences of the lineage. Etiology and treatment focus on individual responsibility; the lineage is held responsible for neither treatment nor remuneration, as was evident in the thanksgiving ceremony.

THERAPEUTIC INTERVENTION

In spiritualist healing, intervention is primarily symbolic, although, as we pointed out earlier, what appears as symbolic intervention may have somatic implications. Unlike the traditional healer, the spiritualist healer is neither particularly concerned with the physiological or behavioral symptoms of the disease nor with matching specific treatments to symptom complexes. In short, spiritualist therapy is concerned exclusively with the treatment of illness. Regardless of the nature of the disorder, treatments are generally similar for all patients and do not include the administration of medicines. Like the traditional healer, the spiritualist therapist utilizes techniques such as shock treatment, dream analysis, confession, and suggestion.

Both verbal and symbolic dimensions of communication play a major part in therapy. Sermons, psalms, and prayers contain direct instructions on preferred behavior, but less direct symbolic communication is also effectively employed. The panoply of symbols includes a number of those that we have encountered in traditional therapy, as well as new ones.

It is not surprising that new symbols, introducing new concepts and meanings, appear in spiritualist therapy. The cross and the depiction of Jesus — pervasive symbols in spiritualist churches — are associated with the universal Christian community on the one hand and individual salvation on the other. Concepts such as "salvation" and "faith," while often having idiosyncratic meanings to the members of the congregation, promote new and radical concepts of the individual — an individual now responsible for his own salvation, differentiated from, and sometimes opposed to the lineage, but linked to the universal Christian community dominated by Europe and the United States.

Although new symbols are important, most striking and perhaps most effective is the continuity of symbolism. Continuity exists on several levels. The indigenous label may be retained with its original interpretation, but other meanings may be added. For example, members of the spiritualist church use the term *bofo* (pl. *bofoi;* literally, messenger) to refer to particular symbols — sometimes stools and calabashes — in traditional religion that are thought to be repositories of nonempirical powers. We find that this term is retained in their own religion to refer on one hand to angels, on the other hand to the altar. On one level of abstraction bofo continues to refer to a repository of a nonempirical being. However, the form of the repository has changed (or a new form has been added), and the relevant nonempirical beings have been transformed. Of course, exegetical explanations differ. The church membership, as opposed to the leadership, tends to give explanations for rituals that are much more within the idiom of traditional religion. For example, while the leaders of the church may say that the Christian god is not localized in the altar, members of the congregation will claim that the altar is, in fact, the repository of the deity. While the form of symbols may change, frequently the meaning for the majority of people retains continuity with the meaning associated with the traditional context of the symbol.

What are perhaps most interesting are those symbols where the form remains the same but the context changes, allowing new meanings and connotations to be added. Water, for example, is a dominant symbol in both traditional and spiritualist therapy. In both forms of healing, the general exegetical view describes water as a cooling force, washing away sickness and evil (perhaps an adaptive cultural belief). In traditional healing, however, sacred water is often gathered from the rivers, lakes, and lagoons said to be the abodes of the traditional gods; it is associated with lineage and town gods, who often are said to act through the medium of water. Water figures prominently in various aspects of healing rituals, often involving participation of kin.

In spiritualist therapy, water continues to have a healthful connotation. But here water, most frequently used in individual bathing and rituals, is associated with personal purification. Water is made sacred not through association with the traditional gods of the lineage and town but by being blessed by the founder.

Similarly, the importance of color symbolism continues in spiritualist healing. White, most prominently displayed in the "pure" white scarf all women must wear to every meeting (occasionally people are asked to wear white clothes) and the candles burned for illness, continues to have auspicious connotations. Red, found in the red candles also burned for illness and in the blood of Christ, remains a bridge, dangerous but powerful. Within the context of spiritualist therapy, black becomes inexorably negative, where the sinful state ("black as sin") is contrasted with the state of salvation ("white as snow").

The extent to which such concepts are associated with skin color among Ghanaians is unclear. It is evident that the association between the negative connotations of black and non-Caucasian skin color exists among the colonialists, the purveyors of Christianity. It appears that this association was elaborated with the development of exploitive relations between Europeans and non-Europeans. Bastide (1967:289) notes that the progressive Aryanization of depictions of Christ started when Christianity came into close contact with other races. The juxtaposition of symbols is illustrated in the text accompanying the portrait of Capitein, an African educated in Europe. As a seven-year-old slave, Capitein was brought to Holland from "Guinea" by the trader Jacobus von Goch. He later became the first African to be ordained in a Protestant church since the Reformation. His portrait, which sold widely in Germany and Holland, was accompanied by the following text in verse (DeBrunner 1967: 66):

> Look at this Moor! His skin is black,
> but white his soul, since Jesus himself
> prayed for him
> as high priest
> He goes to teach Faith, Hope and
> Charity to the Moors,
> that they, made white, might honour
> the Lamb always.

The uses of color symbolism, then, perhaps may be more profitably examined as outcomes of specific social relationships at a given historical point, rather than as reflections of universal, organically based categories. Under Nkrumah, a Pan-Africanist and Ghana's first president, black became one of the three colors in the Ghanaian flag — a positive and inspirational symbol.

CLINICAL REALITY

We turn now to some discussion of the clinical reality of spiritualist healing. Concerned exclusively with the treatment of illness, the explanatory framework within which healing takes place is clearly articulated in the sermons. The perspective on disease is one that is traditional to Christianity. Calestro notes that during the early Christian period:

> Since disease was assumed to be a religious matter, belief in and adoption of Christianity were considered prerequisite to healing. The cure required the sufferer's denunciation of sin and his subsequent absolution at the hands of one believed to be holy. (1972:95)

That disease was held to be the divine punishment for sin, with the cure requiring personal salvation, repentance, prayer, and good deeds, was expressed by the apostle James:

Is any sick among you? let him call for the elders of the church; and let them pray over him, anointing him with oil in the name of the Lord: And the prayer of faith shall save the sick, and the Lord shall raise him up. (James 5:14-15, King James Version)

As I demonstrated earlier, personal salvation, the prerequisite for successful healing in the spiritualist church, involved concrete changes in behavior and social relationships, often focused on expanding individual responsibility.

Again, such concepts are more subtly expressed in the manipulation of symbols. We have pointed out that often the outward form of the symbol remained the same and continued to connote positive physiological associations. The impact associated with the sensory pole, "those *significata* that may be expected to arouse desires and feelings" (Turner 1967:28) remains the same. But the ideological pole — the principles of social organization — is transformed. Thus, such symbols as water and the color white continue to connote auspicious, purifying processes in relation to illness, but the ideological pole no longer refers to the collective form of social organization of the village community, but rather to personal salvation.

Thus, spiritualist healing becomes a means by which people can break kinship ties that they find too cumbersome. Faced with the contradictions of contemporary capitalism, they often utilize the options presented by both forms of healing; while the individualization of the market economy promotes the rupture of reciprocal obligations, the hardships created by colonial capitalism often require the mobilization of reciprocal aid for survival.

PART III

CROSS-CULTURAL
MENTAL THERAPY

Introductory Note

In this section, I am concerned with what the study of these therapeutic systems tells us about the broader issues surrounding cross-cultural mental therapy. In chapter 5, I compare traditional, spiritual, and Western psychiatric therapy with respect to the meaning of illness, treatment, techniques, goals of therapy, and effectiveness. In chapter 6, I draw some relationships between mental therapy and infrastructural relations in Africa and the United States, and discuss the implications of these for the future of indigenous therapy.

A Comparison of
Therapeutic Systems

DESPITE the differences in therapy, the problems patients bring to the traditional and spiritualist therapist are remarkably similar. Witchcraft and sorcery are widely used to describe and explain a variety of syndromes; in this sense, they function as metaphors for social relationships. Sontag (1978:63) has pointed out that descriptions of disease processes are drawn from the negative images of a given epoch. Tuberculosis was described in images of "nineteenth century *homo economicus:* consumption; wasting; squandering of vitality." The metaphors of cancer in the twentieth century, in contrast, are drawn from the language of warfare: invasive, colonizing. Thus, cancer is described in terms of the negative behavior of the twentieth century: abnormal growth, repression of energy.

So, too, witchcraft and sorcery, the idioms through which illness is expressed, embody the negative social relations of contemporary society. Obviously, witchcraft and sorcery are not unique to the capitalist mode of production. But they function to express the negative images of the times and to link social relations to individual misfortune and illness. Thus, in 1970-72 they described, in negative terms, the form of competition and individualization characterizing contemporary relationships. Witchcraft, the most frequently cited instrumental cause of illness, is, like the vagaries of the capitalist marketplace, incomprehensible and mysterious. It is a power that emanates from humans, but its workings are unseen and not controlled by normal means—it implies essence beyond appearance.

Akpaso, the worst of all witchcraft medicines, kills members of the lineage to bring riches to the individual.

In a survey of respondents in Accra, Jahoda (1966) found that three-fourths of those interviewed endorsed the general statement that "witchcraft is often used because of envy and jealousy of the success of others," and one-half of the sample felt that relatives would be jealous of their success. For Mensah and Aba, witchcraft and sorcery, implicated in illness, were expressed around the issues of private property and the conversion of lineage property to objects of commodity exchange. For Mensah and Raymond, envy resulting from their attempts to pursue higher education was implicated. For Adzoa, John, Elizabeth, and Charlotte, witchcraft and sorcery, and consequently illness, were associated with the insecurities and competition of self-employment. In almost all cases, conflicts were phrased in terms of opposition between the patient (or the patient's immediate family) and other members of the lineage.

While this was not a study of illness forms, my case studies are suggestive and do seem to support the studies that point to relationships between economic insecurity and vulnerability to psychosomatic symptoms. The cases I have described are of varying severity. In some instances, the symptom complexes match those of the functional disorders of the biomedical classificatory system; in others, the phenomenon of somatization—"secondary somatic manifestation of minor psychological disorders and interpersonal problems" (Kleinman 1980:361)—seems to predominate. Many of the symptoms we have described among the patients in Ghana appear in the Harvard study: difficulty in sleeping, trembling limbs, nervousness, beating of the heart, shortness of breath, sweating palms, headaches, frightening dreams, being affected by witchcraft (Inkeles and Smith 1970). Further studies should more fully explore the links between patterns of illness and social change in Ghana.

If mental illness in some sense expresses the role contradictions of a society, then mental therapy seeks to resolve these contradictions and recreate a social order; if illness expresses a dilemma about the nature of the self and its relationship to the collectivity, then mental therapy seeks to provide answers to the problems of individual behavior and the articulation of the individual to the social order. Both traditional and spiritualist therapy pose solutions to the problems of illness, both provide an etiological explanation of the disruption involved in an illness episode and project a blueprint for the transformation to normalcy. But they differ radically in the nature of the solution they propose, as a comparison will demonstrate.

THE MEANING OF ILLNESS

As therapies emerge, in part, in response to specific forms of illness, so do the therapies themselves label, identify, and ground the illnesses in their own terms, constructing and ordering the meaning of the illness experience. The assigning of cultural meaning is the first step in molding the course of therapy. This involves setting the cultural construction on the issue of the locus of responsibility. By assigning responsibility for the problem and for the treatment, this process gives us the unit of reference. While all therapies are, in some sense, concerned with the three aspects of the patient—the psyche, the body, and the social being—they differ significantly in how they place their emphasis.

In traditional healing, illness is for the most part *socioatic*—of a social nature—in that the locus of responsibility for the cause and treatment of illness lies with the social group, in this case the lineage. Thus, while the instrumental causes of illness—the agents or vehicles through which the illness occurs—include ancestors, town gods, witchcraft, or sorcery, the ultimate cause of illness, that is, the factor determining why that instrument or agent was able to affect the individual and cause illness, was always to be found through an analysis of conflict relationships. The instrumental causes, then, are merely the vehicles of sanctions against contravening society. The ultimate causes are to be found in the contraventions themselves.

Thus, while illness behavior is often attributed to the soul (kla or susuma) of the individual, the soul may be injured unbeknown to the patient, absolving the conscious individual of responsibility. The cause of illness is externalized; treatment involves the manipulation of external forces, that is, contemporary social relationships.

In its ideal form, traditional healing may be described as sociotherapy, directed toward treatment of the lineage, or perhaps of various segments of the town. The kinship group first becomes involved as the therapy managing group, being responsible for decisions about the course of treatment. Kin are required for participation in rituals at various points in the treatment process, and all major rituals require at least a spokesman for the lineage group. Failure to attend rituals or to visit sick kin incurs suspicion of guilt. In addition, the wrongdoing of one member of the kinship group may result in another falling ill, as in the cases of Mensah, Aba, and Adzoa.

Thus, the focus is on the relationship among members of a kinship group, even if those members are not always present. The struggle against witchcraft and sorcery, which are signs of conflict, is an attempt to maintain and manipulate those relationships. Traditional healing offers a therapeutic community; healing occurs gradually through interaction between the patient and the kin group, along with the healer and, to a lesser extent, members of the healer's family.

The therapeutic community described above is not always achieved. Individuals sometimes furtively consult the healer, arriving on their own without the knowledge of their lineage group. In a case such as that of John, some of the kin are purposely excluded from knowledge of the treatment, lest they cause ill to befall the patient. Yet, however frequently these cases occur, they are seen as exceptions, aberrations from the form in which healing should be practiced, deviations from the basic premises of traditional healing.

Spiritualist healing makes no such claim to the necessity or efficacy of the involvement of kin in healing. While the instrumental causes of illness, as those in traditional healing, point to conflicts in interpersonal relationships manifested in witchcraft and sorcery, the ultimate cause lies in a breach of faith or failing of the individual. The implications for assignment of responsibility are therefore very different: the individual is ultimately responsible for his own illness, treatment, and destiny. While the instrumental causes of illness — witchcraft, sorcery, naturalistic causes — externalize the means, the ultimate cause internalizes the problem: the internal state of the individual determines the extent to which the instrumental agents are able to be effective.

If traditional healing is sociotherapy, spiritualist healing tends toward psychotherapy. To the extent that the cause of illness lies within the individual, the unit of treatment becomes the individual. Some phases of spiritualist healing take place in a group context. If the patient joins the church, she or he participates in certain collective aspects of healing, particularly the dramatic rituals. But while the experience is *in* a group, it is not *with* others: the patient is not required to interact with other members of the congregation, only to meditate within himself or communicate with God. The congregation functions as a backdrop or audience by singing, praying, and the like. The patient uses the same techniques—praying, meditating, saying verses and psalms—that he or she carries out in private. While the congregation may provide support and perhaps increased concentration by its presence, relationships among members of the congregation are not considered to be a major part of the treatment process. Thus, spiritualist healing, too, provides a therapeutic community, but the emphasis is not on the relationship among members of the group, but rather on the individual as the primary unit. While traditional healing includes one-to-one interaction between healer and patient and some individual meditation on the part of the patient, the emphasis of treatment is on group relationships. In spiritualist healing, the patient often participates with the congregation, but the focus is on the psychic processes of the individual.

It is difficult here to avoid drawing some comparisons with Western therapies. While biomedical psychiatric services are generally underdeveloped in much of Africa, the most prevalent model is that of "traditional" (Western) psychiatry[1] (see Higginbotham 1979:12). Most governments adopt Western models for psychiatric care (Collomb 1973b), and interpretations of disease process continue to be based in psychoanalytic premises (Corin and Murphy 1979).

While recognizing the difficulties of attempting to characterize the range of psychiatric therapies as a composite, I will nevertheless indicate some of the important ways in which the biomedical psychiatric therapies as a class compare to spiritualist and traditional therapies with respect to meaning of behavior, processes and techniques, and goals. The similarities between biomedical therapies and others allow such comparisons to be made.[2] The mainstream approaches will be emphasized, primarily the dynamic therapies that predominate in psychiatric practice, leaving aside the behavior-directive therapies.

The mainstream psychiatric therapies, including the psychoanalytic approaches and many of the group therapies, contrast sharply with traditional therapy in their focus on intrapsychic processes in understanding the meaning of illness and in the emphasis on the responsibility of the individual. While the individual may not be to blame for the illness, he or she is "in charge of" the cure; it is the responsibility of the individual to work for change.

The psychiatric therapies and traditional healing have similar means of externalizing the cause of illness. Horton (1961) and others have pointed to the similarities between the psychoanalytic construction of the unconscious and West African views of the soul as possessor of unconscious and suppressed desires and wishes for which the individual is not responsible. (See also Wallace [1958] for a discussion of this view among the Iroquois.) Unlike traditional healing, however, resolution in psychoanalytically-oriented therapies does not always involve the direct manipulation of contemporary relationships. While both forms of healing presume that the ultimate cause of illness lies outside the individual, for the dominant psychiatric therapies the key social relationships are located in early childhood, beyond reach.

The resolution of illness shares the individual responsibility focus of spiritualist healing. It rests with the individual to know and to cure the illness. Kovel (1976:69) aptly remarks that, "the most prevalent model of therapy in America is one in which an individual either strives alone or in a limited association with others to better himself through technical means, hard work and optimism." Unlike traditional healing, where externalization results in people striving together to analyze and manipulate immediate social relationships, psychiatric therapies seek to mobilize the inner resources of the individual. Like spiritualist healing, the individual is clearly the unit of treatment.

These formulations must be qualified to some extent for the group therapies, but even the group therapies tend to be directed toward the individual (Areneta 1977). Many groups are artificial rather than naturally occurring groups. The emphasis is on individual patients as they respond to the group, not on the alteration of relations within the group. Like spiritualist healing, it often becomes the psychotherapy of the individual within a group setting, less often, through the interrelationships of the group. Some of the more recent approaches, such as est, are also similar in form to spiritualist therapy: the experience occurs within a group, but is basically an experience with the self. At the extreme end of the continuum, such approaches might go so far as to assert that each individual creates the world and merely experiences his own subjective creation.

Family therapy, utilizing a natural group, would seem to have significant similarities to traditional healing.[3] However, family therapy includes a range of approaches (see Kovel 1976:66; Brodkin 1980), among them those that focus on the working out of unconscious fantasies as well as those that manipulate contemporary family relationships. Further, the functions of the family in the United States in the twentieth century are not comparable to those of the lineage in Labadi, which was indeed the basic unit of society, holding access to the means of production and to political offices. As is becoming increasingly true in Labadi, to base therapy on nuclear family relationships in today's advanced industrial society is often to avoid those societal forces that directly impinge on the family and its conflicts.

Despite the recent approaches that question some of the older formulations, it is still accurate to say that, in psychiatric perspectives in general, the unit of reference and responsibility is the individual.[4] Indeed, the notion of individual responsibility in biomedicine extends beyond mental health to "voluntary assumption of health risks" for chronic degenerative diseases. Thus, one leading physician states: "The individual has the power—indeed the moral responsibility—to maintain his own health by the observance of simple and prudent rules of behavior relating to sleep, exercise, diet and weight, alcohol and smoking" (Knowles 1977:80). Emphasis on individual responsibility continues to underlie even the counterculture responses of holistic medicine.

TECHNIQUES AND PROCESSES

THE DRAMATIC HEALING RITUAL

Symbols are consciously manipulated in the dramatic healing ritual, a major aspect of both spiritualist and traditional healing. The appearance of the dramatic healing ritual in both forms of therapy results in a perception of continuity on the part of the participants. Although both therapies use the dramatic healing ritual, the play is different and the players have changed.

There are those functions of dramatic healing characteristic of all ritual. As numerous investigators have pointed out, symbols are manipulated to create and inculcate a belief system sanctioning a given set of social relations and promoting certain values and concepts. Clearly, a large degree of teaching of values and belief systems occurs through the dramatic healing ritual, providing the answers to such questions as who has the power to heal and who is responsible for illness. The dramatic healing ritual functions to focus approval on acceptable alternatives and disapproval on unacceptable ones, symbolically creating and resolving conflicts through collective action. These general functions attain a particular salience in ritual healing of mental illness, which is directly concerned with meaning, with appropriate and acceptable versus inappropriate and unacceptable behavior.

As significant as the observation that all healing rituals provide meaning and indicate standards of acceptable behavior, is the analysis of the way in which they differ: the different frameworks for meaning; the various ways in which conflicts are symbolically resolved; which classes or strata have the power to manipulate ritual, to indicate and define acceptable behavior, to influence the cognitive and affective orientations through a power that is nonmaterial, but linked to strategic resources.

In traditional healing, the ritual participants are kin, and they represent kinship relationships. Malevolent forces are removed, and protection is instilled within the framework of the relative equality of access to resources of the village community. When the traditional healer bids the participants to bathe in sacred water, it is the sacred water blessed by the ancestors, lineage, town, and place gods who safeguard the principles of the society. For the participants, on the sensory level water purifies, removes evil, promotes health; on the ideological level it symbolizes the social relationships of the village community. It requires no great leap into the unconscious or collective conscious to make this connection. The healer explicitly states that the ritual will not work and the patient will not be healed unless things are right in the "house." When the ritual participants are marked with white, on the sensory level it guards against evil and signifies victory, on the ideological level it is the white of the ancestors, the elders, the priests of the town gods, of harmonious social relationships.

Equally important is how the symbols are manipulated, who is manipulating them, and how ritual is being used instrumentally to shape social relationships, to accrue or dissipate power. The healer orchestrates the ritual, makes diagnostic decisions, decides who is wrong and who is right, who has to pay and how much. His interests lie in reinforcing a society where the priests and elders are the authorities. The extent to which he is able to use ritual power capriciously and for his own ends is limited by mythoideological constraints: if he does evil, his medicine will go bad, and only unscrupulous patients will frequent him. These constraints, however, are less binding for the medicine owners than for priests, who have strictly defined modes of interaction and compensation. Ordinary people also manipulate symbols and utilize these relationships to mobilize kin and create reciprocity.

In spiritualist ritual, the participants are members of the congregation. On the sensory level, auspicious symbolism continues to refer to purification and protection against evil, but this is facilitated not by reestablishing lineage relationships but often by discarding them. The symbolic conflicts to be worked out are not among lineages or kin, but between ways of life. Such conflicts are resolved by abnegating the old ways and affirming the new ones. Like the traditional healer, the spiritualist healer dashes the congregation with sacred water; however, it is water made sacred by the Christian God.

On one level, perhaps the level that has the most salience for the patients, the meaning remains the same; at the sensory pole, water purifies and protects against evil. At the ideological pole, however, water is no longer the medium of the town and lineage gods. It is, instead, the medium of the Christian God, who demands that participants put away traditional religion, placing individual salvation — in both a secular and sacred sense — above the concerns of family and kinship. At the sensory pole, white continues to be auspicious and purifying. But white is now the white of salvation, the pure white of snow as opposed to the black of sin and the dark things of traditional religion and of Africa; it is the white of the colonialists. Again, the healer makes these relationships explicit in his sermons, directly attaching behavioral prerequisites to healing.

The healer who orchestrates and manipulates the ritual no longer represents the elders of the village community. These healers, often young men, represent a new stratum and, as individual entrepreneurs, are not part of the traditional power structure. Their power derives from their achieved ability to develop a following, not from ascribed position. The spiritualist healer presents new alternatives, new ways of thinking, molding new relationships as prerequisites for healing. He is much less constrained by custom and doctrine and is able to use power more freely for his own ends, as some of the songs composed by the townspeople at homowo attest.[5] He is in a position to challenge, and to persuade others to challenge, the social relationships characteristic of the village community. While the source of the healer's power is ritual, it is linked to strategic resources in a number of ways. Unbeez (unemployment) is a major reason for church membership and is often implicated in complaints of illness. Members may share information about jobs, and the healer is in a position to play a key role in determining the flow of information. In addition the healer often has access to other sources of funding that may be tapped for special purposes.

While the dramatic ritual is not widely used in Western therapies, dramatization and role playing are being increasingly utilized in Gestalt therapy, transactional analysis, and other therapies using psychodrama to promote the acting out of roles (see Michaux 1972 for a comparison of therapeutic ritual and psychodrama). Even in the more traditional therapist-client situation, although manipulation of the environment has not been an organized aspect of therapeutic techniques, certain forms of it are none the less utilized to promote behavior change.

Western dynamic therapies are often considered to be nondirective, particularly when compared with the direct instructions given in non-Western dramatic healing rituals (Kennedy 1973). Yet, as Hobbs notes, "insight is manifested when the client makes a statement about himself that agrees with the therapist's notion of what is the matter with him," pointing to the pivotal role of the therapist (1962:742). Krasner goes so far as to refer to the therapist as a "social 'reinforcement machine,' programmed by prior training and experience" (1961:61). Citing the extensive literature on the controlling role of the therapist indicating that patients changed their moral values in the direction of the therapist, that patients' dreams conformed to the theoretical formulations of the therapist, that increasing similarity in verbal behavior was noted, he concludes, "the evidence is strong that the therapist by virtue of his role has the power to influence and control the behavior and values of other human beings," so that, "the particular response class reinforced or punished will be determined by the therapist's class morality background" (Krasner 1961:70). The healing arena is similarly utilized by the Western therapist to shape relationships that, as discussed in more detail later, are primarily those of an advanced capitalist society. The Western therapist, too, manipulates physical conditions, often in such a manner as to cut down on external stimuli in order to make therapist-originated stimuli more effective: "couch or easy chairs (face to face); room illumination; sound proofing; mood music; heavy carpets; bland clothing" (Krasner 1961:75). Suggestibility is enhanced by belief in the capability of the therapist — reinforced by an impressive office, an assortment of academic degrees, a professional reputation, and a patient waiting list, not dissimilar to the traditional healer's demonstrations of magic and displays of wealth from grateful patients (Calestro 1972:99).

OTHER TECHNIQUES

All forms of healing seem to make use of some form of altered states of consciousness. Following Prince (1980), we can delineate three levels of altered states of consciousness: dreams; mystical states and meditation; dissociation states.

Both traditional and spiritualist healing, as well as the biomedical therapies (particularly those that utilize psychoanalytic techniques), make use of dream analysis. In each of these therapies, such a technique reflects the view that a full explanation of behavior requires reference to levels other than that which is immediately observable.[6] In both traditional and spiritualist healing, analysis of the patient's dreams occurs fairly casually and as a matter of course (see, for example, the discussions of John's or Raymond's dreams). For traditional and spiritualist healers as well as for Freud or the Iroquois (Wallace 1958), dreams represent the wishes of the soul. While dream analysis is not a central feature of the therapeutic system, as is the case in psychoanalysis and derivative systems, dream events are related to illness and curing in a variety of peripheral ways. Both traditional and spiritualist healers make use of the dream state to enhance their powers of analysis. The source of the patient's problems may be revealed to them through their own dreams and meditation, a technique not formally utilized by most therapists (see Prince 1980 for a discussion of possible psychotherapeutic functions of dreams).

Meditation and mystical states are major therapeutic techniques in spiritualist healing. Similar to the mysticotranscendental approaches in U.S. therapies, such a technique is highly subjective and individual. In the spiritualist churches the individual may meditate alone or in the company of the congregation. Like est therapy, the experience may occur within the group, in fact may require a group structure to break down defenses (Kovel 1976), but the experience is not so much with others as it is with oneself. Recitation of prayers and psalms is said to assist the state of meditation. In traditional therapy, patients may casually engage in meditation, but it does not appear to be a central aspect of therapy. However, forms of mild trance, mystical states, and meditation occur during the dramatic rituals, often facilitated by the repetitious praying and chanting.

Dissociation states, in the form of possession, associated with drumming, music, and other sensory stimuli, occur during most of the public rituals of the spiritualist church. The expression of feelings when in the possessed state, whether those feelings are benign or hostile (the influence of a good or evil spirit), is encouraged. As I have pointed out earlier, possession behavior is highly individual and not ascribed. In traditional healing, we find states of mild dissociation, especially after patients undergo a particularly grueling procedure such as nasal installation or an intense ritual procedure, but outright signs of dissociation states among patients are not common. While this is in keeping with traditional religion, where possession is usually limited to ascribed statuses, it contrasts with those healers associated with democratic, or perhaps more accurately, individualistic possession cults, where patients habitually become possessed.

Physical manipulation is a technique used extensively by traditional and spiritualist healers. Its use is limited in most biomedical techniques, with the exception of certain psychodramatic techniques and encounter groups that include physical interaction. Western techniques tend to rely more exclusively on the verbal dimension, verbal exchange being the medium of influence.

COMPARATIVE EFFECTIVENESS

Although specific techniques differ among various therapies, several investigators have suggested that there are underlying mechanisms common to all therapies—supportive patient-therapist relationships, suggestion, confession—and that it is these mechanisms that have implications for the effectiveness of different therapies. These scholars cite studies suggesting that, with the exception of psychopharmacotherapies (drug therapies), all forms of psychotherapy seem to work, or not work, equally well for a wide range of disorders. One study, for example, compared the outcomes of different forms of psychotherapies and found insignificant differences in the proportions of patients who improved. The investigators concluded that "the most potent explanatory factor is that the different forms of psychotherapy have major common elements—a helping relationship with a therapist is present in all of them, along with the other related, nonspecific effects such as suggestion and abreaction" (Luborsky, Singer, and Luborsky 1975:1006). Other studies of patients support similar conclusions (see Prince 1980:339 for a review of such studies).

More recently, the World Health Organization survey of schizophrenic psychoses in nine countries has cast some doubt on the extent to which biomedical treatment positively affects prognosis. The most important outcome of the two-year follow-up was the finding that the patient sample in developing countries had a better course and outcome on all variables than the schizophrenics in the developed countries (Sartorius, Jablensky, and Shapiro 1978:111). The study also suggested that the favorable course and outcome found for schizophrenics may be rooted in social and cultural considerations (WHO 1979).[7]

There is, then, a fairly large body of literature suggesting that it is the common mechanisms in various psychotherapies which are responsible for whatever effectiveness such therapies possess. These include confession and catharsis, client-therapist relationship, and arousal of faith and hope, all of which enhance suggestion (Loewen 1969; Frank 1961a; Kiev 1964; Strupp 1973; Torrey 1972a, b; Calestro 1972; Luborsky, Singer, and Luborsky 1975). Prince (1980) presents a novel approach, explaining the similarity of outcome by the universal "endogenous" self-healing mechanism of the patient, rather than the exogenous influence of the healer. He argues that most treatments offered by healers are simply exaggerations of endogenous mechanisms, specifically sleep, rest, and social isolation; the use of altered states of consciousness, including dreams, mystical states and meditation, dissociation states and "shamanistic 'ecstasy'." Many investigators suggest that traditional healing, which often makes more active use of these techniques, is no less effective than biomedical therapies.

In any discussion of comparative effectiveness of therapies, we are immediately confronted with enigmatic issues on both the conceptual and methodological levels. Taking the less problematic area first, there are considerable methodological problems that are precluded from resolution by the present state of the literature. A cursory glance at the cross-cultural literature immediately reveals the lack of uniformity in reporting such aspects as symptoms, stages, treatment, and behavioral manifestations, making comparison extremely difficult. There is, however, an expanding body of literature that systematically explores the range of information that must be collected to make studies comparable (see Kleinman 1980 and Press 1980 for examples). Nevertheless, problems resulting from the small number of prospective studies and the unreliability of retrospective studies remain significant.

The individual investigator faces considerable problems in attempting to carry out research that can contribute to the cross-cultural literature. Among these are the difficulties of determining the nature of "representative" versus "unrepresentative" cases and the problems of assessing the effects of treatment. In the absence of long-range studies, it is difficult to evaluate outcome in light of the fact that: (1) a significant proportion of illnesses seem to be self-limiting, that is, they will resolve themselves regardless of treatment; and (2) remission, where symptoms disappear only to return at a later date, often occurs.

In the case of mental therapy, the problem of determining treatment outcome is even more complicated. The fact that the etiology of most mental disorders is unknown or unclear makes it especially difficult to assess the results of various modes of treatment. Even when we limit ourselves to Western psychotherapy, numerous scholars have pointed to the inadequacies of present methods of evaluation of outcomes (see Prince 1980:339). Attempts to distinguish symptom-relief from cure become even more problematic in mental disorders, where symptoms are so clearly behavioral, involving values, beliefs, and culture.[8]

Intrinsic to the issue of evaluation are the conceptual difficulties of assessing and comparing various modes of therapy, based on the problem of determining what constitutes the nature of "cure."[9] Basic to this concern is the proposition that different types of healing, particularly ritual and biomedical healing, pursue different goals. The biomedical model tends to focus on symptoms and syndromes—disease—while ritual healing tends to be more holistic in approach, concerned with the state of the patient in reference to a wider social and cosmological framework—illness. One must modify this somewhat in discussing psychotherapy, where the model for therapy is not necessarily based on the biomedical model of disease cure, but rather on the development or education of a person. This, however, brings its own problems of comparison, with its obvious reference to rules of conduct and culturally-prescribed values.

Despite these methodological and conceptual problems of comparison, there seems to be evidence supporting the utility of examining the efficacy of ritual healing. In addition to the indirect evidence of the questionable effectiveness of Western methods discussed above, there are a few studies that attempt to evaluate ritual healing more directly. It is generally suggested that religious healing has its greatest success in psychosomatic, hysterical, and neurotic cases where there is predominant "emotional" involvement (see Bourguignon 1976 for a review of such studies). While it is true that these studies are generally impressionistic,[10] the weight of opinion, if not evidence, seems to indicate that these therapies have areas of effectiveness.

In Ghana, there has been little systematic study of the effectiveness of non-Western therapies. There seems to be, however, a general view among investigators and health workers that traditional healers serve an important function and are effective. Doctors and social workers interviewed by me at the mental hospital in Accra repeatedly stressed their view that patients who had not improved in the mental hospital had often improved when treated by a traditional healer. Jahoda (1961:268) suggests that "the support and reassurance" provided by traditional healers and spiritualist churches "probably often prevents the occurrence of serious breakdowns." In discussing traditional healers and spiritualist churches, Baeta (1967: 242) notes that "the most striking successes so far obtained appear to have been with the mentally depressed." Twumasi (1975) also claims that traditional healers are more effective in treating mental disorders than biomedical healers.

Studies that attempt to explicate the way in which traditional healing is effective fall into two general categories: those that focus on the cultural and social aspects of healing; those that attempt to examine the relationships between the symbolic and the somatic. In the first category, numerous investigators have pointed to the various aspects of the "shared world view," the rallying of group support, and the restructuring of relationships in the treatment process (see Kiev 1972; Kennedy 1973; Harwood 1977; Waxler 1979; Kleinman 1980, to name only a few). Kleinman (1980:361) summarizes this position in his claim that indigenous practitioners heal because they must heal. They maximize the psychosocial and cultural treatment of illness by externalizing the problem and encouraging adaptive behavior by mobilizing group support. It seems fairly clear that this approach is a major factor in the effective treatment of at least some types of disorders, particularly those that might be classified as neurotic problems.[11]

The second, and complementary, line of studies attempts to examine the implications of techniques utilized in traditional healing for the interplay between symbolic and physiological processes. Much of the recent research on the physiological effects of meditation, biofeedback, trance, and placebos points to productive and provocative directions for research into how ritual therapies may affect not only psychological disorders but known biologically based disease as well.

These studies are concerned with the physiological effects of various elements of ritual, particularly dramatic healing rituals. Early research by physiologists concerned itself with the effect of repetitive stimuli on the brain. Neher (1962), for example, investigated the neurophysiological effects of repetitive drumming. Much of this literature is reviewed by Walker (1972), who suggests that these stimuli promote an altered state of consciousness leading to beneficial and healthful results. Jilek (1976) reviews various techniques of sensory deprivation and stimulation implicated in the production of altered states of consciousness: hypoventilation, hyperventilation, hypoglycemia, and dehydration due to fasting, sleep deprivation, exposure to extreme temperatures, rhythmic sensory and acoustic stimulation.

Lex (1979) suggests that the investigation of the effects of ritual trance should not be restricted to brain behavior. She examines the relevance of the concept of CNS (central nervous system) "tuning" and areas of specialization in the brain hemispheres. The two cerebral hemispheres differ in their functions: the "dominant" left hemisphere produces logical functions such as linear, analytic thought and the sequential processing of information; the functions of the "subordinate" right hemisphere are characterized as more emotional, concerned with spatial and tonal perception, the recognition of patterns, holistic thought. "Tuning" of the nervous system, then, refers to the "sensitization of or facilitation of particular centers."

Briefly, she argues that many of the practices associated with ritual situations and which facilitate ritual trance, such as rhythms, chanting, and the like, are in fact elaborate "driving behaviors," which work to "tune" the nervous system, engaging the preeminence and lessening the inhibition of the right hemisphere, producing therapeutic results. Meditation techniques, for example, particularly those that involve repetition, may monopolize the left hemisphere, thus freeing the right hemisphere. Ritual, then, promotes the "readjustment of dysphasic biological and social rhythms by manipulation of neurophysiological structures under controlled conditions" (Lex 1979:144).

Prince argues along similar lines. He suggests that the therapeutic value of meditation practices and mystical experiences is based on the activation of the mode of consciousness associated with the right hemisphere — "holistic, non-verbal, analogical" (1980:313) — which increases the adaptive powers of the individual through greater use of all his coping mechanisms.[12] Prince and Lex suggest that certain ritual, trance, and meditation behaviors produce physiological changes that are possibly related to the physiologically restorative "trophotropic response" (the opposite of Cannon's "flight or fight" response), characterized by decreased oxygen consumption, heart rate, respiratory rate, and arterial blood lactate, as well as increased skin resistance and increased slow wave activity in the EEG.

The placebo effect has long been implicated in studies of ritual and biomedical healing. The salience of the placebo effect has been associated with the therapist (Frank 1961b:5-6) and various other healing practices (Kiev 1972:138). Recent studies now suggest that the placebo may work in a very specific physiological manner, stimulating the production of endorphins, substances recently found to occur naturally in the brain. Sometimes called "natural opiates," they regulate the same body functions that are most strongly influenced by opiate drugs, particularly the relief of pain (see Snyder 1978a, b). Since these findings have not yet been assessed with reference to ritual healing, this may be an interesting area of research to pursue.

While the studies discussed thus far suggest that ritual practices themselves produce therapeutic physiological results, a similar line of studies is concerned with the extent to which ritual practices produce or promote altered states of consciousness, facilitating behavior modification. These generally follow the line of reasoning set out by Sargant (1974; 1957) in his discussion of altered states of consciousness and brainwashing techniques. Similar physiological changes are thought to underlie such phenomena as possession, mystical experience, faith healing, and hypnosis. Excitement and exhaustion lead to alterations in brain functioning, characterized by excessive cortical excitation and hypersuggestibility. These changes promote the breaking up of old (sick) behavior patterns and facilitate the promotion of new ones (Sargant 1974:198; Kennedy 1973:1179; Kiev 1972:137). Prince (1980:313-314) reviews the literature on the therapeutic effects of meditation for "de-automatization" — "a shake up which can be followed by an advance or a retreat in the level of organization," an "undoing to permit a new and perhaps more advanced kind of experience." Kennedy, too (1973:1178), suggests that curing rituals almost always produce an altered state of consciousness, one feature being "deep regression to infantile modes of cognition and action." After this process has occurred, reformation of the personality with respect to the culturally defined conceptual framework can more easily take place. Documenting the occurrence of this process in spirit dancing among the Salish, Jilek claims that "the therapeutic effectiveness of indigenous treatment methods compares favorably with current Western therapies as far as Indian patients are concerned, and with Western correctional management of Indian behavior disorders associated with alcohol or drug abuse" (1976:211). These studies suggest that the practices of indigenous healing may have physiological effects that increase the receptivity of the patient. The cure, however, lies in the behavior modification that occurs as a result of the inculcation of the guidelines for behavior change while the individual is in a state of increased receptivity.

GOALS OF THERAPY

Therapeutic techniques are the means of bringing about behavior change, the vehicles through which content is instilled. Although the techniques may be similar, the content of various therapeutic systems differs significantly. For example, although all therapeutic systems may utilize suggestion as a major force, what is being suggested varies considerably. These differences become most evident when we examine the goals of therapy.

It is these goals that perhaps most clearly reflect the value judgments inherent in all therapeutic systems: "All criteria of improvements ultimately reflect the implicit value judgments of the patient, the people important to him, and the therapist" (Freedman and Kaplan 1972:571). These value judgments are influenced by the ideologies of a given society. In discussing goals of therapy in biomedical systems, the concepts of "face validity" and "construct validity," based on Frank's definitions, have been widely employed.[13] Criteria of face validity are said to be widely shared. They include "subjective comfort, the capacity to establish mutually rewarding relationships with other persons, within and outside the family, the ability to do one's job adequately and to derive some satisfaction from working, and the possession of certain skills" (Frank 1975: 2011). Construct goals, in contrast, are based on improvement measures derived from specific theories and the values upon which these theories are based.

The premises of different therapeutic systems are most manifest in the construct goals. The explicit construct goals of traditional healing have to do with the restoration of cosmological balance: traditional healing seeks to counteract malevolent power causing illness with benevolent power, specifically the gods of the town and lineage. In order for the positive powers to "do their work," however, the patient and family must bring their behavior into line with expectations—the implicit construct goals. Relationships must be restored according to the healer's model of society. Thus, the healer instructs Aba to be more polite, Mensah's father to divest himself of those medicines said to bring him wealth at the expense of his brother, and announces that Afi's wealth is the property of the lineage. Traditional therapy seeks to change the behavior of the patient and those around him or her in such a manner as to reconstruct the social organization of the village community. Traditional healing does not seek a more enlightened individual, but rather the restoration of relationships compatible with the village community mode of production.

Like traditional therapy, spiritualist therapy occurs in a cosmological frame of reference, the explicit goal being to mobilize benevolent power for the cure of illness. Here power is mobilized as the individual increases his or her strength and faith. To produce an individual "right with God" implicitly entails emphasis on individual responsibility and often separation from the kinship group. Bringing the individual into a new therapeutic community—the congregation — which may assist in some of the functions formerly performed by the lineage, further reinforces individual modes of behavior.

The fact that both traditional healing and spiritualist healing utilize religious frames of reference allows them to be categorized as ritual healing. Biomedical therapies differ significantly in that they are secular systems. While they do not rely on a supernatural cosmological system, they are based on a culturally-determined world view. Although the difference between ritual and secular perspectives is important, on one level the construct goals of biomedical therapies may have more in common with spiritualist healing than spiritualist and traditional healing have with each other.

The explicit construct goals of most of the psychoanalytically influenced therapies are concerned with individual responsibility and self-knowledge. Investigators have noted the Western emphasis on the patient's responsibility for his own destiny (Kiev 1972); that the goals of Western therapy emphasize the cultural values of U.S. society centered on the responsibility of the individual (Torrey 1972*a*:80); and that the goals of Western therapy differ from those of non-Western therapy on their emphasis on "ego-strengthening," "instilling self-esteem," and so forth (Kennedy 1973:1175). There seems to be general agreement that "the healing power of psychoanalysis lies in the dictum 'know thyself' " (Kovel 1976:75). Illness or neurotic behavior is seen as a result of early childhood experiences, and the goal of treatment is to remove the underlying basis of neurotic behavior *through the self-reflective process.* Insight, then, has been said to be one of the most firmly rooted assumptions of the therapeutic endeavor, and other strategies, such as catharsis, abreaction, and transference, are valued to the extent that they lay the groundwork for insight (Hobbs 1962). For many, the major explicit goal is behavior change based on insight. The implicit premises that make insight a meaningful goal have much in common with those of spiritualist healing, which is also directed toward the consolidation of the individual, although through self-meditative and ritual techniques rather than insight. In fact, some therapists suggest that insight has been overemphasized, and that there are a variety of corrective experiences, including "connecting" with feelings and self-meditation.

We find, then, that patients consult the traditional and spiritualist healer with similar problems, but the solutions offered by

TABLE 4

COMPARISON OF THERAPIES

	Traditional	Spiritualist	Biomedical
Etiology			
ultimate cause	immediate social relations (externalized) organic	individual failing (internalized) organic	childhood relations (externalized) organic
instru- mental cause	gods, ancestors, witchcraft, sorcery (external)	witchcraft, sorcery (external)	interpsychic process (internal)
Treatment			
respon- sibility	lineage	individual	individual
unit	lineage (sociotherapy)	individual (psychotherapy)	individual (psychotherapy)
Techniques	dramatic healing ritual dissociation states physical manipulation	dramatic healing ritual dissociation states physical manipulation meditation/ mystical states	meditation/ mystical states
	psychopharmaco- therapy dream analysis manipulation of environment verbal directives	dream analysis manipulation of environment verbal directives	psychopharmaco- therapy dream analysis manipulation of environment verbal directives
Goals of Therapy	subjective comfort ability to fulfill roles lineage relations in place	subjective comfort ability to fulfill roles individual salva- tion	subjective comfort ability to fulfill roles individual insight and self-esteem resolution of intra- psychic conflicts

each are radically different. This type of traditional healing strives for sociotherapy. Responsibility for the cause and cure is collective, lying with the lineage. The goal of therapy is to repair and reinforce lineage relationships characteristic of the village community. Spiritualist healing, however, places ultimate responsibility for cause and cure of illness on the individual. The goal of spiritualist healing is individual salvation. Thus, spiritualist healing has much in common with psychiatric therapies, which also focus on the individual and have as their goal individual insight (see table 4).

It is in the area of techniques and processes that we find a great deal of overlap. The use of symbolism, physical manipulation, dissociation states, and the dramatic healing ritual predominate in traditional and spiritualist healing, although we also find these techniques in psychiatric therapies. Verbal directives, manipulation of the environment, and dream analysis are found in all therapies. Suggestion and a special relationship with the healer underlie all therapies, although content differs significantly.

Given the similarities in meaning of illness and goals of therapy between spiritualist and biomedical therapies, dichotomous categories of Western/non-Western and ritual/secular may obscure very important differences. The label of "traditional," generally used to refer to healing based in African cosmological systems, is also problematic. While such a category may be useful, it must be employed with care lest it obscure the fact that there are many varieties of traditional healing (see chapter 2), and that these too are transformed by changes in the mode of production.

Mental Therapy and Social Change

THERAPEUTIC SYSTEMS AND SOCIETIES

Having compared the premises, techniques, and functions of traditional, spiritualist, and Western therapies, we return to our first concern, the analysis of the way in which medical systems are linked to social formations. The typological bases that have been used by scholars to classify medical systems and to relate them to various types of societies have been reviewed by Press (1980). While the study of mental therapeutic systems is not sufficiently well developed to allow us to construct typologies with confidence, I have suggested that we examine the links between therapeutic systems and the production relations, in this case relationships between forms of healing and incorporation into the capitalist world economy and its associated structure of relationships and values.

In chapter 1, I outlined the major changes that had occurred in production relations in the recent period. Briefly, I suggested that we might best understand social relations in Labadi by examining the transformation of the society from the village community mode of production to a capitalist one, within the context of colonialism. Development, geared toward the needs of the metropole rather than internal industrialization, produced features characteristic of many former colonial countries. We find the coexistence and interfacing of modes of production and their attendant classes. The persistence of the village community mode of production is evident in ownership of land by the lineages, the "traditional" political structure, the status of elders, chiefs, and ritual specialists, and others. All this, however, is significantly influenced by the emerging capitalist relations, which create new forms of ownership, status, and values. Individuation, in social relations and ideology, is an integral aspect of capitalist development. These processes are particularly evident among the protoproletariat and service strata which constitute a major sector of the urban population.

Sociotherapy, as found in traditional healing, has its origin in the village community mode of production. The ancestors, the town and lineage gods that provided legitimization for the dominance of the elders and linked them to the land, continue to provide the framework for sanctions in traditional healing. In assigning responsibility for illness, unit of treatment, and goals of therapy, the therapeutic system more or less attempts to deal with the individual by modifying behavior to conform to what it ought to be in a village community.

Ideally, the healers are respected elders, and this form of healing reinforces the power of the elders, chiefs, and priests. Sociotherapy embodies the concept of kin control over resources, particularly choice of and participation in therapy. Kinship-based therapy is buttressed by lineage land ownership and the persistence of the lineage-based political structure.

As the lineage loses control over the fundamental conditions of existence of its members, its hold over therapy weakens. We have discussed the increase in individual gods, "private practice," and the growing number of practitioners who set up shop on the periphery of lineage relationships, treating patients on an individual basis outside the social group. While for "legitimate" practitioners lineage relations continue to be the model of what ought to be, these relations may be and often are manipulated for such individual ends as acquisition of private property.

Thus, while the ideology of traditional healing appears to be antithetical to the emerging capitalist relations, it is directly affected by the dominance of capitalism and can function to perpetuate it. Like indirect rule, traditional healing may foster the illusion of an intact traditional society despite the fact that people are involved in the capitalist economy. Traditional healing, as I have pointed out, exposes some of the ills of the new social relationships through the idiom of witchcraft and sorcery. But it may also mask and gloss over the real relationships in which people are involved by claiming to recreate the reciprocity of the village community (e.g., "She [Afi] will share with those from her mother's family and those from her father's family," when in fact Afi's money is her own).

At the same time, people utilize traditional healing to manipulate the increasingly individual relationships. The emerging economic relationships place a heavy burden on individuals, who must deal with economic insecurity and unexpected threats to health. One way people attempt to increase chances of survival is through sharing of scarce resources, as has been demonstrated in studies of the urban poor all over the world (see Stack 1974; Lomnitz 1977). As we have seen in the case studies, traditional healing, like fictive kin networks, allows people to manipulate relationships in such a way as to create reciprocity and claims on kinsmen. Through participation in such therapy, it is possible to activate sanctions against extreme individualism and to mobilize kin in times of need. The contemporary societal structure necessitates the persistence of traditional healing. The social relations determine the need for reciprocity, and culture history influences the form it takes. While it is true that people are often unsuccessful in mobilizing reciprocity, and that when it does occur it is most likely transient and episodic, through traditional healing, people critique contemporary social relations and assert a less isolated concept of the self.

Spiritualist healing comes into being with the new relations of production, which require the emergence of the individual as the basic unit for wage labor and contract. Inherent in the spiritualist therapeutic system is what Van Binsbergen (1976*b*) refers to as "super-structural reconstruction." Its theoretical premises and preferred modes of behavior move away from the village community and assert a fundamentally different definition of the individual and the correct order of social relationships.

In a sense, the churches are analogous to the small business concerns that are characteristic of this new mode of production. As I have demonstrated, their leaders may be young men who have no authority in the traditional structure but have achieved some formal education. In many ways the churches embody the interests of the large stratum of self-employed small traders and craftsmen. Indeed, spiritualist churches in Ghana experienced their greatest expansion during periods of crisis, which seem to affect such people most sharply because of their marginal position. The introduction of spiritualist churches with the tour through southwestern Ghana of the Grebo prophet Harris in 1914 coincided with the collapse of the timber market in that area. The formation of several important independent churches in the 1920s and Sampson Oppong's tour in 1920-1921, during which he reportedly converted 10,000 people, occurred during the 1920s drop in cocoa prices. The 1960s, which witnessed the greatest period of growth of spiritualist churches, were characterized by falling cocoa prices, inflation, and a precipitous drop in the standard of living: between 1960 and 1963, the Accra price index rose nearly 5 percent annually, and in 1966 the real income of the Accra worker was lower than it had been since 1938 (see Beckmann 1975:129).

The ideologies of people in this stratum seem to be influenced by their marginal status and their hope to do better. We have noted that the sermons in the Church of the Messiah rationalized inequality, but, at the same time, were sympathetic to problems of unemployment and hostile to exploitation of the poor by those better off. In part, they reflect fairly widespread sentiments. Sandbrook and Arn's survey of the attitudes of the urban poor in Greater Accra concludes: "bourgeois aspirations and values among the poor co-exist with resentment and hostility toward the most 'successful' products of the capitalist order. While petty bourgeois aspirations are thus congruent with a populist orientation, they are antithetical to a working-class political perspective" (1977:37). We might surmise that the significant proportion of the population working in the informal sector, where people are not brought together in social production or directly confront owners of the means of production, creates favorable conditions for the development and strengthening of petit bourgeois, individualistic orientations, which are expressed and perpetuated through spiritualist therapy.

Clearly such orientations were perpetuated in the Church of the Messiah — responsibility for one's own destiny, acceptance of inequality and the like help to rationalize and thus promote the new capitalist relations. It is not surprising that Sandbrook and Arn's survey also found that "acquiescent attitudes," which encouraged passivity, (i.e., accepting the current distribution of resources as inevitable and as determined by one's own character or effort), were expressed especially by members of "Spiritual Churches" (1977:49).

The association of Christianity with education and literacy is important in understanding the emergence and popularity of spiritualist therapy. Not only is literacy important to the development of certain sectors of the new labor force but education is perceived as the means to achieving upward mobility, particularly in the numerically significant service sector. Sandbrook and Arn's survey further concluded that, at this stage of semi-industrialization of Greater Accra, populist and class orientations coexist with notions concerning the improvement of life-chances through the permeability of the class structure. While the view that the class structure is open prevails, it is more firmly held by the small businessmen and informal workers than by industrial workers (1977:58). As I have noted, education and literacy have been associated with Christianity from the earliest times. Many schools were mission supervised, and students could gain admission only by becoming Christians. Apparently this relationship continues. Today in the Presbyterian church, which is the denomination most heavily involved in school administration, three-fourths of the members are children, although only one-half of the general population is under sixteen. The imbalance appears to be a result of the exodus of students from church membership upon graduation from school (Beckmann 1975:24).

While Christianity was, to some extent, foisted on Ghanaians through domination, people create new options for themselves. As is the case in traditional healing, people utilize spiritualist therapy to manipulate social relations. Members of the spiritualist churches use these networks to form new relationships, to find jobs, and to make business contacts (see Fiawoo 1959, 1968). They occasionally engage in collective enterprises such as burial insurance but, as we have indicated, these projects have a firmly individual basis. Most important, however, spiritualist therapy gives people the option to break kinship networks and shirk unwanted obligations. For individuals, the options are not necessarily clear-cut; the same patient or family may be involved in consolidating and breaking relationships through traditional and spiritualist therapy, depending on the conditions and strategy at a given time.

In spiritualist healing, then, we have the creation of new understandings about normal behavior, the relationship of the individual to the collectivity, the nature of the person—notions that are more congruent with the emerging structure of capitalist relations. Yet, new forms are created from old forms, and there is much continuity with traditional healing. It is perhaps the very feature of continuity that allows the spiritualist churches to function as more effective vehicles of ideology than the conventional Christian churches or biomedical facilities. The construction of a new symbolic system to recreate a sense of self and restore a sense of meaningfulness involves the use of both old and new symbols. Since symbols are by nature ambiguous, in times of social change old symbols can take on new meanings or can be rearranged to serve new purposes. In spiritualist healing, we see the use of white and water as symbols that now express different relationships, but, because they are traditional ideological forms, to some they may conceal the transformed nature of these new relationships. The "sensory" perception of the symbol might remain the same even while the "message" of the symbol changes. Thus, the domination of colonial culture was much more obvious in the conventional churches, where African forms were prohibited. In the spiritualist churches, ideologies similar to those of the conventional churches may be imparted, but the Africanity of the medium may obscure the similarity of the message.

In spiritualist healing, the dominant themes of individualization, private property, and inequality, are linked with the colonialists and the emerging bourgeoisie, yet certain populist and anticolonial views hold sway. It is perhaps this flexibility that allowed some of the independent churches to be vehicles for the expression of mass resistance to colonial exploitation. Questions still remain concerning the extent to which the availability of this avenue of expression repressed resistance in other arenas. Today, most spiritualist churches actively seek foreign (particularly American) aid, support, and exchange.

Traditional and spiritualist healing, then, constitute two very different modes of therapy, emerging from contrasting patterns of production relations. Each defines, although in contradistinctive categories, the nature of the individual and his or her relationship to the collective. Traditional therapy, in general, seeks to perpetuate an individual as a member of a corporate lineage in a semiegalitarian, agrarian, localized economy. Spiritualist therapy, in contrast, contributes to the process of producing wage laborers, self-employed informal sector and service workers, whose work relationships are individual and contractual in a capitalist economy. Each therapeutic system provides an ideological framework and a context of social relationships, including sanctions, which are overtly utilized to reproduce selected behavioral patterns.

While it is true that these therapies constitute analytically distinct systems of belief and practice, it is also the case that they exist within a single frame of activity, and in both forms of healing the interests of different classes make themselves felt. Just as populist ideologies are found in spiritualist healing, in traditional healing, norms concerning reciprocity and the dominance of the elders stand against interpretations allowing privatization and individuation. These latter are evident in the very practice of the traditional healer. Where the emphasis is placed by the healer, the patient, and the patient's family determines whose interests the healing process serves. Often the collective orientation of traditional healing may be utilized to serve the needs of individual interests. Patients and their families move through a continuum of beliefs and practices, selecting etiologies and treatments they deem appropriate to their life situation at a given moment. Priorities shift as people grapple with illness and attempt to resolve problems and rationalize behavior in a capricious economic context.

This analytic approach is also applicable to Western psychiatry. While spiritualist healing seeks to reorganize the perceptual framework of the individual, producing perspectives and explanations that are more congruent with the emerging system characterized by private ownership, it contains within it contradictory orientations toward traditional and contemporary patterns of social relationships. These are resolved in Western therapy, which also arises from and perpetuates a given social formation; here the underlying premises of spiritualist healing are crystallized and given a theoretical rationale.

Western therapy reflects its origins in the advanced capitalist societies of Europe and the United States. While European psychiatry placed more emphasis on organismic considerations, psychoanalytic technique flourished in the United States. Along with the dominance of psychoanalytic approaches and their followers emerges the firm crystallization of the notion of the individual and individual responsibility in mental therapy.

As numerous scholars have observed, the individual became the basic unit of the society with the consolidation of capitalism (see Bell 1976; Dumont 1965, 1970). Thus, Dubreuil and Wittkower detect at the end of the nineteenth century and the beginning of the twentieth the reflection in psychoanalysis of the "rising ideology of individual self-enhancement." Especially in the United States, "psychiatry and psychology were offered as sciences able to provide principles for enhancing individual autonomy and for a more efficiently functioning society" (1976:126). Early studies such as that by Davis (1938) cite the emphasis on individualism, enhancement of wealth and social status, and self-reliance underlying both Protestantism and the American mental health movement (cf. Albee [1977], who suggests that the rise of psychoanalysis was related to the decline of Protestantism). More recently, Caplan and Nelson reported on the results of their analysis of the first six months of the 1970 *Psychological Abstracts*. They concluded that the mental health movement is characterized by a person-centered preoccupation, favoring explanation based on personal characteristics, disregarding the influence of external or situational forces (1973:209). A content analysis of the dominant themes of mental health pamphlets revealed that the majority of texts contained statements, explicit or implied, that "could be identified as falling within the middle class cultural mold" (Gursslin, Hunt, and Roach 1959:211). The authors concluded that the mentally healthy prototype and the middle-class prototype are basically equivalent (ibid.:63). Thus, the mental health movement is unwittingly propagating a middle-class ethic under the guise of science. These findings are supported by those of Bloch who, based on an analysis of the literature concerning the variables by which therapists evaluate the mental health of their patients, concluded that the mentally healthy stereotype reflected "the desirable qualities of the rising young executive, of the organization man, or of the upwardly mobile middle class citizen" (cited in Buhler 1962:180).

Similar to medical systems in Ghana, therapy in the United States is identified with the emergence and domination of a particular class. However, the use of the term "middle class" is somewhat misleading. Middle class tends to be a "folk" category rather than a scientific one; many Americans identify themselves as middle class despite income and occupational diversity. It is a term that often subsumes workers above the poverty line, small businessmen, professionals, and corporate managers and executives, obscuring the very real differences in resources and power among these categories.

With respect to patients and practitioners, the dynamic therapies seem to be most closely associated with upper-income executives and professionals, but their ideological premises are allied to the interests of the class holding corporate and economic power and seem to function to validate and reproduce that order. Partly this is a result of the emphasis on the individual and the deemphasis on the structure of social relationships within which the individual acts, reinforcing the belief that social relations are not structured by the distribution of wealth, but that success and failure are matters of individual initiative. Hsu (1976:156) notes that the stronger the emphasis on individualism in Western psychiatry, the greater the extent of avoidance of interpersonal networks; Western analysis being "wedded to the Western sacred cow of individualism" does not allow examination of the societal conditions. that generate "deviants." Similarly, Caplan and Nelson (1973:210) claim that the significance of current psychological research is that of "reinforcing social myths about one's degree of control over his own fate," and that it thereby serves to uphold government and primary cultural institutions by freeing them from responsibility for problems.

A glance at the history of the mental health movement tells us that the majority of mentally ill do not participate in this type of psychotherapy. Since it is only available to those who can afford it, upper-income patients may choose to participate in the persuasive techniques, while medication, incarceration, organic and directive treatments are generally the lot of the working-class patient. Nevertheless, the ideological premises of psychotherapy are extended to all classes, through education, social services, and the mass media. The prevalence and dissemination of these views in the United States are evident in Gursslin's analysis of mental health pamphlets (see p. 193). As the emphasis on individual responsibility and power extends beyond the narrow class that, in fact, has the resources to take destiny into its own hands, it plays its part in buttressing "blame the victim" ideology.

As is the case in Ghana, in the United States social transformations give rise to new therapeutic systems. Despite the continued emphasis of the dominant classes on the responsibility and private arena of the individual, the influence of macrosocial conditions has become increasingly obvious as international corporations control ever larger segments of life. One response to the crises of the sixties was new forms of therapy. As the "traditional" family came under attack, and as disillusionment with individual therapy grew, family therapy moved toward the analysis of the relations among family members and away from the emphasis on individual anguish (see Brodkin 1980 for a discussion of this process). New forms of group therapy attempted to deal with alienation, and a number of alternative healing options have arisen in response to the abuses of the medical system. Yet, as in Ghana, these tend to be superstructural reconstructions, often embodying the premises they allege to oppose. Even the community psychiatry programs retain the medical model and to that extent emphasize the individual (Areneta 1977:72). Brodkin (1980:16) described the development of family therapy as an attempt to preserve social order by keeping the balance between the autonomous individual and institutional order. Most solutions to societal pressures are offered in terms of individual mental health measures, with few practitioners following Erich Fromm or Wilhelm Reich in advocating political or economic transformation (Areneta 1977).

The counterculture responses, such as Eastern religion and transcendental meditation, while a reaction to the alienation of the society, continue to embody the basic notions of the dominant society in their emphasis on the individual and their escape from analysis of the interpersonal nexus (see Harris 1974; Hsu 1978:154). This is also true of the most recent response, "healthism," in its various forms, such as holistic health and self-help. True, it is a reaction against the abuses of biomedicine and attempts to challenge the medical establishment and reduce the dependence of individuals on medical practitioners. Yet these movements, whose participants are overwhelmingly professional and upper income, embody the premises of biomedicine; they continue to situate the problem of health and disease at the level of the individual. Individual responsibility in the form of exercise, diet, and relaxation are emphasized, with the implicit assumption that all individuals have the option to choose what they eat, to determine the amount of leisure time they have available, and to amass the resources needed to use it effectively. As Crawford notes, "the ideology of 'healthism' fosters a continued depoliticization and therefore undermining of the social effort to improve health and well-being" (Crawford 1980:368; see also Guttmacher 1979).

In all societies, then, psychotherapies function to mediate between the individual and the society, between the personality and the culture through bridging contradictions. They provide answers to the problem of selfhood and its articulation to society. Whether or not therapies "work" depends on whether they fit a given neurotic situation (Kovel 1976:42). Thus, they relieve the neurotic conflict by restoring order, and by modeling behavior through therapy they define social order. Therapies create order and bridge contradictions in accordance with a theoretical framework, implicit and explicit values that have reference to the dominant class of a given socioeconomic formation.

Both traditional and spiritualist therapy attempt to confront role contradictions and insecurities arising from the contemporary society—the expansion of the capitalist relations of production in the particular form they take in Ghana. Traditional healing does so by subverting the individual and asserting and strengthening reciprocal relationships based on the corporate lineage village community model. While such healing is primarily symbolic, participation does promote some exchange and redistribution. The response of spiritualist therapy is to embrace a new ideological structure and to create a new sort of collective. It is one that elevates the individual, although the patient remains within a therapeutic community. Western therapy takes this orientation still farther, basing its therapy on individuation and resolving conflicts through striving for self-understanding.

All this raises questions about the cross-cultural applicability of Western psychiatry. The defense has been waged on two levels: first, that the values implicit in Western psychiatry are cross-culturally valid, and second, that despite its value content Western psychiatry distinguishes itself from other forms of healing by being "scientific" in approach. The second explanation requires further discussion.

Strupp (1973) gives us a useful point of departure by making a distinction between the theoretical and the practical aspects of a therapeutic system. He suggests that psychoanalysis has made a major theoretical contribution to understanding human development and neurotic and psychotic disturbances, but leaves much to be desired as a therapeutic system. For him, suggestion is the main element in therapy, and suggestion is often more effective in other therapeutic systems. Prince agrees in part with this view, but suggests that only psychotherapy points to the importance of childhood experiences in explaining behavior and is therefore uniquely scientific as an explanatory system. He admits, however, that it is only effective for use with a particular type of individual—urbanized, literate, Western (1980:335). This last point inadvertently indicates a more basic problem. Psychoanalytic techniques offer "insight" and understanding to the extent that one accepts the premises of the explanatory framework—the definition of what constitutes understanding. Not only does this require a certain type of individual (who bears a remarkable resemblance to the "middle class man") but also acceptance of the notion, by no means proven, that the key to modifying behavior lies in the understanding of childhood experiences and in individual insight and action—a view congruent with a social order that emphasizes individual responsibility.

A major contribution made by Freud and his followers, although certainly found in other cultures, was the insistence that personality can be explained—that it is not free to shape itself into any form, but that form is determined by forces that can be known. To the extent that this approach stressed empirical proof, negation, and skepticism, it can be said to be scientific. In a sense, it is also an optimistic view, implying that change is possible, through use of reflective powers. It is, however, the selection of forces said to be dominant in shaping personality that is most culturally bound. While it seems obvious that childhood experiences have some effect in molding adult personality, questions concerning the relative importance of these experiences vis-à-vis the wider socioeconomic relationships—the emphasis on micro versus macro levels of social relationships—remain unanswered. That Western psychiatry generally opts for the former, often to the exclusion of the latter, seems to be a reflection of its own concept of reality, not necessarily of universal scientific truths. This is not to say that the arenas of personality and society are mutually reducible but simply to point out that the way in which a given society conceptualizes these relationships is bound to its own social order.

Just as a particular form of therapy arises from a given socioeconomic formation, it also helps to create it by shaping social relationships. Therapies require the patient's affirmation of their own explanatory framework. In traditional and spiritualist healing patients are told, "Go and sin no more," and we must agree with Calestro (1972:101), who points out that the message is essentially the same for the client in psychotherapy.

I suggest, then, that any analysis of psychotherapeutic systems must deal with therapies as they are constructed within the context of infrastructural relations. The emergence, persistence, and decline of therapeutic systems are related to the progression and imposition of modes of production, with their accompanying classes, ideologies, and values. Therapies are aligned to specific class interests and ideologies. This is not to say that therapies are limited to this or that class or stratum but that they express and perpetuate the interests of a given class or group. In fact, it is the extension of ideologies to people beyond the class whose interests they express that may allow for control and manipulation of the social order. By mediating ideology—promoting certain elements and de-emphasizing others—therapies and therapists reinforce a given social order.

As I have noted in the introduction, this approach to therapeutic systems differs significantly from those stressing the analysis of cultural themes. By maintaining a fundamentally idealist conception of culture, Kleinman, Fabrega, and others (see Introduction) have emphasized the analysis of medical systems as cultural systems, displacing them from social relations. They have shied away from investigation of the sociohistorical conditions that produce and maintain medical systems, despite their insistence on illness and medicine as social products. By omitting exploration of the extent to which medical systems are influenced by relations of production, by avoiding the analysis of medical systems as outcomes of the socio-economic processes of a world system, medical anthropologists often rely on the concept of culture to explain the diversity of medical systems. They easily fall, as a result, into "culture of poverty" explanations for disparities in health status, eschewing examination of the realities of domination and subordination.

IMPLICATIONS FOR INDIGENOUS THERAPY

Because we consider therapeutic systems as embedded in specific social formations, the dialogue on traditional healing assumes dimensions that reach beyond the debate about medical systems. While few investigators suggest that it is practical to institute wide-scale psychoanalytic institutions in developing countries, although many practitioners certainly believe that psychoanalytic formulations are *etic* (in the sense of not being limited to a given culture) principles of human development and psychopathology, any decision to implement therapeutic systems based on the Western model involves significant ramifications for the form of development the society will take. Questions of culture and ideology are especially relevant in the case of psychotherapy, which is premised on cultural representations of what is, and what ought to be, normality.

The implications of this have been summarized by Dubreuil and Wittkower:

> The thesis that both psychiatry and anthropology were and continue to be cultural and even political products of Occidental societies has been well documented. . . . Therefore it is necessary to approach primary prevention not only as a scientific, professional and technical-enterprise, but also as a phenomenon arising from and leading to cultural, social, and even political trends and values. (1976:125)

Thus, the issues involved in the implementation of medical systems are not merely narrow problems of technological change but embrace the basic considerations of what change and development should be about.

Those who oppose the use of traditional healers most frequently do so from the perspective of modernization, arguing that traditional medicine and the practitioners of it have little to contribute to a medical system in modern society. Asuni (1979), for example, is pessimistic about the possibility of cooperation between biomedical and traditional practitioners, noting in passing that the proponents of traditional medicine are usually foreigners to the system, and that indigenes tend to be more cautious. Similarly, Imperato (1979:205-206) argues that higher standards of medical service will gradually phase out traditional practitioners. From this perspective, improved health status of the population is thought to result from the introduction of technology and biomedical resources.

Others seem to accept implicitly or explicitly the premise that, while a greater level of biomedical resources and technology is the ultimate goal, resource deficiencies at the present time necessitate the use of traditional practitioners; that, in the face of the problems of providing modern health services, traditional healers should be used to fill the manpower gap (see Harrison 1979, for example). It is not surprising that there is usually some ambivalence about the use of traditional healers. Dunlop (1979) notes that while it is less costly to the government to include traditional healers, the costs will include the higher risks and the necessity of treating those who have been inappropriately treated. Mburu (1977) opts for education and incorporation of traditional doctors, making them vehicles of change rather than antagonists, but is concerned about the disadvantages involved in their use.

Other proponents of traditional healing cite not only the manpower shortage but the unique contributions offered by the traditional practitioner. Ademuwagun (1979:155) calls for a collaborative relationship between traditional and Western practitioners, given the shortage of medical personnel, but also notes that traditional healers have developed a useful knowledge of health and ecology and are more effective in psychosomatic treatment because communication with the patient is facilitated by a common belief system.

In this last position lie the seeds of a broader critique of biomedicine. The advocacy of traditional medicine may not simply be a matter of manpower shortages, but also a challenge to the underlying principles upon which biomedicine is based. This aspect becomes particularly salient in psychosomatic and mental therapy, where psychiatry has not developed a successful biomedical model, and where culturally constructed normative behavior models are basic to the process of healing.

Thus, several investigators unambiguously call for the use of traditional healers in psychotherapy. Discussing Ghana, Twumasi (1975) notes that "the success of traditional medicine lies in its psychotherapy," which shares the same world view with the patient and calls for utilization of traditional practitioners for "psychological ills." T. A. Lambo, currently deputy director-general of the World Health Organization, is well known for his pioneering attempt to utilize traditional psychotherapists under the direction of psychiatrists in "healing villages" in Abeokuta, Nigeria. He suggests that the treatment of functional disorders be removed from "traditional Western medicine . . . it has become more and more obvious that the Western approach to human health is not entirely acceptable to many people in other cultures" (1977:246).[1]

The subject of "cultural domination" is often an underlying issue in the discussion about traditional healing. Advocacy of traditional healing may reflect not so much a rejection of biomedical technological advances as it does a rejection of the social context, including the ideological system, in which they are embedded. Thus Mburu (1977:166) has described the way in which the introduction of Western medicine with colonialism creates "dependent individuals . . . abrogating their creative potential. By design or otherwise, such is symptomatic of colonial domination." That ideological systems seek to define symbolically the nature of people and the limits of human action has been made abundantly clear by the large body of literature on cultural imperialism.[2] In this volume, I have sought to demonstrate that mental therapeutic systems seek to do so overtly and concretely. Thus, the concern for cultural independence is a very real one. Yet, the key point, often neglected by anthropologists as well as by practitioners, is that culture is not sui generis: symbolic systems are rooted in material relations, which must themselves be addressed.

That the "return to the source" is a basic political process and not simply a cultural event was perhaps most eloquently asserted by Amilcar Cabral[3] who, while recognizing the importance of the reclamation of culture in the independence process, emphasized that truly independent culture can only result from the independence of the productive forces:

> Culture plunges its roots into the physical reality of the environmental humus in which it develops, and it reflects the organic nature of the society which may be more or less influenced by external factors. . . . The objective of national liberation, is therefore, to reclaim the right, usurped by imperialist domination, namely: the liberation of the process of development of national productive forces. . . . The liberation of productive forces and consequently the ability to determine the mode of production most appropriate to the evolution of the liberated people, necessarily opens up new prospects for the cultural development of the society in question, by returning to that society all its capacity to create progress. (Cabral 1973:42-43)

The issue to be addressed is not merely that of retaining or discarding traditional healing. Decisions about the use of indigenous systems will require the systematic evaluation of the weaknesses and strengths of all aspects of the various traditional systems. Complexities and pitfalls inherent in reworking traditional forms are evident in the experience of the *ujamaa* villages in Tanzania. In several countries, herbs, drugs, and specific techniques are being assessed. It might be useful to extend such evaluation to the basic ideological constructs of the system. For example, healing in both traditional and spiritual therapy relies on techniques based in a symbolic and ritual framework. We have demonstrated the way in which the symbolic forms and ritual relationships refer to real socioeconomic relationships and function to shape them by promoting reciprocity, for example, or by removing the individual from the kinship group. Yet, as Van Brinsbergen (1976a) reminds us, for many of the participants it is the ritual relations that are experienced. While accusations of witchcraft and sorcery may function to constrain individual accumulation and perhaps promote reciprocity, people react to fear of witchcraft and sorcery, not to misgivings about stratification and inequality. Thus, such forms of therapy may impede awareness of the nonritual social relations and substitute for a more objective understanding of the social structure.[4]

These considerations become especially important in the treatment of neurotic disorders. Both traditional and spiritualist healing attempt, in different ways and with their vastly divergent solutions, to confront role contradictions arising from the development of capitalist relations. However, neither directly addresses the structure that conditions the role contradictions. To the extent that resolution occurs, it tends to be episodic and on an individual basis because the structural determinants are not removed. Thus, both traditional and spiritualist healing simultaneously express and mask the actual contradictions that people confront. The same may be said of Western psychotherapy. We have suggested that the dominant forms of Western psychotherapy perpetuate and rationalize an individualistic social order. Under the guise of rationality, they often obscure basic problems by drawing attention away from the macrosocial relations that produce individual conflicts to the micro expression of them, from the overhauling of society to the increased coping capacity of the individual. This critique does not preclude consideration of the range of partial solutions. The rewards of individual, temporary therapy may be considerable, broadening the scope of choices available to individuals and increasing their potential to address the social structure.

Such an analysis, however, does suggest that the fundamental problem confronting policymakers may be neither that of modernizing medical systems through the importation of biomedicine nor solely that of reclaiming cultural forms. Rather, it appears that the prior issue to be resolved is that of determining the direction that the society will take—how the wealth of the society will be distributed. The form of the medical system will be conditioned by the way in which the resources, goods, and tasks are to be allocated in the society as a whole. The evolving medical system will both reflect and perpetuate these relations through constructing illness from disease —structuring frameworks for etiology, responsibility, and treatment. The psychotherapeutic system, "the education of the person," will rationalize such relationships. In creating these medical systems, people retain and rework cultural forms, through which they struggle against externally imposed constraints. As they make history, fashioning new forms from old, they transform the circumstances given from the past.

APPENDIXES

Appendix 1

LABADIANS EMPLOYED IN AGRICULTURE IN CENTRAL AREAS

Area	Percentage Labadian	Percentage employed men in agriculture
020	77	14
022	53	11
103	88	22
104	85	28
105	87	28
106	81	14
119	79	12

LABADIANS EMPLOYED IN AGRICULTURE IN OUTLYING AREAS

Area	Percentage Labadian	Percentage employed men in agriculture
020	36	3
023	49	less than 1
100	29	less than 1
101	55	less than 1
102	56	2
107	58	4
118	48	4
120	62	2
121	55	1

Appendix 2

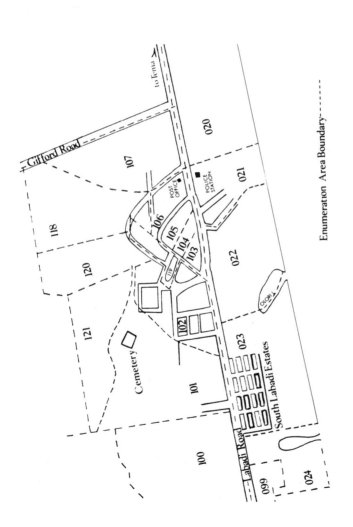

ACCRA MUNICIPAL COUNCIL (21)

Source: 1960 Populations Census of Ghana Special Report A — Statistics of Towns. Census Office, Accra, 1964.

Appendix 3

A. is an example of one of the few farmers involved in commercial farming. These farmers privately own large holdings and hire laborers. Some own cocoa farms in other regions (which might be managed personally or by relatives), other types of businesses, or small industries, or buildings from which they collect rent.

Mr. A is sixty years old, linguist of one of the traditional religious groups, and assistant to the head of his quarter. He has two wives and twelve children; the children are carpenters, clerks, drivers, and the like. He is the son of a farmer and used to farm himself. He now owns a cocoa farm in partnership with his brother, who manages it. Laborers are employed full-time. He individually owns large buildings consisting of multiple dwelling units from which he claims to collect rent of 180 cedis (180 dollars) per month. He does not live in the lineage house, but in one of his own buildings, which takes up almost one square block. Some of the rooms that face the street are rented out as stores. Inside the courtyard of this same unit, he raises livestock for consumption and sale.

B. is an example of the middle stratum who may privately own small pieces of land and hire laborers on a temporary basis. With the exception of rented tractors used to clear the land initially, they primarily employed the traditional iron cutlasses and hoes.

Mr. B is a farmer in his fifties, who also fishes. He represents Abese, his quarter, at the council of the chief fisherman. He owns two pieces of land of about five acres each; the first he inherited from his father and the second he bought from a resident of Teshie. He hires two laborers to help with the weeding and clearing of the land and works together with them. The laborers are from the north of Ghana and are paid 50 pesewas (50 cents) a day. His two wives, who are market women, and some of his nineteen children help during the harvesting. Tractors are used only to clear the land, and hoes and cutlasses are used for the rest of the work. He owns eight hoes and four cutlasses and buys western fertilizer at the market. The majority of the cassava, okra, tomatoes, and watermelon he grows is sold at the market by his wives; the remainder is consumed. Although his financial position appears quite stable at the present time, he states that farming is quite precarious because market prices are unstable. Last year, because of heavy rains, okra was quite scarce, and the market price rose. However, this year there was an overabundance of okra and those who planted it lost money.

D. and E. are examples of the poorest group of farmers who do not privately own their land, and combine farming with other work.

Mr. D is a farmer of sixty years who also does fishing and carpentry. He farms on land that is owned by another man, but is not being used at the present time. He does not hire any laborers and is assisted only by his wife and children. He takes work in carpentry that includes small jobs, such as constructing chairs, boxes, and other small furniture, and larger jobs, such as houses. He usually works with two other men: one is his father's younger brother's son and the other is a more distant kinsman (he does not know the exact relationship). The associations of workers that are necessary for the larger jobs frequently change composition. He has only been working with the present group for three months; the last group disbanded because of disputes concerning the division of the wages. The fee for the work is discussed with the owner of the house before the work is commenced. For a fairly large house, consisting of nine rooms bounding a courtyard, the carpenters may charge about three hundred cedis, which will be divided more or less equally. The work for a house of this size may take approximately five months to complete. Mr. D owns some of the tools, such as the hammer, saw, and level, but must borrow some tools from friends or relatives. He learned carpentry from his father's brother during a three-year period. He usually learns of work from friends. In the past year, his jobs included a complete house, and roofs, windows, and doors on three others.

Mr. E is also a farmer, cultivating four acres over which he has acquired usufructuary rights from the Teshie chief. He is also a fisherman and, in addition, works in the building trade, helping with general construction and plastering. He has worked for the Lands Department and other government agencies, but has been unemployed for four years and is now farming most of the time. He learned his trade from his father's elder brother's son during a three-year apprenticeship period.

Appendix 4

THE following is a document, compiled by the La mangtse, summarizing a case arbitrated by him:

LA MANGTSE WE
15th April 1971

This is a civil action involving first cousins — the Plaintiff and the Defendant.

Claim:

That the Plaintiff was and has been responsible for the sickness of the Defendant, i.e. "SULO".

NC500 damages in case this allegation is not proved.

We heard the evidence of both the Plaintiff and the Defendant. The Defendant admitted before us that he made those utterances on the summons writ and repeated those words, i.e. "SULO DZI BO, BO OGBEO MI NII" (you are a sorcerer, you are killing me).

When we asked the Defendant to substantiate and to prove this allegation he could not do it, but he was told by a Fetish Priest or a herbalist that it was his cousin, the Plaintiff, who had been responsible for his sickness. When asked to bring this herbalist he refused, saying that he was no more asking him to give evidence for him.

I accordingly sought the help of the police to arrest the herbalist before me but he said he does not need his evidence in support of his allegation.

We therefore found him guilty as he could not substantiate and prove his allegation.

The Defendant was therefore asked to pacify his cousin with the following as custom demands:

1. One live sheep
2. One bottle Schnapps and 50 cedis

Up to the time of writing this judgment he has provided one live sheep and the bottle of Schnapps but has asked time to pay the n.c. 50. He has been given three weeks within which to pay this amount.

I will notify your worship when this amount is paid to close the case.

NII ANYETIE KWAKWRANYA II
President, La Traditional
Council

In this case the plaintiff and defendant were brothers' sons. The older brother, the father of the plaintiff, had acquired some land for cocoa farming (as private property) that had previously been farmed by the father of the defendant. Upon the death of the plaintiff's father, the plaintiff went to work on the land. The defendant refused to surrender it, claiming that it was lineage property. The case was settled in the plaintiff's favor by a chief in the area. Soon after this, the defendant claimed to have experienced mild convulsions. He accused the plaintiff of attempting to kill him by sorcery. The plaintiff brought him to court, and the defendant lost the case, since he refused to substantiate his claim by producing the practitioner who had informed him that his father's brother's son was the cause of the illness. (If he had produced the practitioner in "native court," an oracle would have been administered to show which of them was telling the truth; in civil court, it would have been necessary to show actual evidence of poisoning.)

Appendix 5

In order to prepare a protective medicine for a man who complained that witchcraft was causing him illness, the healer selected a piece of cord (*hung*) from a bag containing several such pieces, tied a slipknot in the middle, and attached it to the top part of a small lock. He added two pieces of hair (belonging to the parties concerned), pieces of a red parrot's feather, and some hairs from the tail of a rabbit, then pulled the knot tight and scraped shavings from his nail onto it. After cutting off the excess portion of the string with a knife, he touched the ends together before discarding the other piece. The two ends of the string were then brought together, making a double piece about four inches long. On the other end of this, he tied a key, using the same procedure that he had used for the lock. He then prepared ayilọ (white clay) and tung (red clay), using each to paint a side of the lock.

Appendix 6

In the following case, afole tsofa was brought to the healer for disposal. A young woman, her father's sister and her husband, and her father's mother's sister came to consult the healer. They told the healer that someone had thrown a stone into the window of their house. When they went to the door, they saw a small blue bag in the doorway. They were certain that they were intended to step over it. The bag they brought to the healer consisted of what appeared to be black powder and a charcoal-looking substance wrapped in blue plastic. This was referred to as afole tsofa, meaning medicine that is visible, as opposed to asule tsofa, which is invisible. The medicine was intended to cause the death of the young woman's husband. The healer carefully opened the package and added his own black powder. After pouring a libation with schnapps, he took some in his mouth and spit it onto the package. The package was placed in a hole approximately one foot deep, covered with a stone, herbs, and earth. The healer gathered three types of herbs, to which were applied white clay and a little schnapps. The inhabitants of the house were instructed to bathe themselves in sacred water by placing, in order, small, middle-sized, and large herbs in a bowl of tap water. Libations were then poured by all present.

Appendix 7

Godolaly, a medicine to cure illnesses resulting from witchcraft, sorcery, ancestral spirits, and curses ("these sicknesses can be healed by its medicine and the same medicine can be used to heal many types of illnesses"), was prepared by the healer. This event took place in an outlying Labadi village that had been founded by members of the healer's extended family. Herbs and various other ingredients were brought from town. A large pot, similar to a cauldron, was used to mix and cook the medicine. The following items were placed in a pot: five different types of herbs, including *sulu, kowe,* and *kadoki;* chewed sugar cane; two types of live crabs ("those with red backs and those with yellow backs"); shredded soap; tomatoes; crackers; talcum powder; bread; tobacco; cigarettes; perfume; lavender cologne; hair oil; gunpowder; palm nut oil; and a liquid poured from an insecticide bottle that the healer claimed was a very potent European poison. Schnapps was poured and spit into the mixture. The healer, calling upon Nyongmo, the ancestors, and his personal gods to bless the preparation of the medicine, intoned:

> When I am asked to kill, I must kill, when I am asked to heal, I must heal. All ghosts, witches, bad susuma, or evil gods must be defeated by this medicine. Any bad thing must go into the herbs so that when they are used for something they will work.

He then sacrificed a fowl and dripped the blood on the herbs. "This is your fowl; you must take it and give blessings." The mixture was cooked on an open fire for about ten hours, until it became powder. It was then ground with a pestle and mixed with gunpowder that had in turn been mixed with water. The healer divided it into two portions by putting both hands through the center. A libation was poured into the space in the middle. A special invocation was whispered. This was said to make the portion on the left poisonous and that on the right nonpoisonous and able to be taken by mouth. The portion on the left was put into bottles tied with streamers of red calico, that on the right in bottles tied with white calico. The healer said that the red one was now very dangerous and must be kept at the back of his house. He claimed this special formula, which he had procured in Nigeria, where he had traveled to learn his trade, was very dangerous and should not be in the hands of those who would not use it for good.

Appendix 8

A three-year-old girl had been brought to the healer by her father. She had awakened from sleep, screaming, "They are chasing me; they are going to catch me." The diagnosis was that her behavior meant that witches were pursuing her. This was a result of someone's malevolent intent to harm her parents. She was thoroughly bathed in herbs and water and lifted toward the sky three times. The healer used a sharp knife to make three superficial incisions, approximately one-quarter of an inch long, at each temple, forehead, base of neck, sternum, shoulders, each side of the waist, wrists, knees, and ankles. Ground herbs were rubbed into the openings. Her father was given schnapps with which to pour a libation, and she was given medicine to drink.

Appendix 9

THE following account illustrates the awroke hamǫ. The fact that the participants were not Ga meant that the ritual had to be explained and participants prompted. This case was also somewhat unusual because the patient was living away from home with her husband, who was stationed at a nearby army base.

An Ewe woman who had come to the healer complaining of dizziness, palpitations, and anxiety was declared cured (her symptoms had vanished) at the end of three months. The awroke hamo ritual, which must be performed at the conclusion of a successful treatment, was scheduled and attended by approximately twenty members of her family and her husband's family. The relatives lined one side of the courtyard, and members of the healer's household and I sat in a line on the other side. The husband of the patient, who was a soldier at Burma camp and claimed not to speak Ga well, sat with the relatives.

The patient, dressed in a new cloth and a silk headkerchief, was ceremoniously brought out of one of the buildings and placed at the head of the courtyard, flanked by her mother, the healer, the healer's assistant, and a distinguished visitor who acted as the healer's linguist. The healer prepared some white clay and placed a longitudinal mark on her right arm. He then prepared a calabash of sacred water to which was added some herbs and white clay. The husband presented a bottle of schnapps, a goat, and a shilling. The shilling was put into the bowl, and the goat was slaughtered amid libations and invocations. The blood of the goat was dripped on the representatives of the gods, the feet of the patient, and a few drops into the bowl of water.

The healer was asked what he would charge. He replied that he would charge fifty pounds (one hundred cedis) — apparently the necessary stylized reply. The husband, who claimed not to speak Ga, had to be prompted by the linguist to "beg" to get the price reduced. He finally stood up and thanked the healer for all he had done and then asked him to reduce the price. It was reduced to forty-nine pounds. This stylized bargaining continued for awhile, and then the healer said he would take whatever they wished to give. It was then explained to the family, who claimed to be unfamiliar with Ga customs, that they should come up one at a time and contribute as much as they could to the cure of their kinswoman. (The Ga speakers claimed that the ignorance was feigned.) To demonstrate, members of the healer's compound led the way by walking up to the healer's assistant, telling him their name, and giving him their contribution (about twenty pesewas [twenty cents] each). The linguist then called out the name of each person, the amount of his or her contribution, and dropped it into the water. The rest of the party responded with a chorus of *oyiwaladong* (thank you). The husband and the relatives incurred the displeasure of the household and embarrassed the patient by contributing what was thought to be relatively small amounts of money. After an hour, the money was counted and found to total approximately six cedis. The family was informed of this, and the husband asked for the lowest possible price. The healer set the price at fourteen pounds (twenty-eight cedis), and the patient was ceremoniously handed back to her husband. The patient, the healer, and the linguist took some of the sacred water into their mouths, spit it back into the calabash, and washed their faces and arms with it. Everyone was then ceremoniously served with drink.

Appendix 10

TEXT OF SERMON

Now let us go into the Bible. There was a time when Samaria had not received the word of the Lord. There was a man named Simeon, who went through Samaria preaching, usually sorcering and bewitching the people. There was something behind, but the Bible was on top and all the people believed in him. They accepted the miracles which he performed, and they all thought he was an upright man of God. This man continued with the evil things he was doing. He was regarded as the son of God, and they all bowed to him, and the respect that was to be given Jesus Christ was given to him. But you know, when Peter and the rest went to preach the Gospel, they preached the word vehemently. This man, who had been bewitching the people, believed also. And do you know what happened after the preaching of the Word through the laying on of the hands of the Apostles? The Holy Spirit was given. When Simeon saw that, he went by night to them and said, "Now brother, I saw you laying your hands upon the people and they received the Holy Spirit. Now take this money and give me the power also, so whoever I lay hands on will also get the Holy Spirit." Do you know what happened? Peter looked at this man and said, "Thy money perish with thee because you thought the spirit of the Lord may be purchased with money. But mind you, money is the source of all evil."

Reading from verse eight, it says, "And when Simeon saw that through the laying on of hands of the Apostles, the Holy Ghost was given, he offered them money saying, 'Give me also this power so that on whosoever I lay my hands on, he will also receive the Holy

Ghost.' But Peter said unto him, 'Thy money perish with thee for thou thought the spirit of God may be purchased with money; thou has no part in this matter, for thy heart is not right in the sight of God. Repent therefore of this thy wickedness and pray to God, if perhaps the thought of thine heart may be forgiven thee.'" That is the point—if perhaps thy thoughts may be forgiven thee.

Do you know what happened? Then answered Simeon and said unto them, "Pray ye hard for me that none of these things which ye have spoken come unto me!" So, dear brothers and sisters in Christ, God's grace, God's power is never bought with money but is given to you by grace through faith, and that not by ourselves, not by our beauty, and not by our ability, but it is the gift of God that we should boast of it.

Everybody must get right with God before the year comes to an end, or you will die. Thy laziness perish with thee, thy wickedness perish with thee, because thou thought God would be worshipped with wickedness, thy disobedience would perish with thee because thou thought the gift of God would be purchased with disobedience, thy hard-heartedness will perish because thou thought God would be worshipped with a strong heart. Before the end of the year or before the month of January ends, we must change altogether. Let us show ourselves as true Christians in all things.

But this morning the theme of the sermon is telling you never to think of any property in the world, which will give you trouble, but lay up your treasure for yourself in Heaven, where neither moth nor rust will corrupt. The Bible tells us that we must lay our treasures in Heaven where neither moth, rust, nor thieves break through and steal (Matthew 6:20). The few that have gathered here this morning, you are obliged, you are now being compelled, you are now being forced, you are now being advised, you are now being authorized, you are now being asked, to lay your treasures in Heaven, where there is neither thieves, rust, nor moth. For the Lord God of Israel will keep it safe for you. Amen.

And don't let us feel jealous of what our brother is struggling for; I have no right to struggle for the suit, the shoes, the cloth, headkerchief, the necklaces, and the shoes and the rest that they have and we don't have. Because these are worldly things and they will pass away. But when we lay up our treasures in Heaven through the heart of Jesus Christ, given to us, one day we may go there and find a big mansion for us. Hallelujah!

For instance, now, this morning we have politics in white robes but not politics in black robes, and so when Kwame was in Ghana, he had all the wealth that he could have: one day he went away without the wealth. Now when Busia was in Ghana, he built all the castles he has in Wenchi; now he left them without taking a cloth (Kwame and Busia refer to deposed presidents of Ghana).

Once there lived a rich man with so many lands and farms, and there was a poor man whom the rich man hired. And this poor man had been weeding his farm for him. But whenever this man went to the farm to weed, whenever he found anything strange on the land, the rich man took it out of the poor man's hands. This thing continued and continued for many years. We call this thing anibre [covetousness]. One day this poor man was digging on the farm when he saw a very small box. When he looked at the outside of the box, it looked like an Indian box that contained some gold jewels. So this poor man took the box and brought it home. Then he told his master, this is what I have found when I was weeding the farm. Then the master said, "Ha! Let me see it." Then he brought it. When the master saw it was very precious, he thought it contained a jewel. He said, "Ha! This is mine. This is something which I put under the ground to acquire the land, so don't take it, it is mine."

Now listen to what happened. The poor man said he will not give that thing to the rich man his master, and so, it was a police case and they sent it to the chief of that town. So do you know what happened? Nobody knows what was inside the box. But when they went to court the rich man claimed that the box was his. And the rich man was able to send bribes to all the heads who will judge the case, and they finally judged the case in his favor, saying that he owns that precious thing. So this precious thing was taken out of the poor man's hands. The poor man went to the farm and brought it, they said it did not belong to him; he did not open it.

So do you know what happened? The chief said, "If the thing belongs to both of you, here is what I will do. There is no key to open that box, so whoever can find a key to open this box, he is the owner of this thing." Do you know what happened? This rich man went and bribed the person whose care the box was in until the date of judgment. He went and saw this man, gave him money, and said, "I will bring a goldsmith and give him soap to put in the thing and then when he takes it out he will be able to mold a key for the thing so that I will win the case." The caretaker said, "All right, bring the money." He took the money and then allowed the goldsmith to see the thing, and then the goldsmith was able to mold a nice key for it. But the goldsmith was not able to complete the whole thing until the last minute. It was after the people had gathered that he brought the key to the rich man. When he saw the goldsmith coming, he said, "Yes, this is my boy, my boy is bringing the key to me. I sent him to go under my bed to bring the key. See, now he is bringing the key." And he held the key. Ha! Cunning!

So don't feel jealous of some people's property, wealth, or what they have acquired. Now they placed the box in the middle of the gathering and they made the rich man with all his *kente* sit by the side of the box. Then the poor man with his limp, wretched cloth that was faded by washings; even his sandals were made of tire, and he had used that black ink to cover the whole of them. So the chief said, "Bring me the key." The poor man said, "I have no key because I found it on the ground. I did not say it belonged to me but that I found it on the ground as a gift." Then they said, "Rich man, bring me the key if the thing really belongs to you." Then he dug his hands into his pocket and said, "I have it." Then he handed the key to the chief and the chief said, "When we open it, whatever we see in it is yours."

The rich man said, "Oh yes, it is mine!" "Whether it is good or bad, it is yours," they said. "I say it is mine, it is mine." So they put the key in the box. The person who opened the box saw something in it and closed it. And he went and called the chief to come and see, so when the chief opened the box and saw it, he said, "Ha!" Then he came back. They called seven people, who ran away. The only daughter of the chief had been killed two weeks ago and nobody knew where she was. The unknown person killed the girl and put her head in the box and went to this man's farm and made a hole in the ground and put it there.

So they held secret counsel and said, "Ha, this man killed our daughter, that is why he is claiming the whole box; we shall see." Now the chief came up again and said to the rich man, "Rich man, whatever is in this box is for you, is your property." Then the rich man said, "You are wasting time; it is mine I told you, you give my thing to me and let me go away." "Does it belong to you?" Then he was annoyed. "The thing is mine, give my thing to me." The chief said to his linguist, "Go open the thing." They opened the box and they called the poor man to come and see. He said, "Ha!" Then he went back. Then they called the rich man. They called him, "Mr. Richman, this is your thing, come and look at it, so that you may not say we have taken any part of it." When he came and found it, he could not look at it. He was backing away; the chief told someone to hold up the contents of the box. They found that it was the head of the precious princess of the nation. "Ha! You killed my daughter; we are going to kill you instead." The rich man said, "No, no! How can I have killed your daughter?" "But you said it is yours." Do you know what happened? The rich man was caught and his head cut off.

Take a lesson from this. Don't be jealous of someone's property. because if you follow it, you will surely die one day. Let us lay our treasures in heaven. That poor man laid his treasures in heaven, but the rich man laid his treasures on earth.

Notes

INTRODUCTION

1. The term traditional has been widely used to refer to a range of indigenous medical systems. The advent of modernization theory modified the nineteenth-century usage (see Weber 1964), to pose a questionable dichotomy between traditional and modern.

2. Harwood does, however, discuss the social and economic context in which spiritism ocurs.

3. The failure to analyze societies, and thus their medical systems, as they are conditioned by a world system has also tended to limit those sociocultural approaches that have attempted to identify the social relations linking medical systems to the wider society. For example, interesting directions are indicated by Glick (1967:67), who has suggested that medical systems reflect the sources of power in a society, and by Unschuld's (1975) attempt to classify medical systems on the basis of locus and nature of controls over resources.

4. The inhabitants of the town refer to it as "La," not Labadi. However, since "Labadi" is used in official records, I will use that name.

1. THE SETTING

1. Azu (personal communication with the author) claims that the place of origin is the basis of the original name, La Boni, later corrupted to Labadi. Kropp (1969), on the other hand, suggests on the basis of linguistic evidence that the resemblance to "Bonny" appears spurious.

2. There is some disagreement about the date when the migrations occurred. Field (1940) and Dickson (1969) set the date at around the sixteenth century. Azu (1974:7n) opts for the fourteenth century, citing a Dutch map of the Gold Coast made in 1629 that shows the Ga communities. She asserts that it is unlikely that the level of political organization could have developed so rapidly from farming communities by 1629. DaKubu (1972:100), too, points to Marees's (1912) citation of Labadi,

"Nengo," and "Temina" in 1602. The current chief claims that the present site of Labadi was established around 1640, calculating from the founding of Teshie by Labadians in 1700.

3. Although the term tse is used to refer to father in the kinship sense, its meanings also include owner and controller. When employed as a suffix, tse often indicates a special relationship, linking an individual to an object, connoting mastery, control, or ritual ownership. See LaBarre (1970:163) and Paulson (1964:219) for cross-cultural examples of this phenomenon.

4. I use maximal and major lineage in the sense described by Fortes (1949:4-7). By maximal lineage, I refer to the most extensive group of people of both sexes related to one another by common patrilineal descent, traced from one known founding ancestor through known agnatic antecedents. By major lineage, I refer to all agnates of one of the sons of the founder of the maximal lineage. The seven maximal lineages of Labadi are of diverse generational depth, with those of the more recent settlers being more shallow.

5. Ghana National Archives, "Enquiry into circumstances mentioned in a letter of complaint from the chief of Labadeye," April 18, 1883.

6. The National Redemption Council, formed by Lt. Col. Ignatius Acheampong, deposed Busia on January 13, 1972. In October of 1975, the National Executive Council of the NRC was replaced by the Supreme Military Council, composed of seven police and military heads. A successful coup was led by Flight-Lieutenant Jerry Rawlings in June, 1979. Rawlings formed the Armed Forces Revolutionary Council, which held general elections within a few months. A parliament of 140, headed by Dr. Hilla Limann as President, was elected. In December 1981 Flight-Lieutenant Rawlings once more assumed power as head of a Provisional National Defense Council after a coup d'état overthrew President Limann.

7. The 1960 census is the last to report Labadi data separately from those of Accra as a whole. The employment data for Accra, based on the 1970 census, are not yet available.

8. The concept of "stress" has functioned to conceptualize the relationship between symbolic phenomena and bodily dysfunction. While stress may be defined generally as a stimulus that provokes the organism to respond in a condition of disturbance (e.g., Jaco 1970:211), the term has been used to signify both the stimulus (the environmental agents that disturb the organism) as well as the response (the reaction to such agents); its referents have been physiological, sociological, or psychological. For social scientists, then, the concept of stress is often the magical "black box" that links the *somo* and the *psyche,* the organism and the environment. A stress pattern of response to psychosocial stimuli appears to be pathogenic and may be a major factor in the etiology of several diseases.

Basic to the stress premise of disease are the concepts of change and adaptation. Social incongruity, arising when change demands adaptation that is not made or made inadequately, increases the risk of disease (Kagan 1971:38). Numerous situations associated with social change are thought to provoke stress: situations of transition involving alternative roles and values resulting in ambiguity of choice for the individual (Eisenstadt 1971: 80); migration and unemployment (Levi and Andersen 1971); loosening of primary ties and lack of support system (Eisenstadt 1971); various physical and sociological characteristics of emerging urban societies (Gosta 1971). See Lumsden (1975) for an attempt to use systems theory to look at stress and responses to the Volta River project in Ghana.

2. THE HEALERS

1. Faced with such a diversity of phenomena, the skeptic may well question the existence of medical "systems." It is true that we are not dealing with ideal systems, i.e., functionally integrated entities of intercommunicating parts, where practitioners adhere strictly to a common, consistent body of knowledge. Nevertheless, it is clearly useful to distinguish categories of practitioners without implying complete homogeneity within each category.

2. Among the Akamba in Kenya we find distinctions between herbalists and diviners (Mburu 1977:168); among the Zulu between ethnodoctors and diviners (Ngubane 1977:320); in Lusaka between herbalists and witch doctors (Frankenberg and Leeson 1976:239); in Nigeria, the non-Muslim Hausa distinguish between herbal treatment and spiritual appeasement (Last 1976:147); the Ogori of middle Nigeria make a distinction between herbalists and ritual specialists (Gillies 1976:378); and in western Nigeria we find herbalists and diviner priests (Harding 1973:200).

3. See Christensen (1954) for a discussion of the Tigari cult.

4. Jahoda (1961:254) describes this category as "modern healers" in that they "are characterized by a departure from the traditional pattern, involving the adoption of some of the external trappings of the Western medical man and pharmacist." This distinction, however, is not altogether accurate in that it erroneously implies that "traditional" medicine does not involve innovation and change.

5. Hastings (1979:175) speculates that this striking outburst might be a "reaction of disillusionment with the fruits of the political 'kingdom,'" or, on the other hand, "a sort of carrying across into the religious field of the political achievement." As we will discuss later, the growth in independent churches in Ghana appears to coincide with economic crises.

PART II: INTRODUCTORY NOTE

1. A more systematic application of this approach, which consists of visiting alternately at random hours, is known as "random spot checks" (see Pelto and Pelto 1978:130). My spot checks were not entirely random as I tried to be present, as much as possible, at times when patients were expected.

2. Although I was not always present, I encountered the majority of patients consulting the healer during this period. I recorded a total of

twenty-seven patients for two months, which seems fairly typical. Jahoda's (1961) study of five healers in Accra, in which he collected minimal demographic data on all patients treated, yielded an average of 12.9 patients per month per healer. Comparisons, however, must be approached with caution as his study was conducted in 1954-1955.

3. There are certain difficulties in comparing the school attendance rates with those of the 1960 population census, in that in 1967-1968 free primary education was abolished and school fees reinstituted.

4. Because the diagnostic procedures are so crucial, I did not include patients for whom I arrived too late to witness these procedures.

5. Patients, healers, and relatives graciously allowed me to use a tape recorder. All verbatim material is transcribed and translated from the tape.

3. TRADITIONAL HEALING

1. Because my emphasis was on diseases diagnosed as mental disorders, supernatural explanations tended to predominate. See Warren (1979) for a detailed discussion of naturalistic categories among the Brong, whose classification system is quite similar to that of the Ga.

2. *Abonsam* is probably borrowed from the Twi word for a mythical devillike character (Sasabonsam). Although Ga traditional religion does not include such a character, it is often used to represent the general notion of wickedness. Ga Christians use it to refer specifically to the devils of Christian mythology, while others use the term for evil powers in general.

3. Illness is said to "catch" (*mǫ*) a person's susuma. Susuma, translated literally as shadow, refers to that element of the personality thought to determine the fate or fortune of the individual. Although ritual specialists often have a fairly elaborate explanation of the various components of personality, involving epistemological and ontogenetic questions (see Mullings 1975 for details), all strata of Labadians generally agree on the existence of the susuma. The susuma is believed to have an existence beyond the conscious functioning of the individual: dreams are the result of actions by the susuma. Unbeknown to the conscious mind, the susuma may become offended and cause illness or death. I was told, "If you are accused of witchcraft and not exonerated, the fact that you have said to yourself 'this person has accused me of witchcraft' will result in your susuma becoming unhappy. Your susuma may then say 'let me go to the other world if they do this to me in this world.' You may then sicken and die." The susuma is thought to be the element that is stolen or evacuated from the body in times of illness. Permanent evacuation results in death.

4. Any study of African religion by non-Africans should be premised on the understanding that the way in which Africans conceptualize their religion and what it means in their daily lives on a subjective level is not something easily understood by the investigator. The investigator can collect exegetical data, what people say about what these beliefs and symbols

mean, and, as well, observe what social variables become meaningful in behavior that is considered to be within the realm of religion. These constitute, however, two different levels of analysis; a partial explanation of the former does not negate a rigorous analysis of the latter, which is subject to its own rules of proof and falsification.

5. My understanding of the wong/dzemawong distinctions differs from those of both Field (1937) and Kilson (1971). Field emphasizes the character of each as the main point of distinction: "A *wong,* I am told, is 'something that can act, but not be seen.' A *dzemawong* is the same in nature as a *wong* but differs in having much greater power, intelligence, and scope . . . *dzemawong* is a powerful type of intelligent *wong,* not specialized in his activities, but practically omnipotent and omniscient" (Field 1937:4). "Every *dzemawong* is a *wong* but not vice versa" (ibid.:11). Based on the fact that a dzemawong is thought to act only if it approves of the action, to be ubiquitous, and to demand a high standard of ethics, while the wong is thought to be specialized, limited, defined, and automatic, Field characterizes dealings with the wodzii as medicine and dealings with the dzemawodzii as worship (ibid.).

Kilson (1971:19) does not emphasize this distinction. She focuses instead on one aspect of the definition, translating dzemawong as "place-god" and associating this term with kpele gods (as opposed to those of other cults). Although there are definite associations in some cases between dzemawodzii and topographical features in Labadi, this is not the main distinguishing feature. In addition, gods of cults other than kpele are referred to as dzemawodzii.

6. Professor N. K. Dzorbo suggested this term in a personal communication.

7. Kilson (1971:70) suggests, correctly I think, that adeboo is used to connote the fact that something antedates phenomena of the same class.

8. It is interesting to note that Christians in spiritualist churches refer to the altar as woku.

9. While I am in complete agreement with Turner (1967:118) that such beliefs should not be forced into preconceived categories of witchcraft and sorcery, the two categories as discussed above are quite explicit among the Ga. These appear to be somewhat congruent with the Azande categories that Evans-Pritchard dichotomized as witchcraft and sorcery. "Azande believe that some people are witches and can injure them by virtue of an inherent quality. A witch performs no rite, utters no spell, and possesses no medicines. An act of witchcraft is a psychic act. They believe that sorcerers may do them ill by performing magic rites with bad medicines" (1937:21).

10. It is tempting to interpret Aba's illness as having to do with puerperal psychosis. Corin and Murphy (1979:157) note that such psychoses are responsible for one-third of all female psychiatric admissions, and are clearly precipitated by sociocultural factors.

11. According to Berlin and Kay (1969), not all cultures recognize the triad of red, black, and white, which they refer to as level II. Given that it

is the case that all cultures recognize light and dark, one is tempted to speculate that whatever universal meanings are associated with colors might simply stem from the experiences of night and day, with night being more dangerous and unpredictable.

5. A COMPARISON OF THERAPEUTIC SYSTEMS

1. A notable exception are the attempts by Collomb and his colleagues to modify the cultural assumptions of Western psychiatry.

2. The difficulties in making these comparisons seem to stem more from the fact that those who are attempting to decode the system are caught up and involved with manipulating the symbols of their own society, rather than from intrinsic incomparability.

3. Some investigators have suggested that such therapy is perhaps more effective than therapy focused on individual careers for such groups as children, the mentally retarded, and others (see Gurman and Kniskern 1981:742-777).

4. In many circles, Freudian psychoanalysis has been rejected as a viable therapeutic system. But as the prototype of Western psychiatry, it continues to be very influential in many areas of intellectual life.

5. A number of the spontaneous songs sung during homowo ridicule some founders for being more interested in making money than salvation.

6. See O'Nell (1976:64-66) for some discussion of the cross-cultural use of dream analysis in illness.

7. A critical discussion of methodological problems of this study may be found in Edgerton (1980).

8. See Draguns (1977) for a survey of the problems of transcultural assessment.

9. See Bourguignon (1976) for a discussion of this as it bears on the assessment of ritual healing.

10. Jilek (1974) and Kleinman (1980) are examples of recent notable exceptions.

11. Some investigators have also suggested that social isolation may be a major factor in the outcome of such psychotic disorders as schizophrenia. This view is supported by findings of better outcomes in developing countries (WHO 1979).

12. The implications of hemispheric asymmetry or cerebral lateralization, however, are far from clear. More advanced research points to the interdependence of the hemispheres and a specialization more subtle than was previously thought to be the case.

13. See Harwood's (1977:188 ff.) comparison of spiritism and psychotherapy.

6. MENTAL THERAPY AND SOCIAL CHANGE

1. As mentioned earlier, there have been several notable attempts to integrate African and European therapy (see Corin and Murphy 1979:

168). These range from efforts to integrate elements such as group meetings, participation of family, African housing (Collomb 1973*a*), to the more extensive integration pioneered by Lambo in Nigeria. Nevertheless, most psychiatric care is based on Western models (Collomb 1973*b*).

2. Franz Fanon (see *The Wretched of the Earth* [New York: Grove Press, 1963]) was one of the earliest in this tradition, linking colonial war and mental disorders.

3. Amilcar Cabral was the first Secretary-General of the African Party for the Independence of Guinea and Cape Verde Islands (PAIGC), which waged a successful armed struggle to wrest Guinea-Bissau and Cape Verde from Portuguese colonialism. Before his assassination by Portuguese agents on January 20, 1973, Cabral wrote extensively about the necessity of a dynamic concept of culture.

4. This critique is particularly relevant to the solution often voiced, perhaps somewhat paternalistically, by Westerners — that the biomedical specialist treat the symptoms and refer the patient to the traditional healer, who would function autonomously "without his values or image being adulterated" (see Comaroff 1981, for example).

References Cited

Acquah, Ione. 1958. *Accra Survey.* London: University of London Press.

Adams, Robert McC. 1966. *The Evolution of Urban Society: Early Meso-potamia and Prehistoric Mexico.* Chicago: Aldine Press.

Ademuwagun, Zaccheus A. 1979. The Relevance of Yoruba Medicine Men in Public Health Practice in Nigeria. *African Therapeutic Systems,* edited by Z. A. Ademuwagun, J. A. A. Ayoade, I. E. Harrison, and D. M. Warren. Waltham, Mass.: Crossroads Press.

Albee, George W. 1977. The Protestant Ethic, Sex, and Psychotherapy. *American Psychologist* 32(2):150-161.

Alland, Alexander. 1970. *Adaptation in Cultural Evolution: An Approach to Medican Anthropology.* New York: Columbia University Press.

Appiah-Kubi, Kofi. 1981. *Man Cures, God Heals: Religion and Medical Practice Among the Akans of Ghana.* New York: Friendship Press.

Areneta, Enrique, Jr. 1977. 'Scientific' Psychiatry and 'Community' Heal-ers. *Traditional Healing: New Science or New Colonialism. See* Singer 1977.

Armstrong, W. R., and T. G. McGee. 1968. Revolutionary Change and the Third World City: A Theory of Urban Involution. *Civilisations* 18 (3):353-376.

Asuni, Tolani. 1979. Modern Medicine and Traditional Medicine. *African Therapeutic Systems. See* Ademuwagun 1979.

Azu, Diana G. 1974. *The Ga Family and Social Change.* Leiden: Afrika Studie-centrum.

Baeta, C. G. 1967. Aspects of Religion. *A Study of Contemporary Ghana: Some Aspects of Social Structure,* vol. 2, edited by W. Birmingham, I. Neustadt, and E. N. Omaboe. London: George Allen and Unwin, Ltd.

Bannerman, R. H. 1977. WHO's Programme. *World Health* November: 16-17.

Barbot, Jean. 1732. *A Description of The Coasts of North and South-Guinea.* London: printed for H. Lintot and J. Osborn. (Also in Churchill, Awnsham, comp. *A Collection of Voyages and Travels....* London: 1732.)

Bastide, Roger. 1967. Color, Racism, and Christianity. *Daedalus* Spring 96(2):312-327.

Beckmann, David M. 1975. *Eden Revival: Spiritualist Churches in Ghana.* St. Louis: Concordia Publishing House.

Beiser, M., et al. 1978. Author's abstract. *Transcultural Psychiatric Research Review* 15:86-87.

Beiser, Morton, and Henri Collomb. 1981. Mastering Change: Epidemiological and Case Studies in Senegal, West Africa. *American Journal of Psychiatry* 138(4):455-459.

Bell, Daniel. 1976. *The Cultural Contradictions of Capitalism.* New York: Basic Books.

Berger, Iris. 1976. Rebels or Status-Seekers? Women as Spirit Mediums in East Africa. *Women in Africa,* edited by N. J. Hafkin and E. G. Bay. Stanford: Stanford University Press.

Berlin, Brent, and Paul Kay. 1969. *Basic Color Terms: Their Universality and Evolution.* Berkeley and Los Angeles: University of California Press.

Bibeau, Gilles. 1979. The World Health Organization in Encounter with African Traditional Medicine: Theoretical Conceptions and Practical Strategies. *African Therapeutic Systems. See* Ademuwagun 1979.

Bond, George, Walter Johnson and Sheila S. Walker, eds. 1979. *African Christianity: Patterns of Religious Continuity.* New York: Academic Press.

Bourguignon, Erica. 1976. The Effectiveness of Religious Healing Movements: A Review of Recent Literature. *Transcultural Psychiatric Research Review* 13(1):5-21.

Brodkin, Adele M. 1980. Family Therapy: The Making of a Mental Health Movement. *American Journal of Orthopsychiatry* 50(1):4-17.

Brown, A. P. 1936. An Account of the Fishing Industry at Labadi with Some Reference to Teshie and Accra. *Teachers' Journal* (Gold Coast) 8(3):135-138, 9(2):124-127, 9(3):78-83.

Buckley, Anthony D. 1976. The Secret—An Idea in Yoruba Medicinal Thought. *Social Anthropology and Medicine,* edited by J. B. Loudon. A.S.A. Monograph 13. New York: Academic Press.

Buhler, Charlotte. 1962. *Values in Psychotherapy.* New York: The Free Press of Glencoe.

Cabral, Amilcar. 1973. *Return to the Source.* New York: Africa Information Service.

Caldwell, J. C. 1967. Population: General Characteristics. *A Study of Contemporary Ghana,* vol. 2: *Some Aspects of Social Structure. See* Baeta 1967.

———. 1968. *Population Growth and Family Change in Africa: The New Urban Elite in Ghana.* Canberra: Australian National University Press.

Calestro, Kenneth M. 1972. Psychotherapy, Faith Healing, and Suggestion. *International Journal of Psychiatry* 10(2):83-113.

Caplan, Nathan, and Stephen D. Nelson. 1973. On Being Useful: The Nature and Consequences of Psychological Research on Social Problems. *American Psychologist* 28(3):199-211.

Carlestam, Gösta. 1971. The Individual, the City, and Stress. *Society, Stress, and Disease.* See Eisenstadt 1971.

Christensen, James. 1954. The Tigari Cult of West Africa. *Papers of the Michigan Academy of Science, Arts and Letters* 29:389-398.

————. 1959. The Adaptive Functions of Fanti Priesthood. *Continuity and Change in African Cultures,* edited by W. Bascom and M. Herskovits. Chicago: University of Chicago Press.

Cohen, Robin. 1976. From Peasants to Workers in Africa. *The Political Economy of Contemporary Africa,* vol. I, edited by Peter Gutkind and Immanuel Wallerstein. Beverly Hills, Ca.: Sage Publications.

Collomb, H. 1973*a*. Rencontre de Deux Systèmes de Soins. À propos de Thérapeutiques des Maladies Mentales en Afrique. *Social Science and Medicine* 7:623-633.

————. 1973*b*. L'Avenir de la Psychiatrie en Afrique. *Psychopathologie Africaine* 9(3):343-370.

Comaroff, Jean. 1981. Healing and Cultural Transformation: The Tswana of Southern Africa. *Social Science and Medicine* 15B(3):367-378.

Corin, Ellen, and H. B. M. Murphy. 1979. Psychiatric Perspectives in Africa. Part I: The Western Viewpoint. *Transcultural Psychiatric Research Review* 16:147-178.

Crawford, Robert. 1980. Healthism and the Medicalization of Everyday Life. *International Journal of Health Services* 10(3):365-88.

Daaku, Kwame Yeboa. 1970. *Trade and Politics on the Gold Coast: 1600-1720: A Study of the African Reaction to European Trade.* London: The Clarendon Press.

DaKubu, M. E. Kropp. 1972. Linguistic Pre-history and Historical Reconstruction: The Ga-Adangme Migrations. *Transactions of the Historical Society of Ghana* 13:87-111.

Davis, Kingsley. 1938. Mental Hygiene and the Class Structure. *Psychiatry* 1(1):55-65.

DeBrunner, Hans. 1967. *A History of Christianity in Ghana.* Accra: Waterville Publishing House.

Dickson, Kwamina. 1969. *A Historical Georgraphy of Ghana.* London: Cambridge University Press.

Draguns, Juris G. 1977. Advances in the Methodology of Cross-Cultural Psychiatric Assessment. *Transcultural Psychiatric Research Review* 14(2):125-143.

Dubreuil, Guy, and Eric Wittkower. 1976. Primary Prevention: A Combined Psychiatric-Anthropological Appraisal. *Anthropology and Mental Health,* edited by J. Westermeyer. The Hague: Mouton Publishers.

Dumont, Louis. 1965. The Modern Conception of the Individual: Notes on its Genesis and that of Concomitant Institutions. *Contributions to Indian Sociology* 8:12-61.

———. 1970. Religion, Politics, and Society in the Individualistic Universe. *Proceedings of the Royal Anthropological Institute of Great Britain and Ireland for 1970.* 31-41.

Dunlop, David W. 1979. Alternatives to "Modern" Health Delivery Systems in Africa: Public Policy Issues of Traditional Health Systems. *African Therapeutic Systems. See* Ademuwagun 1979.

Dupré, G., and P. P. Rey. 1973. Reflections on the Pertinence of a Theory of the History of Exchange. *Economy and Society* 2(2):131-163.

Dzobo, N. K. 1978. Personal communication.

Edgerton, R. B. 1971. A Traditional African Psychiatrist. *Southwestern Journal of Anthropology* 27:259-278.

———. 1980. Traditional Treatment for Mental Illness in Africa: A Review. *Culture, Medicine and Psychiatry* 4(1):167-189.

Ehrenreich, Barbara, and John Ehrenreich. 1974. Health Care and Social Control. *Social Policy* 5(1):26-40.

Eisenstadt, Samuel N. 1971. Problems in Theories of Social Structure, Personality and Communication in Their Relation to Situations of Change and Stress. *Society, Stress, and Disease,* edited by Lennart Levi. London: Oxford University Press.

Evans-Pritchard, Edward. 1937. *Witchcraft, Oracles and Magic Among the Azande.* London: Oxford University Press.

Eyer, J. 1975. Hypertension as a Disease of Modern Society. *International Journal of Health Services* 5:539-558.

Fabrega, Horacio, Jr. 1974. *Disease and Social Behavior: An Inter-Disciplinary Perspective.* Cambridge, Mass.: Massachusetts Institute of Technology Press.

Fiawoo, Dzigbodi. 1959. Urbanization and Religion in Eastern Ghana. *The Sociological Review* 7:83-97.

———. 1968. From Cult to Church: A Study of Some Aspects of Religious Change in Ghana. *Ghana Journal of Sociology* 4:72-87.

Field, M. J. 1937. *Religion and Medicine of the Ga People.* London: Oxford University Press.

———. 1940. *Social Organization of the Ga People.* London: The Crown Agents for the Colonies.

———. 1960. *Search for Security: An Ethno-psychiatric Study of Rural Ghana.* London: Faber and Faber.

Forster, E. F. B. 1972. Mental Health and Political Change in Ghana 1951-1971. *Psychopathologie Africaine* 8(3):383-417.

Fortes, Meyer. 1949. *The Web of Kinship Among the Tallensi.* London: Oxford University Press.

———. 1959. *Oedipus and Job in West African Religion.* Cambridge: Cambridge University Press.

Frake, C. 1961. The Diagnosis of Disease Among the Sunbanum of Mindanao. *American Anthropologist* 63(1):113-132.

Frank, Jerome. 1961*a*. *Persuasion and Healing: A Comparative Study of Psychotherapy.* Baltimore: Johns Hopkins University Press.

——. 1961*b*. The Role of Cognitions in Illness and Healing. *Research in Psychotherapy,* vol. 2, edited by Hans H. Strupp and Lester Luborsky. Chapel Hill, N.C.: American Psychological Association.

——. 1975. Evaluation of Psychiatric Treatment. *Comprehensive Textbook of Psychiatry,* edited by E. Freedman and H. Kaplan. Baltimore, Md.: Williams and Wilkins.

Frankenberg, Ronald, and Joyce Leeson. 1976. Disease, Illness and Sickness: Social Aspects of the Choice of Healer in a Lusaka Suburb. *Social Anthropology and Medicine. See* Buckley 1976.

Freedman, Alfred M., and H. Kaplan. 1972. *Comprehensive Textbook of Psychiatry.* Baltimore, Md.: Williams and Wilkins.

Fustel de Coulanges, Numa Denis. 1901. *The Ancient City,* translated by Willard Small. Boston: Lothrop, Lee and Shepard.

Gillies, Eva. 1976. Causal Criteria in African Classifications of Disease. *Social Anthropology and Medicine. See* Buckley 1976.

Gish, Oscar. 1979. The Political Economy of Primary Care and "Health by the People": An Historical Exploration. *Social Science and Medicine* 13C:203-211.

Glick, Leonard. 1967. Medicine as an Ethnographic Category: The Gimi of New Guinea Highlands. *Ethnology* 6(1):31-56.

Goody, Jack. 1957. Anomie in Ashanti? *Africa* 27(4):356-363.

Gugler, Josef, and William Flannagan. 1978. *Urbanization and Social Change in West Africa.* New York: Cambridge University Press.

Gurman, Alan, and David Kniskern, eds. 1981. *Handbook of Family Therapy.* New York: Brunner Mazel.

Gursslin, Orville R., Raymond G. Hunt, and Jack L. Roach. 1959-1960. Social Class and the Mental Health Movement. *Social Problems* 7(3): 210-218.

Guttmacher, Sally. 1979. Whole in Body, Mind and Spirit: Holistic Health and the Limits of Medicine. *Hastings Center Report* 9(2):15-21.

Harding, T. 1973. Psychosis in a Rural West African Community. *Social Psychiatry* 8(4):198-203.

Harris, Marvin. 1974. *Cows, Pigs, Wars, and Witches.* New York: Vintage Books, Random House.

Harrison, Ira E. 1979. Traditional Healers: A Neglected Source of Health Manpower. *African Therapeutic Systems. See* Ademuwagun 1979.

Hart, Keith. 1973. Informal Income Opportunities and Urban Employment in Ghana. *The Journal of Modern African Studies* 11(1):61-89.

——. The Politics of Unemployment in Ghana. *African Affairs* 75(301): 488-497.

Harwood, Alan. 1977. *Rx-Spiritist As Needed: A Study of a Puerto Rican Community Mental Health Resource.* New York: John Wiley and Sons.

Hastings, Adrian. 1979. *A History of African Christianity 1950-1975.* Cambridge: Cambridge University Press.

Higginbotham, Howard. 1979. Culture and the Delivery of Psychological Services in Developing Nations. *Transcultural Psychiatric Research Review* 16:7-27.

Hobbs, Nicholas. 1962. Sources of Gain in Psychotherapy. *American Psychologist* 17(10):741-747.

Hopkins, A. G. 1973. *An Economic History of West Africa.* New York: Columbia University Press.

Hopper, Kim. 1979. Of Language and the Sorcerer's Apprentice: A Critical Appraisal of Horacio Fabrega's Disease and Social Behavior. *Medical Anthropology Newsletter* 10(3):9-14.

Horton, Robin. 1961. Destiny and the Unconscious in West Africa. *Africa* 31(2):110-116.

———. 1971. African Conversion. *Africa* 41(2):85-108.

———. 1972. Stateless Societies in the History of West Africa. *History of West Africa,* edited by J. F. A. Ajayi and M. Crowther. New York: Columbia University Press.

Hsu, Francis L. K. 1976. Rethinking Our Premises. *Anthropology and Mental Health.* See Dubreuil and Wittkower 1976.

Imperato, Pascal J. 1979. Traditional Medical Practitioners among the Bambara of Mali and Their Role in the Modern Health Care Delivery System. *African Therapeutic Systems.* See Ademuwagun 1979.

Inkeles, Alex, and David Smith. 1970. The Fate of Personal Adjustment in the Process of Modernization. *International Journal of Comparative Sociology* 11(2):81-114.

Jaco, E. Gartly. 1970. Mental Illness in Response to Stress. *Social Stress,* edited by Sol Levine and Norman Scotch. Chicago: Aldine Publishing Company.

Jahoda, Gustav. 1961. Traditional Healers and Other Institutions Concerned with Mental Illness in Ghana. *International Journal of Social Psychiatry* 7(4):245-268.

———. 1966. Social Aspirations, Magic, and Witchcraft in Ghana: A Social Psychological Interpretation. *The New Elites of Tropical Africa,* edited by P. C. Lloyd. London: Oxford University Press.

Janzen, John M. 1978. *The Quest for Therapy in Lower Zaire.* Berkeley, Los Angeles, London: University of California Press.

Jilek, W. G. 1974. *Salish Indian Mental Health and Culture Change: Psychohygienic and Therapeutic Aspects of the Guardian Spirit Ceremonial.* Toronto: Holt, Rinehart and Winston of Canada.

———. 1976. "Brainwashing" as Therapeutic Technique in Contemporary Canadian Indian Spirit Dancing: A Case in Theory Building. *Anthropology and Mental Health.* See Dubreuil and Wittkower 1976.

Kagan, Aubrey. 1971. Epidemiology and Society, Stress and Disease. *Society, Stress and Disease,* vol. 1. See Eisenstadt 1971.

Kennedy, John. 1973. Cultural Psychiatry. *Handbook of Social and Cultural Anthropology,* edited by J. J. Honigmann. Chicago, Ill.: Rand McNally.

Kiev, Ari, ed. 1964. *Magic, Faith and Healing: Studies in Primitive Psychiatry Today.* New York: Free Press of Glencoe.

———. 1972. *Transcultural Psychiatry.* New York: Free Press.

Killik, Tony. 1966. Sectors of the Economy. *A Study of Contemporary Ghana. Vol. I: The Economy of Ghana.* Edited by Walter Birmingham, I. Neustadt, and E. N. Omaboe. Evanston: Northwestern University Press.

Kilson, Marion. 1971. *Kpele Lala: Ga Religious Songs and Symbols.* Cambridge, Mass.: Harvard University Press.

Kimambo, I., and C. K. Omari. 1972. The Development of Religious Thought and Centres among the Pare. *The Historical Study of African Religion.* See Ranger 1972.

Kimble, David. 1963. *A Political History of Ghana: The Rise of Gold Coast Nationalism, 1850-1928.* Oxford: Clarendon Press.

Kitching, Gavin. 1972. The Concept of Class and the Study of Africa. *African Review* 2(3):327-350.

Kleinman, Arthur. 1973. Medicine's Symbolic Reality: On a Central Problem in the Philosophy of Medicine. *Inquiry* 16:206-213.

———. 1980. *Patients and Healers in the Context of Culture.* Berkeley, Los Angeles, London: University of California Press.

Knowles, John. 1977. The Responsibility of the Individual. *Daedalus* 106 (1):57-80.

Kovel, Joel. 1976. *A Complete Guide to Therapy: From Psychoanalysis to Behavior Modification.* New York: Pantheon Books.

Krasner, Leonard. 1961. The Therapist as Social Reinforcement Machine. *Research in Psychotherapy,* vol. 2. See Frank 1961b.

Kropp, M. E. 1969. A Note on "La." *Research Review* 5(2):27-32.

LaBarre, Weston. 1970. *The Ghost Dance.* Garden City, New York: Doubleday.

Lambo, T. A. 1977. Traditional Healing and the Medical/Psychiatric Mafia: An Interview. *Traditional Healing: New Science or New Colonialism? See* Singer 1977.

Landy, David. 1974. Role Adaptation: Traditional Curers under the Impact of Western Medicine. *American Ethnologist* 1(1):103-128.

Last, Murray. 1976. The Presentation of Sickness in a Community of Non-Muslim Hausa. *Social Anthropology and Medicine. See* Buckley 1976.

Leslie, Charles M. 1977. Pluralism and Integration in the Indian and Chinese Medical Systems. *Culture, Disease, and Healing,* edited by David Landy. New York: MacMillan Publishing Co.

Levi, Lennart, and Lars Andersen. 1971. Psychosocial Stress: Population, Environment, and the Quality of Life. *Society, Stress, and Disease. See* Eisenstadt 1971.

Lévi-Strauss, Claude. 1963. The Sorcerer and His Magic. *Structural Anthropology.* New York: Basic Books.

Lewis, I. M. 1971. *Ecstatic Religion: An Anthropological Study of Spirit Possession and Shamanism.* Harmondsworth, England: Penguin Books.

Lex, Barbara. 1979. The Neurobiology of Ritual Trance. *The Spectrum of Ritual: A Biogenetic Structural Analysis,* edited by E. d'Aquili, C. Laughlin, Jr., and J. McManus. New York: Columbia University Press.

Loewen, Jacob A. 1969. Confession, Catharsis, and Healing. *Practical Anthropology* 16(2):63-74.

Lomnitz, Larissa. 1977. *Networks and Marginality: Life in a Mexican Shantytown.* Translated by Cinna Lomnitz. New York: Academic Press.

Luborsky, Lester, Barton Singer, and Lise Luborsky. 1975. Comparative Studies of Psychotherapies. *Archives of General Psychiatry* 32(8):995-1008.

Lumsden, D. Paul. 1975. Towards a Systems Model of Stress: Feedback from an Anthropological Study of the Impact of Ghana's Volta River Project. *Stress and Anxiety,* vol. 2, edited by I. Sarason and C. Spielberger. Washington, D.C.: Hemisphere Publication Company.

Macklin, Ruth. 1973. Values in Psychoanalysis and Psychotherapy: A Survey and Analysis. *American Journal of Psychoanalysis* 33:133-150.

MacLean, Una. 1976. Some Aspects of Sickness Behaviour Among the Yoruba. *Social Anthropology and Medicine. See* Buckley 1976.

Magubane, Bernard. 1976. The Evolution of the Class Structure in Africa. *The Political Economy of Contemporary Africa. See* Cohen 1976.

Marees, Pieter de. 1912. *Beschryvinghe ende historische verhael van het Gout Koninckrijck van Gunea.* London: Hakluyt Society.

Marshall, Judith. 1976. The State of Ambivalence: Right and Left Options in Ghana. *Review of African Political Economy* 5:49-62.

Mburu, F. M. 1977. The Duality of Traditional and Western Medicine in Africa: Mystics, Myths and Reality. *Traditional Healing: New Science or New Colonialism?* See Singer 1977.

McKown, R. E., and David J. Finlay. 1976. Ghana's Status Systems: Reflections on University and Society. *Journal of Asian and African Studies* 11(3-4):166-179.

Meillassoux, Claude. 1964. *Anthropologie Économique des Gouro de Côte d'Ivoire.* Paris: Mouton.

Messing, Simon. 1958. Group Therapy and Social Status in the Zar Cult of Ethiopia. *American Anthropologist* 60(6):1120-1126.

Michaux, Didier. 1972. La Démarche Thérapeutique du Ndöp. *Psychopathologie Africaine* 8(1):17-57.

Mullings, Leith. 1975. Healing, Religion and Social Change in Southeastern Ghana. Ph.D. Dissertation, University of Chicago.

———. 1976. Women and Economic Change in Africa. *Women in Africa. See* Berger 1976.

———. 1979. Religious Change and Social Stratification in Labadi, Ghana: The Church of the Messiah. *African Christianity: Patterns of Religious Continuity,* edited by G. Bond, W. Johnson, and S. Walker. New York: Academic Press.

Neher, A. 1962. A Physiological Explanation of Unusual Behavior in Ceremonies Involving Drums. *Human Biology* 34(2):151-160.

Ngubane, Harriet. 1976. Some Aspects of Treatment Among the Zulu. *Social Anthropology and Medicine. See* Buckley 1976.

———. 1977. *Body and Mind in Zulu Medicine: An Ethnography of Health and Disease in Nyuswa-Zulu Thought and Practice.* New York: Academic Press.

Nypan, Astrid. 1960. *Market Trade: A Sample Survey of Market Traders in Accra.* Legon, Ghana: Economic Research Division, University College of Ghana.

Ogot, Bethwell. 1972. On the Making of a Sanctuary: Being Some Thoughts on the History of Religion in Padhola. *The Historical Study of African Religion. See* Ranger 1972.

O'Nell, Carl. 1976. *Dreams, Culture and the Individual.* San Francisco: Chandler & Sharp Publishers, Inc.

Onoge, Omafume F. 1975. Capitalism and Public Health: A Neglected Theme in the Medical Anthropology of Africa. *Topias and Utopias in Health,* edited by Stanley R. Ingman and Anthony Thomas. The Hague: Mouton Publishers.

Opoku, K. A. 1970. A Brief History of Independent Church Movements in Ghana 1862-1969. Unpublished paper.

Oppong, Christine. 1974. *Marriage Among a Matrilineal Elite: A Family Study of Ghanaian Senior Civil Servants.* Cambridge Studies in Social Anthropology, No. 8. Cambridge: Cambridge University Press.

Owusu, Maxwell. 1970. *Uses and Abuses of Political Power.* Chicago: University of Chicago Press.

Parsons, Talcott. 1951. *The Social System.* Glencoe, Ill.: The Free Press.

Patterson, K. David. 1979. Health in Urban Ghana: The Case of Accra 1900-1940. *Social Science and Medicine* 13B(4):251-268.

Paulson, Ivar. 1964. The Animal Guardian: A Critical and Synthetic Review. *History of Religions* 3(2):202-219.

Peil, Margaret. 1972. *The Ghanaian Factory Worker: Industrial Man in Africa.* Cambridge: Cambridge University Press.

Pelto, Pertti, and Gretel Pelto. 1978. *Anthropological Research: The Structure of Inquiry.* Cambridge: Cambridge University Press.

Press, Irwin. 1980. Problems in the Definition and Classification of Medical Systems. *Social Science and Medicine* 14B(1):45-57.

Prince, Raymond. 1960. The "Brain Fag" Syndrome in Nigerian Students. *Journal of Mental Science* 106:559-570.

———. 1964. Indigenous Yoruba Psychiatry. *Magic, Faith and Healing: Studies In Primitive Psychiatry. See* Kiev 1964.

———. 1979. Symbols and Psychotherapy: The Example of Yoruba Sacrificial Ritual. *African Therapeutic Systems. See* Ademuwagun 1979.

———. 1980. Variations in Psychotherapeutic Procedures. *Handbook of Cross-Cultural Psychology: Psychopathology,* vol. 6, edited by H. Triandis and J. Draguns. Boston: Allyn and Bacon.

Ranger, T. O., and I. N. Kimambo. 1972. Introduction. *The Historical Study of African Religion,* edited by T. O. Ranger and I. N. Kimambo. Berkeley, Los Angeles, London: University of California Press.

Reindorf, Carl. 1966. *The History of the Gold Coast and Asante*. Accra: Ghana Universities Press.

Reynolds, David K. 1976. *Morita Psychotherapy*. Berkeley, Los Angeles, London: University of California Press.

Robertson, Claire. 1976. Ga Women and Socioeconomic Change in Accra, Ghana. *Women in Africa*. See Berger 1976.

Rodney, Walter. 1972. *How Europe Underdeveloped Africa*. London: Bogle-L'Ouverture Publications.

Sai, F. A. 1971. The Market Women in the Economy of Ghana. Master's thesis, Cornell University.

Sandbrook, R., and J. Arn. 1977. *The Labouring Poor and Urban Class Formation: The Case of Greater Accra*. Montreal: Centre for Developing Area Studies, McGill University.

Sanjek, Roger. 1982. The Organization of Households in Adabraka: Toward a Wider Comparative Perspective. *Comparative Studies in Society and History* 24(1):57-104.

Sangree, Walter. 1966. *Age, Prayer and Politics in Tiriki, Kenya*. London: Oxford University Press.

Sargant, William. 1957. *Battle for the Mind*. New York: Doubleday.

———. 1974. *The Mind Possessed: A Physiology of Possession, Mysticism and Faith Healing*. Philadelphia: Lippincott.

Sartorius, N., A. Jablensky, and R. Shapiro. 1978. Cross-cultural Differences in the Short-term Prognosis of Schizophrenic Psychoses. *Schizophrenia Bulletin* 4(1):102-113.

Schoffeleers, Matthew. 1972. The Resistance of the Nyau Societies to the Roman Catholic Missions in Colonial Malawi. *The Historical Study of African Religion*. See Ranger 1972.

Sharpston, M. J. 1972. Uneven Geographical Distribution of Medical Care: A Ghanaian Case Study. *Journal of Development Studies* 8(2):205-222.

Singer, Philip. 1977. Introduction. *Traditional Healing: New Science or New Colonialism?* edited by Philip Singer. New York: Conch Magazine, Ltd.

Snyder, Solomon. 1978a. The Opiate Receptor and Morphine-like Peptides in the Brain. *American Journal of Psychiatry* 135(6):645-652.

———. 1978b. The Body's Natural Opiates. *Yearbook of Science in the Future*. Encyclopaedia Britannica, Inc.

Sontag, Susan. 1978. *Illness as Metaphor*. New York: Farrar, Strauss and Giroux.

Stack, Carol. 1974. *All Our Kin: Strategies for Survival in a Black Community*. New York: Harper and Row.

Steel, William. 1977. *Small-scale Employment and Production in Developing Countries: Evidence from Ghana*. New York: Praeger.

Strupp, H. 1973. Needed: A Reformation of the Psychotherapeutic Influence. *International Journal of Psychiatry* 10(2):114-120.

Swift, C., and Tolani Asuni. 1975. *Mental Health and Disease in Africa*. New York: Churchill Livingstone.

Szereszewski, Robert. 1965. *Structural Changes in the Economy of Ghana 1891-1911.* London: Weidenfeld and Nicolson.

———. 1966. The Macroeconomic Structure. *A Study of Contemporary Ghana,* vol. 1.

Torrey, E. Fuller. 1972. *The Mind Game: Witchdoctors and Psychiatrists.* New York: Emerson Hall Publishers.

———. 1972. What Western Psychotherapists Can Learn from Witchdoctors. *American Journal of Orthopsychiatry* 42(1):69-76.

Turner, Victor. 1967. *The Forest of Symbols: Aspects of Ndembu Ritual.* Ithaca, New York: Cornell University Press.

Twumasi, Patrick. 1972. Scientific Medicine—The Ghanaian Experience. *International Journal of Nursing Studies* 9(2):63-75.

———. 1975. *Medical Systems in Ghana: A Study in Medical Sociology.* Tema: Ghana Publishing Corp.

———. 1977. Medicine: Traditional and Modern. *Insight and Opinion* 7(1):20-50.

———. 1979a. Ashanti Traditional Medicine and Its Relation to Present-day Psychiatry. *African Therapeutic Systems.* See Ademuwagun 1979.

———. 1979b. A Social History of the Ghanaian Pluralistic Medical System. *Social Science and Medicine* 13B(4):349-356.

United Nations, Department of International Economic and Social Affairs, Statistical Office 1980. *Compendium of Social Statistics: 1977.* Statistical Papers, Series K, No. 4. New York.

Unschuld, Paul. 1975. Medico-cultural Conflicts in Asian Settings: An Explanatory Theory. *Social Science and Medicine* 9:303-312.

Van Binsbergen, Wim M. J. 1976a. Ritual, Class, and Urban-Rural Relations: Elements for a Zambian Case Study. *Cultures et Développement* 8(2):195-218.

———. 1976b. Religious Innovation and Political Conflict in Zambia: A Contribution to the Interpretation of the Lumpa Uprising. *Africa Perspectives,* vol. 2. Leiden: Afrika Studie-centrum.

Walker, Sheila. 1972. *Ceremonial Spirit Possession in Africa and Afro-America.* Leiden: E. J. Brill.

Wallace, A. F. C. 1958. Dreams and the Wishes of the Soul: A Type of Psychoanalytic Theory among the Seventeenth Century Iroquois. *American Anthropologist* 60(2):234-248.

Wallerstein, Immanuel. 1976. The Three Stages of African Involvement in the World Economy. *The Political Economy of Contemporary Africa,* I. See Cohen 1976.

Ward, Barbara. 1956. Some Observations on Religious Cults in Ashanti. *Africa* 26(1):47-61.

Warren, Dennis. 1978. The Interpretation of Change in a Ghanaian Ethnomedical Study. *Human Organization.* 37(1):73-77.

———. 1979. The Role of Emic Analyses in Medical Anthropology: The Case of the Bono of Ghana. *African Therapeutic Systems.* See Ademuwagun 1979.

————. 1979*b*. Indigenous Healers and Primary Health Care in Ghana. *Medical Anthropology Newsletter* 11(1):11-13.

Waxler, Nancy. 1977. Is Mental Illness Cured in Traditional Societies?: A Theoretical Analysis. *Culture, Medicine and Psychiatry* 1(3):233-253.

Weber, Max. 1964. *The Theory of Social and Economic Organization.* New York: The Free Press.

Weber, Max. 1930. *The Protestant Ethic and the Spirit of Capitalism.* London: George Allen and Unwin, Ltd.

Wintrob, Ronald M. 1973. The Cultural Dynamics of Student Anxiety: A Report from Liberia. *Psychopathologie Africaine* 9(2):267-283.

Wittkower, E. D., and Hector Warnes. 1974. Cultural Aspects of Psychotherapy. *American Journal of Psychotherapy* 28:566-573.

World Health Organization. 1979. *Schizophrenia: An International Follow-Up Study.* Chichester, N.Y.: Wiley.

Zborowski, Mark. 1952. Cultural Components in Responses to Pain. *Journal of Social Issues* 8(4):16-30.

Index

Abeokuta, Nigeria, 200
Abonsam, defined, 228 n. 2. *See* Demons, as cause of illness
Abortion, 64
Accra, 18, 19, 58, 165, 189, 190
Accra Mental Hospital, 49, 51-52, 99, 100, 141, 178
Acheampong, Lt. Col. Ignatius, 226 n. 6
Acquah, I., 38, 50
Adams, R., 71
Adeboo. *See* Creation
Ademuwagun, Z., 200
African Party for the Independence of Guinea and the Cape Verde Islands (PAIGC), 231 n. 3
Agbaafoi. *See* Society of medicine owners
Agriculture: in Labadi, 21-25; case studies, 208-210; farming, 20, 22, 23-24, 33; fishing, 13, 24-25; effects of religion on, 76
Akamba, of Kenya, 50, 227 n. 2
Akan, of Ghana, 128
Akonnedi medium, 40
Akpaso, "witchcraft medicine," 111, 112, 165
Akutso. *See* Lineage
Alland, A., 5
Altered states of consciousness, 174, 176, 179, 181. *See also* Dissociation states; Dreams; Meditation; Possession
Ancestors, 68, 76; as cause of illness, 67, 68, 85, 86; in traditional therapy, 98, 118, 187
Ankarful, 49

Anxiety, 30, 35, 100. *See also* Stress
Armstrong, W. R., 31, 32
Arn, J., 189, 190
Ashanti, of Ghana, 122, 128
Asuni, T., 2, 199
Ataa Naa Nyongmo. *See* Supreme Being
Awroke hamo. *See* Ritual, of thanksgiving
Aye. *See* Witchcraft
Azu, D., 25, 26, 27, 34, 123, 225 n. 1

Baeta, C. G., 178
Bannerman, R. H., 2
Barbot, J., 16
Basel mission, 16-17
Bastide, R., 158
Behavior modification, 181
Beiser, M., 35
Berlin, B., 124, 229 n. 11
Bible, 154, 160
Biofeedback, 179
Biomedicine: cross-cultural applicability of, 2, 200; and curative versus preventive services, 48-49; ideology and values in, 2, 4; and treatment of choice, 49-50, 51; use of, 96, 133. *See also* Biomedical therapy
Biomedical therapy, 37, 47-49, 192-195; in Africa, 168, 198-199, 230 n. 1; and class, 173, 193-194; cross-cultural applicability of, 196-197; effectiveness of, 175-176; goals of, 173-174, 178, 183; and group therapies, 169-170, 194, 195; responsibility in, 168, 169, 170, 183, 192-194, 196, 197; techniques, 173-174

Ghana, 181; goals of, 110-120, 182; government policy toward, 7, 43; practitioners, association of (*see* Society of medicine owners); practitioners, characteristics of, 79-81, 120, 121, 171; practitioners, compensation of, 42, 80-81, 102-103, 114, 121, 219; practitioners, range of, 38-43; role of kin group in, 36, 84, 89, 94, 103, 109, 110, 112-114, 115, 116, 120, 121-122, 129, 166-167, 187, 188; therapeutic community in, 167; as treatment of choice, 51-52, 200. *See also* Classification of disease, Ga categories; Diagnosis, in traditional therapy; Divination, in traditional therapy; Divinities; Etiology of disease, in traditional therapy; Medicine; Ritual; Treatment

Transcendental meditation, in U.S., 195

Treatment: in spiritualist therapy, 138-150; in traditional therapy, 94-120. *See also* Medicine; Ritual

Trophotropic response, 180

Tsɛ (father, owner), 13, 39, 226 n. 3

Tsofa, defined, 62. *See also* Medicine

Tsofatsɛ, defined, 62. *See also* Traditional therapist

Turner, Victor, 123, 124, 126, 127, 128, 160, 229 n. 9

Twumasi, P., 48, 49, 50, 52, 122, 128, 178, 200

Ujamaa, villages in Tanzania, 201

Unemployment, 152, 173, 189; in Accra, 33; in Ghana, 19; in Labadi, 33; as reason for church membership, 153-154

UNICEF, 1

United Africa Company (UAC), 18

Unschuld, P., 37, 225 n. 3

Urbanization, 18, 35

Village community mode of production, 14, 16, 186

Van Binsbergen, W. M. J., 188, 202

Visions, in spiritualist healing, 45-46

Walker, S., 179

Wallace, A. F. C., 169

Warnes, H., 4

Warren, D., 50, 62, 228 n. 1

Water, use in therapy, 102, 106, 120, 123, 140, 158, 171, 172

Witchcraft, 26, 60, 61, 147, 167, 187, 217; as cause of illness, 67, 73-75, 88, 93, 97, 134, 135, 136, 142, 145, 146; as cause of mental illness, 78-79; and competition, 96, 165, 202; defined, 72-73, 134, 229 n. 9; in dreams, 110; and kinship (*see* Kinship, and witchcraft); legal ramifications of, 61, 73-74, 88; medicine, 111-112; as metaphor, 164; protection from, in churches, 152; and social change, 74-75

Woleiatse, 13

Women, employment in Ghana, 31; and marketing, 30-31, 57, 110, 149; membership in spiritualist church, 131; as patients, 57

World Health Organization (WHO), 176, 200; classification of illness, 63; position on traditional medicine, 1, 2

Wottkower, E. D., 4, 192-193, 199

Woyei. *See* Spirit mediums

Wulomei, 38. *See also* Priests

Yellow fever, 65, 99

Yoruba, of Nigeria, 51

Zaire, 50

Zborowski, M., 63

Zulu, of South Africa, 51, 107, 126, 127, 227 n. 2

Designer: UC Press Staff
Compositor: Janet Sheila Brown
Printer: Braun-Brumfield
Binder: Braun-Brumfield
Text: Baskerville 11/13
Display: Baskerville and Deutsch Black

Date Due